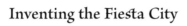

Inventing the Fiesta City

Inventing
the Fiesta City
Heritage and Carnival in San Antonio

LAURA HERNÁNDEZ-EHRISMAN

Published in cooperation
with the William P. Clements Center for Southwest Studies,
Southern Methodist University

UNIVERSITY OF NEW MEXICO PRESS   ALBUQUERQUE

13 12 11 10 09 08   1 2 3 4 5 6 7

Library of Congress Cataloging-in-Publication Data

Hernández-Ehrisman, Laura, 1972–
Inventing the fiesta city : heritage and carnival in San Antonio /
Laura Hernández-Ehrisman.
p. cm.
"Published in cooperation with the William P. Clements Center for Southwest Studies,
Southern Methodist University."
Includes bibliographical references and index.
ISBN 978-0-8263-4310-9 (cloth : alk. paper)
1. Fiesta San Antonio (San Antonio, Tex.)
2. Festivals—Texas—San Antonio.
3. San Antonio (Tex.)—Social life and customs.
I. William P. Clements Center for Southwest Studies.
II. Title.
GT4811.S25H47 2008
394.269764'351—dc22
2007042908

Book design and type composition by Melissa Tandysh
Composed in 11/13.2 Garamond Premier Pro | Display type is Brioso Pro

CONTENTS

List of Illustrations

vii

Acknowledgments

ix

INTRODUCTION:
San Antonio's Pedestrian Rhetoric

1

CHAPTER ONE:
Battle of Flowers: Women and San Antonio's Public Culture,
1891–1900

18

CHAPTER TWO:
The Order of the Alamo: Heritage and Spring Carnival,
1900–27

44

CHAPTER THREE:
Night in Old San Antonio: The San Antonio Conservation Society,
1924–48

73

CHAPTER FOUR:

Juan Q. Public: Reynolds Andricks and the Fiesta San Jacinto Association,

1950–70

103

CHAPTER FIVE:

Rey Feo and the Politics of Inclusion,

1970–2000

135

CHAPTER SIX:

Fiesta Rowdiness: La Semana de Carnaval

169

Conclusion

194

Notes

199

Bibliography

226

Index

233

LIST OF ILLUSTRATIONS

Cover.   Miss San Antonio rides in the 1980
         Rey Feo People's Parade.
Figure 1.   The Alamo decorated for the Battle of
            Flowers Parade, 1893.   19
Figure 2.   "Save the Alamo" float in the Battle of Flowers
            Parade, 1904.   37
Figure 3.   A duchess processing in the Order of the Alamo's
            coronation, 1988.   45
Figure 4.   Duchesses of the Order of the Alamo riding in the
            Battle of Flowers Parade, 1990.   46
Figure 5.   King Antonio reception before Fiesta, 1934, within
            the Alamo chapel.   57
Figure 6.   Nighttime view of San Fernando Cathedral decorated
            for Spring Carnival. In the background are city hall
            and city market, ca. 1904.   67
Figure 7.   Joyce Boothe and Joanna Hull in costumes for the
            San Antonio Conservation Society's Indian Harvest
            Festival, 1939.   87
Figure 8.   Reproductions of the puppets from the Conservation
            Society's puppet show, originally used in 1924. On the
            left are the mayor and city managers. On the right are
            Mr. and Mrs. San Antonio, the Stage Manager, and
            the goose that represents San Antonio.   89
Figure 9.   María, the famous tortilla maker for the Conservation
            Society's first NIOSAs.   100

Figure 10. The display of the grotesque at a recent Cornyation.   113

Figure 11. Miss Fiesta crowned by Rudolph Richter, with
Reynolds Andricks holding her wand on the right, 1956.   118

Figure 12. Peterie Guerra, a Miss Fiesta in the 1950s, in her
"western wear."   127

Figure 13. Queen of Soul contest, 1973, with the emblem of
a crown over an Afro hairstyle in the background.   139

Figure 14. Rey Feo I, Logan Stewart, and King Antonio LIX,
David Steves, 1981.   157

Figure 15. Parade crowd at the Fiesta Flambeau, 2002.   175

ACKNOWLEDGMENTS

I owe a tremendous debt of gratitude to many friends and colleagues who have helped me through the process of writing this book. This study began as a short research paper for a graduate school class, became a master's thesis, and then a dissertation. In many ways, its evolving character is closely tied to my development as a scholar. Several members of the faculty of the American Studies Department at the University of Texas first encouraged this development. As my dissertation advisor and mentor, Steven Hoelscher guided my understanding of heritage, place, and festival. I benefited from his scholarship and from his patient readings of my many rough drafts. Janet Davis also deserves praise for her insights on carnival and popular culture. Desley Deacon, my master's thesis advisor, gave me much valuable material and insights on women's culture in the Southwest as well. Shirley Thompson's questions and comments on my dissertation also helped my understanding of race and community in the South. In addition to my professors in American Studies, faculty from the Anthropology and English Departments in Austin also aided me. Richard Flores was a continual source of support and mentorship. His own scholarship of San Antonio's public culture was crucial for my work. José Limon's work was also a great influence, and his advice played an important role in shaping this book.

After I completed my dissertation, I was very fortunate to receive support from the Clements Center for Southwest Studies at Southern Methodist University. During my year there, I received invaluable support from Clements Center faculty and associates, including David Weber, Sherry Smith, Suzanne Bost, Alexis McCrossen, Benjamin Johnson, Michelle Nickerson, Brian Frehner, and Andrew Graybill. I owe particular thanks to the visiting scholars who traveled all the way to Dallas to review my work. Sylvia Rodríguez gave me wonderful advice about analyzing social relationships in public space, and Joy Kasson offered many insights about analyzing visual materials and women's culture in the South.

The research for this project was conducted in numerous archives. In particular, I thank the staff at the University of Texas at San Antonio Archives, who have compiled a wonderful collection of materials about Fiesta San Antonio. I also benefited from the material at the Center for American History at the University of Texas at Austin, the Institute of Texan Cultures, the Daughters of the Republic of Texas Library, the San Antonio Conservation Society, and the San Antonio Public Library. I also wish to sincerely thank editor David Holtby and the staff at the University of New Mexico Press for their guidance in this project and Meredith D. Dodge, who meticulously edited my manuscript.

I would also like to thank the many Fiesta organizers and participants who gave me their time and insights. Michaele Haynes, who has written her own wonderful book on the Order of the Alamo, was a great help in the early stages of this project. Several former Fiesta presidents, Carol Canty, Ralph Lehr, Peter Hennessey, Don Moyé, and Jorge González, also gave me important insights, as did Chuck Blische, Anne Keever Cannon, Gracie Poe Griffin, Elysiana Cantú, Rose Kozmetsky, Nicolas Hollis, Socrates Ramirez, and Mary Begia. A special thanks to Diane Bozorgi for her ideas and personal mementos of her time as Miss Fiesta. Other San Antonians who are not directly involved in Fiesta but who gave me generous insights are Carlos Guerra, Mario Salas, Miguel de Oliver, Santiago García, Jim Mendiola, Lizzie Martínez, Ramona Dávila, and Eli Rios.

Finally, a big thanks to my family, who have helped me in this process for almost ten years. My parents, Wayne and Emilie Ehrisman, gave me their own perspective about Fiesta and San Antonio, as well as free room and board on my many research trips. They introduced me to Fiesta, with many trips to Night in Old San Antonio (NIOSA). My sister, Sarah Ehrisman, took wonderful photographs of Cornyation. My husband, Gustavo Hernández, has been a constant source of support as well. He has accompanied me to numerous Battle of Flowers and Flambeau parades, NIOSAs, Miss Fiesta pageants, and Carnivals through the years. He has also read many drafts, offering a refreshing and sometimes critical point of view. I am continually grateful for his consistent love and support. This book is dedicated to my daughter, María Isabel, who arrived as I was completing this manuscript. She has made my life a continual celebration.

Introduction

San Antonio's Pedestrian Rhetoric

MY STORY BEGINS WITH MY FIRST MEMORY OF WALKING THE CITY. During my senior year of high school, I participated in San Antonio's Battle of Flowers Parade, one of the central events of the city's annual Fiesta. Each year, parade organizers sponsor four of the city's public high schools, providing the float, costumes, and all the decorations. As a class officer in one of these selected schools, I could ride in this prominent city spectacle. Some of my friends, who were members of the school band, marched in the parade every year, but this was my sole opportunity. The Battle of Flowers Association (BFA) chose the theme and the outfits. This year, they chose musicals, and so my high school float was designed for *Oklahoma!* A few months before the parade, I was fitted for a "pioneer" dress—a long, yellow skirt, puffy shirt, and a big, white bonnet. I walked alongside the float in my frumpy outfit, chosen to be one of the hardy pioneer children, while my taller friends rode in a mock wagon above heaps of plastic yellow flowers.

I was thrilled to be in the parade. The day of the Battle of Flowers was an annual, citywide holiday, so I knew most of my friends and family would be in the stands. We arrived at the preparation area several hours before the start at eleven in the morning, and I spent this time watching hundreds of costumed people preparing. Band members tuned their instruments. Horses were fed. Cars were decorated with wreaths and flowers. Giant floats emerged from trucks and warehouses and traveled to their designated spots. When we finally began to process down the parade route, I started my first "long poem of walking" through downtown San Antonio, spatializing the city with my footsteps.[1] As I continued in the parade, I traveled south on Broadway, passing by the four-dollar seats and families with coolers on the back of their flatbed trucks, with lawn chairs and legs pushed into the free spaces in between. Young kids stood in the front rows, tossing confetti and blowing whistles. I then passed the large bleachers and the main reviewing stand, directly in front of the Alamo. We paused in front of the judges, smiled, and then traveled past denser crowds, over the river, past Joske's Department store, the Menger Hotel, and Frost Bank, with small crowds watching from their balconies. We turned west onto Commerce Street, and then north onto Santa Rosa Street, and finished before we hit the highway. I waved for more than two hours.

Like the participants in hundreds of other urban parades, I had a brief chance to perform in the middle of a citywide audience. I enjoyed the opportunity of "going public"—momentarily becoming the center of attention. As a young child, I sat in those same flatbed trucks, eating snow cones and watching bands, mayors, police officers, and festival queens pass by. Through the act of "passing by" myself, the myriad glances, waves, and hellos were my "pedestrian enunciations."[2] My entry into the center of San Antonio's public culture was an act of weaving buildings, people, and streets together, and acting the space of the street as a speaker acts through language.[3] Within the limitations of a particular spatial and social order—the boundaries of the route and the context of the parade—I could establish my own relationships with other participants and people who shared this space. Every year, hundreds of San Antonians take their own footsteps in this parade, forming relationships on this public stage and enacting the social forces of the city.[4] In this spectacle, social actors both create and challenge boundaries, and social contradictions become clear. This parade is a framed event, set aside from the daily traffic of downtown San Antonio. Yet parade participants also enact the everyday practices of walking the city. This parade is a special circumstance, a distinct opportunity for public visibility, but those who walk its path also speak the pedestrian rhetoric of the city.

In the years since my brief role in the parade, I have come to a new understanding of the significance of my performance. Dressed as an Anglo pioneer in a musical version of Manifest Destiny, I participated in a popular narrative of western history. The parade is full of such references, but the most important story it tells is of the modern city itself. The Battle of Flowers Parade is as unique and as ordinary as any other urban parade, shaped by national and transnational cultural currents, yet articulated through distinct local traditions and histories as well. The event is an annual part of a citywide festival called Fiesta. This civic festival began in 1891 and continues to this day and is a time to celebrate the city and articulate a distinct community identity.[5] Throughout Fiesta, both San Antonio natives and visitors actively shape a distinct civic culture. Fiesta reflects many regional and national cultures yet also demonstrates the particular social relationships of San Antonio. Over its long history, as various social actors struggled to enter Fiesta through parades, pageants, and street fairs, they became part of larger structures of power, but their particular footsteps often transgressed these boundaries and continually transformed the city itself.[6] As a cultural performance Fiesta provided a more flexible space for these social orders to be challenged.[7] Through the twentieth century, Fiesta has expanded dramatically. What began as a single parade has now become a ten-day calendar of more than two hundred events, which various civic and commercial organizations in the city sponsor. Now Fiesta has three parades, which attract more than two hundred thousand spectators each. Large street fairs monopolize the entire downtown area every night of the week, and community organizations stage their own parties throughout the city. In this work, I trace the significance of these changes and how they are connected to social change in San Antonio and the nation.

In order to understand Fiesta, though, one should first understand San Antonio before the city's modern era. In the almost two hundred years before the first Fiesta parades, San Antonians created a distinct civic culture within two intersecting routes, its waterways and its roadways. The San Antonio River and its tributary a few miles west, the San Pedro Springs, was the basis for the first human settlements in the region.[8] Groups of nomadic Indians who had been camping for thousands of years along its banks named the waters Yanaguana. The streams wound all the way down to the Gulf of Mexico, a hundred miles to the southeast.[9] In 1691, Spanish explorers began to arrive to the area, and in 1718 the first mission, San Antonio de Valero (later called the Alamo), was founded. Five missions were eventually built along the path of this river, flourishing between 1730 and 1755. San Antonio became a community of Franciscan missionaries and the Coahuiltecans who lived and worked at the missions, creating an intricate acequia water system that remains to this day. When more citizens from New Spain came to the area in 1730, founding the Villa de San Fernando de Béxar, they built a new church on the opposite side of the river from the mission. The plaza at the western side of the church, the Plaza de las Islas (named for the fact that most of the settlers were originally from the Canary Islands), became the center of their community life. Another plaza, on the eastern side of the cathedral, was the center for military exercises and the presidio.

After Mexico's independence from Spain, San Antonio de Béxar was an isolated village with a struggling economy. The missions were secularized, and conflicts with Native Americans hindered ranching and farming. Leaders of the town began to promote it as a trade center, with links to Louisiana and the northern Mexican regions of Coahuila, Chihuahua, and New Mexico. The native Tejano population declined, and more Americans came to settle in the city.[10] The Mexican government, newly freed from Spanish rule, encouraged this flood of new American colonists by offering grants to empresarios, managers who were responsible for recruiting immigrants and distributing land.[11] Soon, Anglo immigrants outnumbered Tejanos by ten to one in Texas. These new immigrants and native Tejanos had a relationship marked by both conflict and cooperation, forming economic and political alliances, while Tejanos also made efforts to check increasing Anglo influence in the region. In San Antonio these communities also fostered a blending of customs.[12] San Antonio formed a three-tiered society, with clear residential patterns. On the west side of the river, the prominent "first families" lived, descendants of the Canary Islanders, who guarded their elite status by preventing marriage with "mixed races." On the east side of the river, the descendants of Indians and Spanish soldiers lived. Anglos who came to the region quickly recognized and assimilated into the higher ranks of this social structure.[13] The Tejano rituals prevailed, though, in public ceremonies. December was fiesta season, as Roman Catholic celebrations included the feast of the Immaculate Conception, Our Lady of Guadalupe, and Christmas. The town plaza was filled with games and booths during these feast days. San Antonio also began a celebration of Mexican Independence Day on September 16, which included church bells, gun salutes, patriotic speeches, and processions through the city streets.[14]

Conflicts soon developed between Anglos and Tejanos, however, particularly over the question of Texan independence. When the Mexican dictator, Antonio López de Santa Anna, seized dictatorial powers and threw out the Constitution of 1824, Anglo Texans and Tejanos alike protested, but Tejanos were much more ambivalent about Texan independence, torn between their loyalty to Mexico and their Texan home. For Tejanos, the Texas Revolution was a civil war, as divided families fought on both sides at the Alamo and other major battles.[15] For several years after Texan independence, San Antonio was physically marked by continuing conflict. The military plazas were filled with bodies; houses punctured by cannon shot or in ruins.[16] In the first year after independence, Texan Gen. Felix Huston even insisted that the mayor of San Antonio, Juan Seguín, abandon and destroy the town in order to prevent further Mexican attacks. Seguín refused and successfully petitioned Sam Houston to rescind the order, but Mexican forces briefly reoccupied the city twice in 1842. Because of murder threats, Seguín himself was forced to flee to Mexico that same year. At least two hundred other prominent Tejano families left the city during this period as well.[17]

As law and civic order were eventually reestablished in the new republic, many Tejanos lost political and economic power, even in San Antonio with its majority Tejano population.[18] Throughout the state, ex-soldiers carried out raids and claimed Tejano lands and lives, accusing all Tejanos of betrayal of the Texas Republic.[19] At the same time, Indians and African Americans were denied the rights of full citizenship. African American freedmen who resided in Texas at the time of independence were required to flee the state. Anglo American control of San Antonio was fostered through a new "peace structure," a political accommodation that placed Anglos atop the existing hierarchy of San Antonio's society.[20] Now, interethnic marriages aided Anglos in gaining land and status while allowing Tejano elites to protect their own familial interests.[21] This structure took shape in municipal government as San Antonio's Texas-era mayors were consistently Anglo, while most of its city council remained Tejano. This new alliance promoted a shift in public celebrations as well. For example, the Roman Catholic feast of Our Lady of Guadalupe continued in public processions, but Anglos would be included as well. Anglos would also join in other public events such as the fandangos and celebrations given in honor of Texan Pres. Mirabeau Lamar. Even the celebration of Mexican Independence Day continued.[22] The local Tejano population was able to continue many cultural celebrations even though they no longer controlled the city's public space.

When Texans debated U.S. annexation, Tejanos largely opposed the effort, realizing that statehood would only further diminish their social status. They also opposed the Mexican War (1846–48), often seeing it as an act of U.S. aggression on their cultural motherland.[23] For many Anglo Texans, however, who were largely Protestant and from the American South, Texan independence was a step closer to integration into the economy and culture of their homeland of the United States. As Texas was officially annexed in 1845, it became part of an expanding American southern cotton industry based on slavery. Anglos had great influence in San Antonio's political and economic life, and Anglo immigration escalated after the conclusion of the Mexican War. As the population increased, Tejano political power further diminished. In some parts of Texas, Tejanos were driven away by Texas posses who sometimes evicted entire towns. These expulsions were based on charges of being horse thieves and aiding slave insurrections.

In San Antonio, there was an effort to expel part of the local Tejano population, but it failed because the German community failed to support these efforts.[24] Trade and commerce increased, but Tejanos became a minority for the first time in the city's history and lost representation in the city council. The Tejanos' new diminishing numbers deeply affected their social status in the state and the city. San Antonio neighborhoods became segregated by ethnicity as well as class. In 1860, the town was divided into four wards. Almost 80 percent of Tejanos and newly arrived Mexicanos lived in two of these four wards. By 1860 Tejanos owned only 7.8 percent of the city's real estate. In terms of economic power, Tejanos began to form a working underclass, with the 1860 census showing that 65 percent of the Tejano population were laborers.[25]

The U.S. Army began to increase their presence in the city during the Mexican War, establishing quarters that outnumbered the local population.[26] They later established San Antonio as a military outpost, setting up their headquarters in the old Spanish barracks on Military Plaza and then leasing the Alamo from the Roman Catholic Church as a supply depot and beginning an arsenal complex across town. New immigrants from Germany, France, Italy, England, and Denmark would also arrive in enough numbers to raise the city's population to more than eight thousand by 1850.[27] This census revealed the largest groups of the city's free residents: 42 percent had Spanish surnames, 25 percent were Anglo Americans, and 16 percent were of German descent.[28] As Anglos took over municipal government, they also formed a merchant elite that began transporting supplies to forts along the Rio Grande and on the Indian frontier and to mule trains passing through from Texas coastal ports to gold and silver mines in territories to the west and along established routes into Mexico. San Antonio may have also had the nation's first cross-country transport service to the west coast; in 1857 Concord stagecoaches drawn by four-horse teams began carrying mail and passengers between San Antonio and San Diego.[29] San Antonio's roadways were also connecting it to the Gulf coast. In this new mercantile economy, local Germans became most of the mechanics and small shopkeepers; Tejanos, now usually identified as "Mexicans," worked in this industry as cartmen.[30]

Though Anglos clearly controlled San Antonio's politics and economy by the Civil War, visitors still regarded it as a place unlike most American cities. Travelers who encountered this walking city at mid-nineteenth century often described its odd jumble of languages, peoples, and customs. Richard Everett, who came through from the Texas coast with a mule-drawn supply train bound for Arizona silver mines, wrote that "walking about the city and its environs, you may well fancy yourself in some strange land . . . the narrow streets, the stout old walls."[31] This, he recognized, was not organized like any American town. Each night, San Antonio's plazas would be filled with lively markets, cockfights, and indoor fandangos playing both boleros and polkas. Tejanos continued their Roman Catholic feast days and processions; one particular celebration, part of the feast of San Juan, featured El Gallo Corriendo (the running rooster). A contestant was given a brightly decorated rooster to ride on his horse over the main streets of the town, while others rode alongside and attempted to take the rooster by any means possible.[32] Anglo celebrations of the Fourth of July and Texan independence and German dances joined these festivities.

As each of these celebrations developed, however, each community began to operate separately from the others. In the 1850s, newspaper reports indicated that with the exception of a few public balls, each ethnic group kept to itself: "The German has his soiree attended by his Teutonic friends; the Mexican party is rarely visited by the American male; and in private American assemblages the fair señorita is no longer visible."[33] Anglo American participation in Guadalupe celebrations ceased after annexation, and Tejano rituals received greater criticism as well. Anglos were increasingly critical of the fandangos, considering them a public nuisance and issuing taxes on licenses. Some even petitioned the city council to abolish these dances because they believed that they were violent and degenerate. In 1853, fandangos were banned despite Tejano protests. Sometimes Tejanos simply ignored these ordinances, and on one occasion, Tejanos assaulted the local constable after he appeared to stop their dance.[34] Though there was some limited social mingling among the Tejano, Anglo, and German elite, this rarely extended to lower classes, which were characterized by residential and cultural separation.[35]

Anglos, Tejanos, and Germans were also divided on the issue of slavery and southern secession. Some Tejanos had purchased slaves during Spanish and Mexican rule and also aided Anglos in circumventing Mexican antislavery laws. Often, however, they objected to the Anglo definition of slavery as a race-based, inherited, and permanent condition, preferring the labor of servants under a peonage system instead. Anglos often accused Tejanos of aiding runaway slaves.[36]

The war also furthered divisions between Anglos and Tejanos. San Antonio was highly ambivalent about the Civil War, the city voting to secede by only 3 percent. Sam Houston, Texan liberator and revered governor, opposed secession and said so from the balcony of his plaza house while Robert E. Lee, who had been based out of San Antonio as a regimental commander at frontier forts for five years, made his final decision to join the Confederate Army. Many in the German community, who opposed slavery, found themselves shot or hanged when they disputed Confederate conscription laws. Despite the internal debates about entering the war, the city fared relatively well because of its status as a transport hub. Before the Union blockade of the Mississippi River and the Gulf coast, San Antonians drove cattle east to feed Confederate armies and shipped gunpowder up from Mexico to produce ammunition. Southern cotton also made its way into Mexico.[37]

After the war, San Antonio's importance as a transportation center increased. It became the center of a cattle empire, as trail drivers moved out of Texas north to railheads in Kansas. As usual, the plazas were the center of the city's social life, but by 1870, Military Plaza became an open-air market for cowboys, wagon trains, and longhorn cattle. Leather merchants, saloons, and vaudeville theaters opened up throughout downtown, and Plaza de las Islas, now called Main Plaza, became the center of a thriving red light district.

Then the railroad came, the trail drives ended, and modern San Antonio began to take shape. The Galveston, Harrisburg and San Antonio Railway and its later linkage with the Southern Pacific's Sunset Route arrived in 1877 and transformed the city's political, economic, and social life. Paradoxically, the railroad also encouraged a distinct longing for the "San Antonio of yore." As in so many other towns and cities, modernization fostered both desire for industrial progress and nostalgia for a quickly disappearing past. In an era of rapid economic and cultural transformation, San Antonians sought continuity through the creation of new cultural forms that defined and celebrated the city's past, inventing traditions that would also become the basis of the city's modern tourist industry.[38] San Antonio boosters would increasingly "sell the city," commodifying the experience of being in the city by promoting San Antonio's unique qualities, its "distinctness" as a place. Fiesta became the center of this new tourism with its first parade in 1891 and also aided in the reorganization of the city's public space. As Fiesta grew, its organizers gradually constructed a more permanent sense of the city as a perpetually "festive" place.[39] In the only comprehensive account of the festival, Jack Maguire says that San Antonio has "the fiesta spirit," or an "ambiente." He, like many other city boosters, chronicles Fiesta in order to portray San Antonio as a harmonious place that welcomes its visitors.[40] Throughout this study, I trace the connections between Fiesta performances and the larger construction of San Antonio's tourist industry.

San Antonio's festival was similar to events in several other American cities, particularly New Orleans's Carnival. For the first twenty years of its existence, San Antonio's festival was called the Spring Carnival. Given the long history of commercial and social ties to the Gulf coast, it is not surprising that San Antonians would be influenced by these neighboring carnival traditions. New Orleans and San Antonio share a history as part of the territories of New Spain. Both cities had native populations—Creoles and Tejanos—who had to negotiate American political and social norms. Even the elite natives had to struggle to maintain their religion, language, and cultural celebrations. Like the fandango in San Antonio, New Orleans's Creole dances and Carnival balls became the focal point for Anglo American criticism in the early nineteenth century.[41] These communities also fostered a limited blending of social customs, however.

In the late nineteenth century, both cities also shared the regional history of the American South, and both were trying to reinvent themselves. In New Orleans, the city was in an economic decline. In 1840, the city was the third largest in the country. By 1880 it had slipped to ninth. New Orleans faced a huge debt, had few manufacturing industries, and relatively poor linkage to the railroads.[42] During this time, New Orleans boosters chose to focus on developing tourism by reinventing their city as "the city that care forgot," featuring the romance of iron balconies, trailing wisteria, and the gaiety of the local population. Their Carnival, which had its origins decades earlier, was celebrated as the manifestation of this carefree attitude, and railroads and hotels cultivated this image in order to attract more visitors to the city. New Orleans's image was based on two desires: the nostalgia of native whites for the slave-based prosperity of the antebellum era and the exoticism that northern visitors longed for in their travels.[43] Through Carnival, and Mardi Gras in particular, organizers created an image of a "Latin" city, which to Anglos meant "gay, wicked, sophisticated, and subtly lascivious."[44] Like San Antonio, New Orleans boosters developed a modern, "New South" economy based on invented traditions, selling the city by mythologizing its exotic past.

New Orleans's Carnival and San Antonio's Fiesta have many other similarities, a few of which will be traced throughout the book. San Antonio's celebration is not merely a copy of its more famous predecessor, however. There are important differences between the two celebrations, some of which have to do with San Antonio's position as not just a southern city, but a western city as well. In many ways, San Antonio, and Texas in general, straddles southern and western identity. The two industries that define the state are cotton and cattle. Most of the Anglos who came to Texas during Mexican rule were American southerners, who took their cotton and slavery with them. The children of these immigrants became part of the Confederacy, and their descendents later enforced Jim Crow segregation on both African and Mexican Americans. At the same time, Texas's Anglo immigrants were also part of the story of Manifest Destiny, playing a vital role in the U.S. annexation of the West. Texas had a nineteenth-century cattle industry and incorporated Mexico's ranching culture even as the state subjugated the Mexican population.[45] Thus, San Antonio's modern cultural celebrations also connected the city to its legacy as part of the American West.

Many western cities in the United States have staged their own "fiestas." The event that bears the closest resemblance to San Antonio's early celebrations is the Fiesta de Los Angeles.[46] No doubt late nineteenth-century San Antonians were influenced by California's Spanish revival that began with the publication of Helen Hunt Jackson's *Ramona* in 1884. This revival focused on what Carey McWilliams famously identified as the "Spanish Fantasy Past" that promoted a nostalgic vision of a leisurely Spanish colonial society devoted to little more than fiestas and fandangos (ignoring the contempt that Anglo immigrants expressed at the time, not to mention their often violent overthrow of this native elite).[47] As Anglos reinvented Creole Carnival in New Orleans, this romanticized Spanish history became the subject of numerous pageants throughout the Southwest. In 1893, two years after San Antonio's first Fiesta parade, Los Angeles city boosters created a Fiesta de Los Angeles featuring a parade and royal court.[48] Los Angeles also was successful at creating a distinctive civic identity based on this mythicized past, one that drew many tourists westward. The city, which at the time was still primarily an agricultural center, also used this invented tradition to promote the main products of the region, displaying grapes, oranges, and olives.[49]

The fiestas of San Antonio and Los Angeles have several other features in common, including an emphasis on historical pageantry over raucous revelry (unlike Mardi Gras). Los Angeles residents soon grew tired of the romance of old Spain, however. Critiques of this "un-American" festival proliferated, as various local publications opposed the celebration of foreign manners and customs.[50] The fiesta was discontinued by 1900 and replaced by a much vaguer Fiesta de las Flores. Anglo boosters chose to create more cultural distance between themselves and their Mexican past.[51] San Antonians' Fiesta, by contrast, continued to expand, for reasons that will be elaborated in the next chapter.

San Antonio, in more ways than one, is between New Orleans and Los Angeles, positioned in the middle of an imagined South and West. Through looking at San Antonio's public culture, one can see a negotiation of both southern and western identity. Two years after San Antonio's first Fiesta parade, Frederick Jackson Turner gave his legendary address, "The Significance of the Frontier in American History," at the 1893 Chicago World's Fair. In this speech, he defined the Anglo American western frontier even as he announced its closure. For Turner, and for hundreds of western historians afterward, American westward expansion was the best expression of American identity itself. According to Turner, Anglo Americans exercised the principles of democracy, independence, and ingenuity through settling the West. The frontier was not just a boundary between East and West but also between savagery and civilization. As Anglos pushed westward, they continually encountered the primitive and relived the stages of industrial progress, and these ventures strengthened and renewed American identity. After Turner's address, the American West continued to be associated in popular literature with democracy, newness, and progress. In San Antonio's Fiesta parades, echoes of Turner's thesis are clear in the orderly procession of floats representing Indians, Spanish, and then Anglo pioneers.

As Turner's frontier popularized western identity, the Civil War and its aftermath defined southern identity and history. While the image of the West was fused with American identity, the white South was often represented as its antithesis. In the aftermath of the Civil War, northerners portrayed Anglos in the South as poor, lazy, and culturally backward. Some southern historians, most notably C. Vann Woodward, suggested that southerners were marked by the experience of defeat and became guilt ridden and humiliated.[52] While westerners looked to the future, southerners were said to be preoccupied with the past, in the nostalgia for antebellum prosperity. They were also rigidly conscious of caste and class, wedded to notions of white racial superiority.[53] In San Antonio's Fiesta pageantry, with its elaborate and exclusive carnival societies, one can see this attention to maintaining white supremacy and the social elite.

This story should also sound familiar to any reader of Edward Said. These binaries of American regional identity are a form of "othering." Said first defined this process where western European culture gained identity by setting itself off from "the Orient," and this other region became "an underground self" for western civilization.[54] The Orient became a symbolic space for western European writers to project the characteristics their culture repressed, including dishonesty, violence, and excessive sexuality.[55]

Through a similar process of national "internal orientalism," both the American South and West have been described as regions that oppose the values of the North and East by being less industrious, more sexual and disorderly.[56] In many narratives, Northerners came as agents of civic order to "reconstruct" the excessive violence of the South, and easterners moved to tame the "savagery" of the West. Even as these regions are "othered" by such identifications, however, they become crucial for defining a northern-eastern "self." Peter Stallybrass and Allon White elaborate this dependency. As the agents of order attempt to reject disorder, they find they are dependent on this low-other culture for their own sense of self. In this way, what is made socially peripheral becomes symbolically central, a space of desire for the repressed.[57]

As he traveled through the country, Buffalo Bill drew thousands of spectators who enjoyed his depiction of a lawless, violent West. In the late nineteenth century, some looked to the region as remedy for civilization, not a confirmation of it. Teddy Roosevelt articulated this most clearly in his cult of the "strenuous life," promoting the vitality and labor of life in the West as an antidote to a complacent, overcivilized East. At the same time, many northerners looked to the South with longing as well. They imagined the South as a region whose leisurely rhythms were a relief from their fast-paced, industrial world. During the Gilded Age, both the South and West became symbolic repositories for anxieties about urbanization and social change. One of the most interesting aspects of San Antonio's Fiesta is that its multiple performances play with both these polarities—East and West, North and South. Fiesta boosters represented San Antonio's history as both frontier outpost and refined southern city of leisure.

The most important polarity in this discussion of the American West and South is one that revolves around race. While white westerners and southerners may have been portrayed as the negative self-images of a northern-eastern American self, white Americans of all regions participated in the process of defining "whiteness" through the deprecation of various "nonwhite" ethnic groups.[58] White southerners portrayed African Americans as degenerate, impulsive, and childlike, incapable of social equality with whites. White westerners depicted Native Americans, Mexicanos, and the Chinese as primitive, untrustworthy, and deserving of their subjugation in the Anglo conquest of the region. In Texas, what united both white southern and western identity was the depiction of "the Mexican," both as defeated enemy in the story of Manifest Destiny and a subjugated population under the southern practices of Jim Crow. In San Antonio's public culture, Mexicanos were both socially displaced and symbolically centralized. The city's growing tourism industry depended upon images of Mexican culture to market the city to visitors even as Mexicanos themselves were marginalized.

To trace Fiesta's place in the selling of the city, though, one must begin at the Alamo. The Alamo is a small fortress that has become a colossal figure in the local and national imagination. For those of us who grew up next to this "shrine," the Alamo seemed particularly pervasive. For most of the twentieth century, San Antonio has been nationally known as the Alamo city. The site, and the 1836 battle, cast an enduring shadow on most accounts of the city's past and its present. In her analysis of Alamo myth and ritual, Holly Beachley Brear argues that Fiesta is a secular Easter following the Good Friday of the Alamo's fall.[59]

Brear's insights are valuable to understanding Fiesta. The festival is deeply entangled in Alamo memory. Fiesta commemorates the anniversary of the battle of San Jacinto that won Texan independence and thus redeems the sacrifices of the Alamo battle. Richard Flores has described the Alamo as a master symbol of what he calls the Texas Modern, the period between 1880 and 1920 when economic, social, and cultural changes transformed Texas from a Mexican cattle-based society to an Anglo-dominated industrial and social order.[60] Fiesta San Antonio, also introduced during this period of the Texas Modern, articulated many of the same emerging social relations as the Alamo. Commemorating Texan independence, like remembering the Alamo, shaped a distinct racial hierarchy between an Anglo self and Mexican other.

I owe particular gratitude to Richard Flores's work on San Antonio and the Texas Modern. His analysis, in many ways, was the inspiration for this book. I modify his ideas through my study of Fiesta, however, to demonstrate that this festival, unlike the Alamo, expresses a more complicated picture of this period and the eras that follow. Central to my analysis of "inventing the fiesta city" is how this is distinct from inventing the Alamo city. The Alamo codified racial separateness and emphasized the binary racial lessons of a new social order. The cultural memory of racial stratification at the Alamo was fixed at the site of its stone-fortified church. Fiesta, an ephemeral, multivocal spectacle, was always more ambivalent. Fiesta performances moved between repulsion and desire for the Mexican other and was more openly riddled with anxiety.[61] As a set of performances that included hundreds of social actors and subjects, Fiesta was a more contradictory space, a fuller articulation of the complexities of modernity.

The process by which Fiesta expressed both repulsion and desire for a Mexican other is a form of carnival logic. Mikhail Bakhtin was the first to translate medieval carnival practices into a discussion of power and resistance among social classes. Peter Stallybrass and Allon White reformulated Bakhtin's ideas to fit the realm of literary studies. The most popular carnival practice is one of "inversion," where people of the lower social strata are temporarily elevated to the top. Ordinary citizens become temporary carnival kings. Inversion is also used to describe the temporary social acceptance of behaviors that are usually considered vulgar or deviant, or "low" culture. During carnival season, the grotesque overpowers classical (high culture) ideals, as participants eat and drink excessively, expose their bodies, and openly engage in taboo social practices. At various moments, one can see these practices of inversion in Fiesta, and this study highlights their social significance.

Another theory that Stallybrass and White define is Bakhtin's idea of "hybridization, " which is a merging of the binary categories of high and low culture.[62] The resulting mixtures are hybrid cultural forms. Stallybrass and White argue that hybrid cultural formations challenge social order in more fundamental ways than inversion. While inversion merely temporarily reverses the social order, hybridization has greater potential to provoke social transformation. By combining elements that are usually seen as incompatible, hybrid forms expose social contradictions in ways that potentially destabilize the social order. The only way to make sense of these theoretical constructions, though, is by tracing their significance through history. In this study, I look at various hybrid performances and examine their potential for encouraging social change.

Though Fiesta was clearly a spectacle for tourists, its biggest audience was always local. Fiesta drew visitors but never in the numbers that came for New Orleans's Mardi Gras or Pasadena's Tournament of Roses Parade. Fiesta was a story that San Antonians told themselves, articulating a civic identity involving negotiations among multiple communities. There have been very few academic studies of Fiesta. The most notable are those of Holly Beachley Brear and Michaele Haynes. Both of their histories of Fiesta formed the foundation for my initial understanding of the festival, but these accounts are part of their larger projects on Alamo memory and the city's debutante culture. My purposes are a little different. I describe the various changes in Fiesta as part of the larger history of changing power relations between women and men and Anglos and Mexicanos in defining the city's public culture. At its beginning, Fiesta celebrated a new social order in San Antonio, a German and Anglo elite who controlled the newly modernizing city. Through the language of Texan independence, this new elite celebrated their social prominence and white racial superiority. The social elite who organized the first

Fiesta parades, whom I call the "heritage elite," used this commemoration to legitimize their own social dominance in the city. Connecting themselves to the Alamo defenders through their heritage, whether ancestral or symbolic, this elite made themselves modern heirs to reign over San Antonio.[63] San Antonio's heritage elite marked the anniversary of Texan independence in order to naturalize their own positions of power; they connected the certainty of historic commemoration with the continuation of their own roles as cultural guardians. They were never entirely successful in their efforts, however. Throughout this study, I examine the extent to which this heritage elite could control this festival's performances and meanings. As Fiesta grew into the citywide spectacle it is today, its history is not merely that of the dominant class seeking to impose certain values upon the greater San Antonio public. Instead, it is a complex series of negotiations among competing interests.[64]

My story is also about the continued relevance of "going public" for women. Like Mary Ryan, I am in search of women in public and for the ways they merged women's culture with public culture. This story, then, is part of a larger effort to understand the power of dividing public and private social spaces and how these terms are continually marked by gender.[65] I have also found that these categories are relevant to race and ethnicity. The culture of segregation, with its careful divisions of public streets and facilities, was a pervasive social reality for both African Americans and Mexicanos in much of San Antonio's twentieth-century history. Through Fiesta, many Mexicanos struggled to move into the middle of the city's public space. As both women and Mexicanos went public, they shifted the boundaries of San Antonio's civic culture. These groups put themselves "in place" in Fiesta by stepping "out of place"—transgressing the boundaries of home and segregated neighborhood.[66]

In the first chapter, I look at the first ten years of Fiesta parades, called the Battle of Flowers. Organized by women's voluntary organizations, these parades featured upper-class white women pelting flowers at each other in mock battles in front of the Alamo.[67] Through these parades, women created a space between the binary spheres of public and private. Acting as matronly custodians of culture, these women were able to secure a role for themselves in the city's public culture. I also examine these parades as they were performed at the boundary of one economy and the emergence of another. The parade presented the city as a site of "antiquated foreignness." At the same time, Fiesta featured modern technology, spectacle, and temporary pleasure. Fiesta crowds were thrilled with the first electric lights on Commerce Street at the turn of the century, and boosters sold the city for its modern conveniences as much as its rustic charm.

As Fiesta expanded, its elite pageantry developed in the first two decades of the twentieth century. While the founders of the Battle of Flowers Association strained the boundaries of womanhood through the parade, their daughters were initiated into a more secluded privatized sphere, focused on the southern beauty. These changes represent not only an expansion of the festival but also an increasing emphasis upon social order in San Antonio. The city modernized, and Jim Crow laws proliferated. The various communities that made up its public were increasingly segregated into separate events. Greater immigration from Mexico increased Anglos' fears about social order. The new "royal" roles of the kings and queens of Fiesta reigned over this new society. At the same time, the carnival grew as a space to express underlying anxieties about disorder, racial difference, and desire.

In my third chapter, I begin to trace the slow unraveling of Jim Crow, with a new generation of San Antonio elite women who defined the city's tourist industry through its Spanish colonial past. The San Antonio Conservation Society (SACS), from the mid-1920s through World War II, increasingly challenged municipal authorities who were destroying the remnants of San Antonio's Spanish colonial architecture.[68] Through the language of cultural conservation, the SACS, unlike previous voluntary associations, articulated a local form of the Spanish heritage fantasy. Restoring the mission buildings, hosting tamale dinners, and dressing in elaborate Mexican dresses, these women exemplified the modern search for authenticity through the elevation of "the primitive." Their Fiesta event, called a Night in Old San Antonio, represented this nostalgia. They also, however, performed a transitional ambivalence between the social segregation of the previous era and the post–World War II model of social integration. While previous festival pageantry emphasized a longing for the Old South, these women shifted the festival's emphasis to South of the Border.[69]

After World War II, as the city boomed into a center for the growing defense industry, Fiesta assumed the rhetoric of cold-war democracy and interethnic equality. Although San Antonio's heritage elite asserted some continuing control over Fiesta traditions, for the most part they lost the battle. This shift reflected changes in the city, especially its phenomenal postwar growth, and it also changed the model for Fiesta participation. A middle-class ethic of inclusion became the dominant promotional language of the festival. At the same time, Anglos in the city "played Mexican" to articulate this new civic identity. Anglos' social relationships with Mexicanos themselves were not as friendly, but Mexican American organizations, like the League of United Latin American Citizens (LULAC), sought inclusion in the city's public culture as they did in the national social fabric.[70] While this generation had only token membership in Fiesta events, they began a long effort to control their cultural productions within Fiesta.

From the mid-1960s to the 1980s, Fiesta organizers received the most direct and public challenges to its events and membership. Many of these challenges came from Mexican American activists, who protested both the lack of participation and the stereotypes of Mexican culture. A new generation of these reformers also had greater power in local politics, and they demanded greater symbolic power as well, openly challenging the Anglo-dominated Fiesta. As a result, Fiesta included a new king, Rey Feo, who symbolized a new politics of negotiation between middle-class Anglos and Mexicanos.

As Fiesta organizers broke down previous boundaries, though, they also solidified others. At the turn of the twenty-first century, San Antonio's middle-class civic culture is certainly multicultural. Yet Fiesta organizers and participants alike vilify the city's poor and working-class Mexicano youth. Their fears center around the Carnival, the most inexpensive (and popular) event. I look at how middle-class anxieties about the Carnival reveal deeper contradictions in Fiesta organizers' rhetoric about inclusion and the public. The continuing marginality of the Carnival presents a larger question about the place of these communities in the city's public culture. Their struggle to reshape Fiesta's boundaries will be the challenge of the next century.

At times my analysis will view the city from a distance, as if I were looking at the view from atop the Tower of Americas on Hemisfair Plaza. These occasional views are necessary, in order to catch a glimpse of the city in its entirety. Most of the time, though, I will try to make my analysis at ground level, to follow the complicated paths that so many San Antonians took as they made their way.

. 1 .

Battle of Flowers

Women and San Antonio's Public Culture, 1891–1900

AS TOURIST DESTINATIONS, CITIES AND THEIR LONG HISTORIES ARE often reduced to a particular defining moment. For San Antonio, that moment was the battle of the Alamo for Texas's independence from Mexico. In the most popular story, the outnumbered Texans fought valiantly within that crumbling Spanish mission, even when they knew they would not survive. The Mexican army invaded the Alamo and killed most of the men, but their martyrdom was redeemed only a few weeks later when Sam Houston and his Texan army defeated Santa Anna and won Texas independence at the Battle of San Jacinto. Years later, the remains of the Alamo would be partially restored and transformed into a "shrine of Texas liberty," and San Antonio would become known as the Alamo city.

Yet the journey from battlefield to shrine was longer than one might expect. For decades after the 1836 battles for Texan independence, the Alamo remained in ruins. Travelers and historians often bemoaned the crumbling site or took souvenir stones from its bloodstained walls, but San Antonians made no concerted effort to restore the mission. By the time of the Texans' struggle, the Alamo had been converted into a military fort; later, two German architects transformed the main façade of the church. From the 1850s to the 1880s, the Alamo complex was used as a quartermaster depot for the U.S. Army and a warehouse for a wholesale grocer.

Finally, in 1883, a group of San Antonians convinced the Texas state legislature to buy the Alamo. At this point, the Alamo began the transformation from battlefield ruins to tourist destination. At this particular historical moment, remembering the Alamo became more important not only to the aging veterans of the Texan Revolution but also to those who wanted to script the future of San Antonio. In the next twenty years, Alamo memory would be performed as the center of the city's public culture, and the process began with a small flower parade.

FIGURE 1. The Alamo decorated for the Battle of Flowers
Parade, 1893. UTSA's Institute of Texan Cultures at San Antonio.
Courtesy of the San Antonio Conservation Society.

Origins

In March 1891, a group of prominent San Antonio women organized a meeting to discuss a "flower-celebration that would keep Texas history fresh in the minds of future generations."[1] In a flurry of subsequent meetings, they arranged an elaborate parade of flower-decorated carriages to ride through the city. According to the ladies' plan, carriages would process through the main business district and then would end at Alamo Plaza, next to the historic battlefield of the Alamo. When the procession arrived on the plaza, the carriages would divide in two, with each half going the opposite direction, so that in passing they could pelt each other as well as the bystanders with flowers.

Sources conflict about who came up with the idea of a flower battle. A history printed in the 1899 program states that Colonel Alexander, a prominent member of the San Antonio Club, proposed the idea to honor the first presidential visit to the city.[2] President Harrison was scheduled to arrive by train on April 20 and spend a few hours touring the city. Other sources state that weeks before the president's visit was scheduled, a visitor from Chicago, W. J. Ballard, suggested that the city hold a celebration for the bicentennial of the first naming of San Antonio de Padua, as well as honoring the fifty-fifth anniversary of the San Jacinto battle.[3] The Battle of Flowers records, which Helene Von Phul first wrote in 1931, credit Ellen Maury Slayden as the first with the idea of holding a parade to celebrate the April 21 anniversary of the San Jacinto battle, which was then proposed to Alexander and the San Antonio Club. I am inclined to believe the third version, for reasons that will become clear throughout the chapter. Letting the ambiguity remain for the moment, however, these three origin stories also reveal the three main groups involved in the parade's invention—businessmen, tourists, and elite white women.

Their three differing emphases are also revealing. For the men of the San Antonio Club, who wrote that President Harrison's visit inspired the parade, the event was a most important symbol of the city's integration with the nation. The rapidly growing city was becoming a military and commercial metropolis. For Ballard, the tourist, the anniversary of San Antonio's founding as a Spanish colonial outpost was a marker of the city's "exotic" history. Many visitors viewed San Antonio's remnants of Spanish missions and its Mexicano population as part of its "quaint charm." For many of the city's elite women, though, Texas history took primary importance. Official histories of the Battle of Flowers Association claim that plans for a parade were already under way when President Harrison announced his visit. The date of the parade was merely modified by a day to coincide with his arrival. In fact, the parade was actually scheduled to begin at five in the afternoon, after the president's train would have left the city.

Whoever came up with the initial idea, the ladies did most of the organizing. They planned for an elaborate, genteel celebration. They recommended that many of the city's hotels, offices, and government buildings decorate their exteriors with ribbons and banners. Each carriage in the parade would be filled with fresh flowers. They invited "every citizen with a vehicle and flowers" to participate.[4] The street car company promised to stop running the trains during the procession, and the organizing committee set clear rules: Carriages would maintain at least a twelve-foot distance between them; no flowers would be thrown until the bugle call; and participants should avoid throwing anything at horses or drivers.[5]

The parade did not turn out as planned, however. First, torrential rains forced organizers to cancel the April 20 celebration, and President Harrison could not even leave his car during his visit. For the next several days, the committee debated whether to have the parade at all. Finally, on April 24, they staged the procession in the late afternoon, and the *San Antonio Daily Express* described the event. As the procession began, mounted police officers cleared the way for the military band, followed by a cavalcade of ladies and their "squires."[6] Next came the bicycles, part of the "cycling rage" imported from Paris, immensely popular among the elite.[7] Then came the carriages, all elaborately decorated with natural flowers. The parade was considered a great success, and the ladies decided that this parade would become an annual celebration, held each year on April 21, the anniversary of the Battle of San Jacinto.[8]

In most popular histories of the Battle of Flowers Parade, the story of the first procession ends here. The parade that quickly became a city institution would continue with little controversy. On closer scrutiny, however, the first flower battle was not quite as calm as previously described. According to the less established Republican newspaper, the *San Antonio Light*, the first Battle of Flowers Parade was really quite a battle. The paper describes an anxious crowd, pressing closely to the carriages and waging a furious fight. As soon as the carriage occupants threw their first flowers, the waiting crowd "began picking the fallen roses from the pavement, and even tore off the trimmings of the carriages and soon had the best of the fight." In response, many of the passengers defended themselves with carriage whips.[9]

From this description, the flower battle was a chaotic display of social disorderliness. Men, women, and members of all races, ethnicities, and social classes began striking each other. For example, one lady struck Mr. Doc Fitzgerald, a passive spectator, a severe blow on the face with her whip, but did not see fit to apologize for her mistake. Mr HP Drought made an ugly cut with his whip into the crowd, struck a Negro and the boy ran into a carriage horse in front of the Menger [Hotel] and nearly caused a runaway. A Negro, driving in a phaeton by himself in the procession, struck Loms Glaeser, a white boy, in the right eye with the ends of his reins . . . One young angel with white wings appealed to the crowd for protection from the missiles saying "I wish you men would make them quit."

Apparently the electric cars caused conflict as well. One team of carriage horses was so frightened that they dashed into Alamo Street, overturning a buggy and dragging their driver under the carriage by the lines.[10] In one of the most interesting social disruptions,

one of our tender dudes, completely carried away with the enthusiasm of the occasion, started a flowery duel with a damsel of color and considerable stoutness, under the impression that he was showering tender missiles upon his best girl. No words can portray his embarrassment when the boisterous laughs of the bystanders rudely broke him the realization.

In a social world in which the lines of race, gender, and class were rigidly defined and enforced, such confusion was considered quite noteworthy. The young man was rewarded with carnival laughter, an ambivalent sound that mocks and revives, denies and asserts.[11] His transgression was an embarrassment, yet it was also made possible in such a chaotic context. For the moment of the parade, Alamo Plaza became a world where social boundaries were both transgressed and affirmed. Most important, Alamo Plaza became a crossroads, a space where the people who were normally kept separate were juxtaposed. For in this event, the city's elite exposed themselves to the forces of a diverse public.

Such rowdy battles would not continue at the same pace. After the first year, organizers decided that only parade participants would take part in the flower battle. The crowd would merely watch. Mounted police would monitor and segregate them from the procession. Yet the difficulties of the parade were more than the result of poor planning. They reflected the tensions of a social world in transition. The ladies of the parade committee assumed that the parade could display a city that was less isolated and more modern than ever before. The parade would present a city with railroads, pavement, and streetcars that were absent only twenty years earlier. Parade organizers, like other local elites, felt that these changes benefited the city as a whole. The rowdy crowd that awaited the procession, however, suggested that such rapid modernization came with many dislocations as well.

The Texas Modern

On his travels through San Antonio in 1892, Richard Harding Davis wrote that

> the citizens of San Antonio do not, as a rule, appreciate the historical values of their city, they are rather tired of them. They would prefer that you should look at the new Post Office and the City Hall, and ride the cable road [the electric streetcar]. But the missions which lie just outside the city are what will bring the Eastern man or woman to San Antonio, and not the new waterworks.[12]

As it turns out, Davis was only partly correct. Many San Antonians were quite aware of visitors' interest in San Antonio's past. For several decades, travelers had noted the ruins of the missions, the old plazas, and marketplaces that made the city unique, but San Antonians, like most other Americans of the time, were preoccupied with "progress." They were also well aware that travelers were as interested in modern conveniences as they were with old Spanish buildings. From the late 1870s onward, San Antonio city boosters articulated a rather sophisticated vision of the city as a combination of old and new, of ancient ruins and modern commerce. Promoters described the city as a place for "the historian, the pleasure seeker, the invalid, and the capitalist seeking profitable investments."[13] They frequently invoked the mythology of the Alamo battle: "every street and plaza . . . marks the grave of a hero, friend or foe . . . every stone baptized in human blood shed in the defence of liberty." In the late nineteenth century, San Antonio was also known as a haven for consumptives, who sought its warm, dry climate. Promoters noted the city's climate, the river, its mines and quarries. San Antonio was already a large trading center for wool and other agricultural products. To emphasize both the history and the modern conveniences of the city, promoters described San Antonio as having "a future as marked and distinctive as its past, notable as it has been."[14] San Antonio, in their terms, was a historic city possessed of all the conveniences and comforts of modern civilization, ancient ruins, modern residences and business houses, old plazas and streets laid out by the early Spanish conquerors, traversed by irrigation ditches built by the early Franciscan fathers side by side with the mains of the water works company, with fire hydrants at convenient distances, with the streets lighted by gas lamps and electric light, the street cars running to distant points and the telephone annihilating spaces, modern parks, beautiful drives, numerous churches, fine educational advantages, hotels, boarding houses, fine residents, the most cosmopolitan of all the old cities in America.[15]

For city boosters, the late nineteenth century was a promising time for the city. Many of their ambitions would not materialize; the city would not develop into a center for manufacturing and industry. San Antonio's economy would continue to be based on tourism, trade, and the military. The city, however, had transformed in many significant ways.

In 1877, the Galveston, Harrison and San Antonio Railroad arrived in the city. Six years later, it would link up to the Southern Pacific and form a transcontinental connection between San Antonio, New York, and San Francisco. The International and Great Northern Railroad also arrived, forming a north-south route into Mexico, and in 1887 the San Antonio and Arkansas Pass Railway further linked the region to the Gulf of Mexico. San Antonio was now much more accessible from the rest of the United States and from Mexico. Transportation within the city improved as well, when the San Antonio Street Railway began in 1878. By 1890, four major lines of electrified streetcars spanned the city. The first telegraph line was established in 1876, and the first water pumping station was established in 1878. By 1890, the San Antonio River would also be traversed by fifteen bridges.

In 1891, on the eve of the first Battle of Flowers Parades, the city elite was celebrating a modernizing city, whose population had grown to more than thirty-seven thousand the previous year. These new railroads, streetcars, and bridges transformed the physical development of the city. In the early nineteenth century, the town's life centered around the Plaza de las Islas (now Main Plaza) and Plaza de Armas (now Military Plaza). The Plaza de Armas had been a training ground for the Spanish and Mexican army, but by mid-century several residences were built around the area, and the space became an open market and commercial center. Plaza de las Islas, by contrast, was the social center for the city's festivals. Next to the cathedral, the plaza hosted many religious and civic festivals such as Mexican Independence Day and the feast of Our Lady of Guadalupe.[16]

By the end of the century, though, the social and commercial center had definitively moved to Alamo Plaza. The railroad depots of St. Paul Square on the eastern and Cattleman's Square on the western edges of the city pulled stockyards, lumberyards, and warehouses from the center of the city. Streetcar lines linked to these depots and sent visitors directly to Alamo Plaza, where a flurry of new hotels, boarding houses, and businesses developed. The grand opera house opened on the plaza in 1886, and in 1890 the new post office moved to the north end of the plaza, along with retail druggists, liquor stores, saloons, meat stores, a physician, an attorney, a dentist, a bank, two real estate offices, boarding houses, and hotels.

City officials also restructured the other two plazas. They officially designated Military Plaza as the public market for the city in 1888 but in 1889 began building the new city hall in the center of the plaza, transforming the space from an open market space to a space dominated by the imposing city building. They also constructed the courthouse and garden on Main Plaza. These new buildings covered the plazas, disrupting the daily commerce, religious festivities, and other social practices that happened there previously.

The Battle of Flowers Parade confirmed this transition. When the San Antonio Club first began discussions for the parade, they unanimously chose Alamo Plaza.[17] As the first Battle of Flowers participants paraded through the city, they navigated a rapidly changing urban landscape. The procession moved westward through the newly vibrant business district on Houston Street, then moved to St. Mary's, onto Main Plaza, and back down Commerce Street to Alamo Street and Alamo Plaza, where the flower battle occurred and the greatest crowd gathered.

> There were signs on the streets that something unusual was to be accomplished. From the various arteries of the city leading to Alamo plaza a steady, persistent flow of animated and enthusiastic beings poured itself onto the scene of the battle. By every known method of conveyance and principally by pedalistic action from every quarter of the city the people came. Arriving at the plaza they chose their vantage points. Windows were gradually filled, balconies were occupied and awning and roof tops received their living, expectant burdens . . . The central portion of the plaza was bright with its living crowd . . . It was a cosmopolitan, metropolitan crowd and it swelled until it numbered 10,000 people.[18]

As the papers described, the parade performed the centrality of Alamo Plaza to this new city. In these descriptions, the crowd acted as one. The parade not only transformed the image of the city but also depicted its residents as a cohesive social body.[19] This image did not reflect the displacements of such rapid modernization, however.

Richard Flores has called this transition the Texas Modern, the period between 1880 and 1920, when the introduction of the railroad, the closing of the range, and the rise of commercial farming occurred alongside a new ethnoracial and class order.[20] During this period a new consolidation of non-Hispanic white groups displaced an Anglo-Mexican bicultural ranching society. As I discussed in the introduction, this process had its origins in the Texan independence movement and its annexation to the United States in 1845. After the Civil War, Anglos acquired the best business sites and began to form partnerships with a prosperous German community, which had benefited from its pro-Republican stance during the war and received many political appointments in the state. A non-Mexican, "white" elite began to work together for mutual benefit.[21] At the same time, the region's Mexicano population occupied a liminal position in this new racial order, between the nonwhite Indian and the marginally white Spaniards.[22] While some upper-class families with social standing were able to claim whiteness, Anglos treated most Mexicanos as racial inferiors. Through this period, the Mexicano upper classes maintained a certain level of power and participation in an expanding ranch economy. Anglos and Germans, though maintaining greater power, had to be "Mexicanized" to live successfully in south Texas. Many married into Mexicano families and conducted business in Spanish.[23]

This changed with the decline of ranching and the rise of commercial farming. Both the railroad and the invention of barbed wire destroyed the cattle drives that had been the foundation of the region's economy. The arrival of the railroad gave access to new markets as farm goods could be transported much farther and faster than before. Fencing of ranch lands also ended the cattle drives from Texas to the North. The closing of the cattle trails displaced the local and regional markets of this industry.[24] These changes were particularly devastating to Mexicanos. For example, during the ranching period, cartmen transported goods along a network of roads through the state.[25] In 1856, 60 percent of Mexicanos drove the carts that carried most of the supplies to the region. Railroad lines displaced this service. A new Anglo-dominated economy based on commercial farming took its place. During this transformation, San Antonio became a boomtown that attracted eastern capital, and these new, nationally controlled markets effectively displaced older regional political economic structures.[26] The change to farming was not achieved without battles, and the Texas Rangers violently suppressed Mexicano rebellions. By 1900, Mexicanos performed most of the menial labor in the city, with 54.5 percent of Mexicanos classified as "unspecialized labor."[27]

In the decades immediately following the Civil War, conditions for San Antonio's African American population changed as well. After emancipation, former slaves had one of the earliest migrations from Texas farms and plantations to the cities. San Antonio saw its population of black residents double by 1870.[28] In this decade, German Americans also settled in large numbers in the city and established residency in the eastern part of downtown. African Americans lived predominantly in the German part of town or among Mexicanos on the west side. Still in too few numbers to establish neighborhoods of their own, they often lived in housing their white employers provided.[29] During and after Reconstruction, military installations also offered some protection from hostile whites and some Mexicanos, who saw them as competition for labor. The cattle industry offered greater freedom than farming, and African Americans made up 25 percent of those employed in cattle drives in 1870.[30]

Yet the railroad lines increased and solidified racial discrimination for African Americans as well. After 1877, most were forced into unskilled labor positions such as janitors, sweepers, porters, and servants. They worked in competition with unskilled white and Mexicano laborers. In particular, they were concentrated in the domestic service trades, work considered demeaning for whites and out of character for Mexicanos (as opposed to agriculture and light manufacturing).[31] As the city grew toward the end of the century, and elite whites moved to suburbs further east, south, or north, blacks often occupied their former homes, and many worked for the railroad. They formed several distinct neighborhoods by the turn of the century, most scattered to the west or east near the central commercial district. Though their population decreased between 1870 and 1890, from 16 percent to 12.5 percent in 1890, they had already formed distinct communities in the center of the city.

On the eve of the first Battle of Flowers Parade, San Antonio was a multiethnic city but clearly controlled by an emerging Anglo and German elite. A decrease in Mexicano population, stemming in part from low immigration, and a heavy influx of Anglos from the American South and Midwest, substantially restructured race relations in the city. In 1881, the establishment of the San Antonio Club represented the most important marker of this growing unification of non-Hispanic citizens. As of 1887, the membership list included only one Spanish surname.[32] The Mexicano elite who remained continued to have a small role in the city's social life but only at its edges. Life and labor were increasingly segregated along racial and ethnic lines.

When the wives of the San Antonio Club members staged the first Battle of Flowers Parade, they were participating in this emerging racial order. The parade commemorated a battle that had occurred fifty-five years before, yet it was also a symbol of a united, white, non-Hispanic elite of the present.[33] Directing the city's memory toward the Texas Revolution avoided the more controversial history of the Civil War. Many of the city's German families had opposed secession and were loyal to the Union during the war. San Antonio's white elite had tangled ties to both sides of the conflict. This Anglo-German community preferred to revive a history of a cause that did not bring up those bitter memories.

Still, it is easy to see the connections between reverence for the Alamo heroes and the Confederacy's cause. After all, the Texas Revolution assured the continuance of slavery. Many prominent Texans who had fought for their republic were also fighting to maintain their "peculiar institution," and their victory eventually led to Texas's integration into the agrarian economy of the American South. The focus on Texan martyrdom at the Alamo was also not so different from the "lost cause" movement that began in the Reconstruction-era South, with its portrayal of noble rebels fighting despite overwhelming odds. At the same time, the Alamo was a celebration of a western identity and part of the story of Manifest Destiny that connected the city's history to American expansion. The Alamo battle served as a marker of both southern and western identity, closely tied to the distinctiveness of both American regions.

Most important, though, the Alamo was relevant to the late nineteenth-century present. By the end of the 1870s, Reconstruction was defeated, and white southerners were rapidly remaking old racial boundaries. Just as pioneers had earlier, eastern capital was now moving westward and integrating western cities like San Antonio into the national economy. The parade also marked the time when the Mexicano elite had lost much of its power in the city.[34] When the surviving veterans of the San Jacinto battle were honored at the parade, organizers drew lines between real battles and this mock flower event. Though most of the parade participants were not direct descendants of the Texan forces, through this celebration they identified themselves as the heirs to the Texan victory.

Battle metaphors were also appropriate because the military represented one of the groups that had transformed the city from the days of the Mexican War in the 1840s to the 1890s. U.S. soldiers quartered in San Antonio during the Mexican War later became permanent residents when the headquarters of the Eighth Military District was established. During the 1850s, the city based much of its economy on the presence of these headquarters.[35] In 1878, the army established Fort Sam Houston, which played an active role in the first Battle of Flowers parades, loaning horses to pull the floats and sending official representatives as well. Often, high-ranking officers would act as official coordinators of the procession.

Fiestas Patrias

As much as the parade celebrated an emerging Anglo-German elite, however, it relied on the language and imagery of a Spanish-Mexican city. In a distinct form of what Renato Rosaldo has called "imperialist nostalgia," the Battle of Flowers Parade consistently recalled the people and the culture of the defeated, even as it celebrated the Texan victory.[36] In the discourse of civilization prevalent at the time, such a nostalgia would be understandable. Combining ideas of progress with social Darwinism, civilization marked a stage of human evolution, a departure from savagery.[37] Yet this did not preclude interest in those others who were believed to be at earlier stages of human development. For San Antonio, this process took two forms, as both a particular past and a particular people were both displaced and symbolically centralized. A growing tourism industry depended upon images of both cattle ranching and Mexicanos to market the past to visitors. Battle of Flowers programs featured pictures of log cabins (with the label "home sweet home") alongside images of "quaint" Mexicano candy vendors.

Such images were actually portraying many relatively new practices, not ancient customs. Though Mexicano vendors had been on the plazas for many decades, they developed a series of new services oriented toward visiting Anglo tourists. *Vendedores* created a growing form of outdoor salesmanship, peddling products like candies, flowers, and birds. The chili stands continued to be a unique part of San Antonio's nightlife. Arranged in small tables around wood fire, "chili queens" sold bowls for ten cents.[38] They even drew tourists to the margins of the city. In the "Mexican quarter" west of San Pedro Creek, families made homes into makeshift restaurants for Anglo consumers. These urban entrepreneurs contributed to the tourism industry and to the image of the city itself, ensuring that visitors would imagine the city as a Spanish-Mexican village.

San Antonio's festival was also part of a national movement. Across the country, cities were constructing civic pageants and parades that presented and mythologized local history. David Glassberg, writing of this movement, argued that the historical imagery helped spectators define the boundaries between tradition and modernity.³⁹ For San Antonians, the key difference between the past and the present was the position of Mexicanos. The Battle of Flowers processions marked and naturalized the social order. While they offered visions of pomp and progress, they also displayed marginalized groups. From the first parade, along with the decorated carriages and military bands, came a "fun-maker," a broken down carriage with shabbily dressed occupants, drawn by an old horse with patched harness carrying a banner reading "Poor but in it."⁴⁰ The program from the 1896 parade makes this clear.⁴¹ The parade was organized into four divisions. First, mounted police cleared the crowd. The bicycles followed, visions of modern leisure and technology. The second division was the United States Army band and military processions from Fort Sam Houston. In the third division, the carriages came with the officers of the Battle of Flowers Association, veterans of San Jacinto, and eight floats of various patriotic organizations in the city. One float presented "Our Nation" with girls dressed as each state.⁴²

In the fourth division, parade organizers put the symbols of an earlier age. A Mexican band was followed by carts like the ones cartmen had driven before the railroad put most of them out of business. In the parade, these were driven by children. What was once the main source of goods for the city now became an object of child's play. Cowboys and Indians followed, "dressed in costumes as blood-curdling as knives, pistols, red paint and feathers." These displays were the comic part of the parade, the fun-makers. The most popular of these forms was the donkey brigade. These "quaint beasts" were intertwined with Anglo ideas of Mexicanness. The local press described this group as "the brigade of unhurried, sinister-eyed burros and their sombreroed young riders." They became an object of mockery. This division was described as "a striking foil to all the pomp and pageantry."⁴³ Placed at the end of the parade, they were meant to demonstrate the superiority of Anglo culture by contrast.

As such an example makes clear, carnival practices often stigmatize groups of low social status rather than offer a critique of social power. Along with these groups came the devils, members of the Young Men's Christian Association dressed in red, white, and blue. This parody was an inversion, when social roles were reversed and those in power portrayed those without. The members of the donkey brigade were also "playing Mexican." Sam H. Woodward, "colored, that is artificially colored," who spent his time doing circus pranks, performed another comic element. In such examples of racial cross-dressing, the city's white upper and middle classes demonstrated African Americans as a source of both desire and repulsion. As stigmatized groups were mocked, they were also objects of fascination.[44]

Many western historians have also noted the irony that at this moment, as Mexicano populations were stigmatized, their cultural practices became part of Anglo imagination. Two years after the first Battle of Flowers Parade, Los Angeles boosters created a very similar fiesta of their own, including a parade and royal pageantry. The description of these parades is remarkably similar to San Antonio's event, though there is no evidence that parade organizers were directly influenced by San Antonio's events. The Los Angeles fiesta features the same orderly progression of floats, imitating the city's transition to modernity, and a very similar fascination with an exoticized Spanish heritage.[45] The Los Angeles event had a much shorter history, however. As a result of continuing criticism of this display of "foreignness" and low culture, the parade was discontinued by 1900, replaced by a much more Americanized Fiesta de los Flores that, outside of the name, dropped most references to the city's Spanish past.[46]

It is difficult to know precisely why San Antonio's Fiesta thrived while Los Angeles residents grew increasingly intolerant of such displays. A significant difference, perhaps, is that San Antonio and Los Angeles were becoming very different cities. Los Angeles was experiencing an exponential population boom, and fewer of these migrants were interested in celebrating a Spanish or Mexican past. San Antonians, by contrast, continued to make use of its "Mexicanness." Angelenos also seemed to be less uncertain about the future, embracing the newness of the West and defining the city as a "city of destiny."[47] San Antonians, at least the Fiesta organizers, were much more ambivalent. The parade was an event that looked back as often as it looked forward, and the city itself would also operate on this paradox. In the process of San Antonio becoming an American city, the city's tourism industry celebrated it for its remnants of the Spanish-Mexican past. Its vehicle for entering modernity was a commemoration. Although these elites were enjoying most of the benefits of these new social changes, they were also expressing anxiety about their future prominence in such a rapidly changing city. The Battle of Flowers Parade spoke with a double tongue, expressing uncertainty and excitement about the pace of modernization.

The story becomes even more interesting, though, when considering its inspiration. Where did the idea for a flower battle come from anyway? Oddly enough, the most likely source of the flower processions were very similar parades in Mexico City.[48] At the same time as San Antonio's parades, the Mexican dictator, Porfirio Díaz, used flower battles and processions to celebrate Mexico's own entry to modernity.[49] As San Antonians celebrated their historic freedom from Mexico, the city also demonstrated its continuing modern ties to its ancestral country. Elite San Antonians had many personal ties to Mexico's elite. Ellen Maury Slayden and her husband, U.S. Rep. James Slayden, were close friends of Porfirio Díaz and made frequent trips to Mexico City. These visits possibly inspired Slayden's idea for the flower battle.

San Antonio's story also paralleled Mexico's in many ways, and this becomes clear when considering San Antonio as an intersection of the regions of the American South and greater Mexico, rather than as a city on the north side of the U.S.-Mexico border.[50] Of course, the most obvious confluence was the continuing social life of the city's Mexicano residents. Yet there were other mergings as well. Economic ties between the United States and Mexico were important during this era—railroads linked Mexico City to San Antonio, and American companies invested in mining, industry, and transportation.[51] Comparing these two sets of flower battles, and the meanings for their simultaneous occurrences, reveals how much the two cities had in common.

Like Texas, Mexico became more industrialized and urbanized during this period. The Díaz regime, from 1876 to 1911, welcomed foreign investment, especially from the United States, which funded and controlled expanding railroad lines and the silver-mining industry. As in south Texas, investors from the U.S. Northeast were connecting the country to the world economy. The profits of these investments were benefiting relatively few groups—the foreigners themselves and the native elite who allied with them. By contrast, *rurales*, mounted rural militia, broke strikes and assured greater numbers of landless peasants for factories and large farms by evicting Indians en masse from their communal landholdings.[52] These rurales bore some resemblance to the Texas Rangers who exercised violent forms of land dispossession and social control in the first two decades of the twentieth century in Texas and carried out displacements of Mexicano ranchers. The changing Mexican economy also solidified a particular ethnoracial order, as European, Spanish culture was elevated at the expense of indigenous cultures. Mexican elites put this starkly in terms of modernity. Rural, traditional culture was associated with backwardness, and urban, modern culture with whiteness and progress.[53]

The urban elite of Mexico City wanted to create a culture consistent with their notions of a progressive society.[54] A new social order was developing both there and in San Antonio, and the upper class wished their public rituals to reflect this process. The Americanization of Alamo Plaza, described above, also occurred in Mexico City. One writer describes late nineteenth-century Mexico City as a foreign place: "This is not a Mexican city. It was built by foreigners and is now run by foreigners."[55] As American and European capital came to the city, investors made major changes as well, transforming the urban environment. Both San Antonio and Mexico City were hybrid, multiethnic places, experiencing modernizing transformations at the same time. Mexico City was much larger than San Antonio and the center of an emerging national culture, rather than a small western outpost of the United States. It was, however, significantly less industrialized than cities of the same size in the United States. Thus, while Mexico City's transformation was on a much larger scale, the elites of both cities were eager to distance themselves from a far too recent rural past.

One of Mexico City's elite's first goals was to bring greater order to the city's festivities. Municipal police and fire departments expanded, and many of the social traditions of previous decades were pushed to the margins of the city's central districts. Mexico's "flowery war" was part of this process. Held on the Paseo de la Reforma, the main avenue for social promenading, the aristocratic class had similar passing carriages, hurling bouquets and caval-cades.[56] They also staged bicycle parades along the Paseo during the carnival season. These events displaced other celebrations to the streets of working-class neighborhoods. European culture, particularly French culture, appealed to both the San Antonio and Mexican elites. Ironically, in order to promote a more unified national culture, Mexico City's elites looked to Europe, as did San Antonians. Like other urban elites in the late nineteenth century, Mexico City's upper class shopped for Swiss watches and dined at Parisian cafés. They looked to Europe to rescue Mexico from its "backward" past.[57]

At the same time, both San Antonians and Mexico City elites pushed "native" cultural performances to the city margins. While San Antonio elites staged its Battle of Flowers Parade, its Mexicano community held separate festivals at the edge of the city. The center of these events became San Pedro Creek, the eastern edge of what had become known as the Mexican quarter. Arnoldo De León writes that the *fiestas patrias de diez y seis* had assembled on Military Plaza before 1890; after that, they began further west at Washington or Paschal square.[58] Military Plaza remained an important social space for the Mexicano community, but the new city hall, which occupied most of the plaza, made this a difficult festive gathering place. Anglos considered other events such as the fandangos (dances) that occupied the plazas throughout the century too rowdy for public space by the 1880s.[59] The fiestas patrias, considered the most refined of Mexican festivities, were tolerated, but over-all, public space in the city was more closely policed and monitored.

In such processes it was difficult to draw the boundaries between what was "Anglo" and what was "Mexican," as processes of modernization displaced many traditional cultural practices and communities on both sides of the border. What is clear in terms of the Battle of Flowers Parade, though, is how it became different from previous civic parades in San Antonio. On other days and during other events, the city's downtown streets would be filled with carriages and parade bands. Throughout the nineteenth century, San Antonio's many ethnic and social groups staged their own events through the center of the city. The city's German citizens held *Volksfests*, known for their elaborate floats. Local Mexicanos hosted a parade for diez y seis, the commemoration of the first call for Mexico's independence from Spain on September 16, 1810. African Americans celebrated their freedom during Juneteenth parades, and city leaders organized Fourth of July parades.

In many ways, the Battle of Flowers was similar to these other events, drawing large, diverse crowds. Unlike the other parades, however, the Battle of Flowers was intended to represent the history of the city itself. Like many civic boosters of their time, the Battle of Flowers Parade organizers were redefining the purposes of public processions. Diez y seis, Juneteenth, and the Volksfests represented important anniversaries for San Antonio's multiple ethnic communities; the Battle of Flowers Parade, unlike these community parades, played a crucial role in displaying the city to itself, articulating a vision of its future within a narrative of its past.

Like other urban parades of the time, this was advertised as a public event for the entire community, not just a particular social group.[60] Pictures and descriptions of these early parades demonstrate that those who rode in carriages were members of the San Antonio Club, city leaders, and military commanders, led by African American coachmen. Newspaper reports also indicate that at least one hundred carriages and floats participated, so apparently residents of more moderate means also took part in the procession. Newspapers also mention an ethnically and racially diverse procession. Mexicano *mutualistas* (benevolent associations) rode in the parade, as well as African American volunteer firemen. Perhaps the most surprising possibility is that African Americans rode as independent participants.[61] In their efforts to promote civic unity, San Antonio's elite included a diverse public in their first parade.

By the end of the nineteenth century, these trends could be seen across the country. American urban parades featured more symbolic representations of local history and the city, rather than the histories of particular ethnic groups. These parades were public rituals of common citizenship, including new flags, banners, and seals. The icons were intended to promote the city to an outside national public while encouraging civic loyalty among city residents.[62] For the Battle of Flowers organizers, this celebration of Texan independence would also become the foundation for celebrating the city itself. These early parades would feature San Jacinto veterans, but they would also highlight other aspects of the city's history. No other group would so deliberately fuse the city's public memory with the memory of Texan independence. San Antonio history, in their representations, would be conflated with the Texans' fight.

The turn-of-the-century Battle of Flowers parades had quickly become the foundation for Fiesta San Antonio, and these early years articulated the key social struggles in a modernizing city. The Battle of Flowers parades would represent the city, though not always in the ways organizers planned. Like other urban parades of the time, the Battle of Flowers was an intersection—an event in the economic and cultural center of the city. The parade celebrated more than Texas history. It was a space for commodities to be sold, residents and travelers to encounter each other—a place of economic and cultural exchange. In the central market space of the city, spectators and parade participants gathered in multiple, unpredictable negotiations. Surrounding the procession, street peddlers and entertainers went through the crowd; small businessmen set up stands. Parade time and space provided a site of new forms of exchange among various communities.

The parade occurred at a historical moment when large city fairs and parades flourished in hundreds of urban centers. As Stallybrass and White note, these events transformed the relationship between local and national markets.[63] Bringing eastern tourists to what was still considered a frontier town, the Battle of Flowers Parade tied the city's local economy to the nation. The parade also communicated new meanings to San Antonio residents themselves.

Glassberg synthesizes the purposes of these new spectacles. Downtown businessmen wanted to attract tourists; politicians wanted a larger venue to associate themselves with a growing commercial culture, and the elite wanted a new forum for presenting their ideas to the public. Parade organizers designed these celebrations to present a unified portrait of the city, yet the bringing together of diverse communities created fears as well. Elite patrons (with some cause) talked about the possibility of rioting crowds and the loss of civic control.[64] The Battle of Flowers Parade offered new possibilities for communicating to a large urban public and new anxieties about how this public might impact civic order. While parades are designed as highly ordered events, they are much more unstable than their organizers often wish. The Battle of Flowers Parade was no different. The parade occupied multiple intersections; mock battles participated in the real battles as the city's many communities struggled through the transition to modernity.

The women who invented the Battle of Flowers Parade claimed public space as well. Like many elite women of their time, turn-of-the-century San Antonio women shaped public space through the language of cultural custodianship. At a time when the ideology of separate spheres continued to define political and civic activities as part of men's public sphere, women created ways to assume a limited public role by carrying their custodial duties to the world outside the home. Women crafted their own conceptions of citizenship and constructed "a public space located between the private sphere of the home and public life of formal institutions of government."[65] They used the parade to place themselves in the center of the city's public life.

Women's History

In the days before the 1896 Battle of Flowers Parade, the *San Antonio Daily Express* noted that

> it is a tribute of noble womanhood to heroic manhood; for the women are its promoters, the custodians of custom. They do the work; they are the generals, the majors and the captains of the battle, and the men are only privates under orders. . . . The weapons are those tender flowers, . . . poems of peace and nature's lesson of fraternity to man.[66]

The local press made a play on the social inversions of this parade, as women took on the masculine roles of warriors and flowers became weapons. Indeed, it became clear from the first year that the Battle of Flowers Parade was a women's event. In the years after the initial parade, the Battle of Flowers Association became an exclusively women's organization and would maintain control over the parade. For years, this distinguished the parade from similar processions across the country. Although many cities were articulating community identities at this time, few had parades run exclusively by women.

When Helen Von Phul wrote a history of the association, she noted the unusual reaction of San Antonio Club members to women's presence at their first meeting.

The ladies met at the home of Colonel Andrews, San Antonio Club president. He then presented their idea to Club members . . . the startled gentlemen, who had not up to this time had a woman at one of their meetings, listened with attentive interest to Col Andrews . . . tell what the ladies had in mind.[67]

The physical presence of women in the men's club represented a larger intrusion of women into the city's public affairs. Although negotiated through and financed by their husbands, these women defined a distinct public space for themselves, one centered on the moral purpose of public events. The local press, in a rather patronizing tone, recognized the women's role in this first parade by stating that

the gentlemen of course are going to do all the heavy work such as employing the bands, having stands erected on the plaza and other such things as the feminine mind fails to compass, but it remains for the ladies to make it a success or a failure in the way of a parade.[68]

FIGURE 2. "Save the Alamo" float in the Battle of
Flowers Parade, 1904. UTSA's Institute of Texan Cultures
at San Antonio, Courtesy of Virginia Essington.

Of course, when they proposed a flower battle and procession to commemorate the Texan victory at San Jacinto, they were also entering what many considered a distinctly male domain—the site of the Alamo. Women entered this space of male martyrdom through cultural custodianship. In the same year that the Battle of Flowers Association staged its first parade, elite San Antonio women also organized the Daughters of the Republic of Texas (DRT), dedicated to the preservation of historic sites and the memory of men and women responsible for the independence of Texas. Modeled after the Daughters of the American Revolution, the DRT was a patriotic organization of elite women (many of whom were also part of the Battle of Flowers Parade) who used heritage to claim power in the city. Women temporarily occupied this space through a gendered discourse of mourning for the male martyrs. As San Jacinto veteran Captain McMasters commented the following year, women never forgot those who sacrificed for their country. Men, consumed with the business of daily commerce, did not take time to honor the dead.[69] Mourning was a discourse of Victorian womanhood, so women took on the duty of memory, using another popular symbol of their "delicate" sensibility, flowers. Women commemorated the male martyrdom of the Alamo battle with a battle of flowers. San Antonio's elite women were employing the familiar terms of the private feminine sphere to enter the public realm. As "custodians of culture," the wives of San Antonio Club members sought to redefine their social position.

In order to find this place, they focused on Texas history and how it should be remembered. Like other white southern women during this period, they were "expanding the conception of voluntarism to include matters of history," and in the process, "a generation of white women acquired expertise in and influence through public history."[70] Limited in their abilities to directly shape the political economy of the New South, white women looked to history and used this cultural authority as an instrument of power.[71] The Battle of Flowers Parade became a vital part of the city's tourist industry, and the pageantry of Texas history played an important role in how its residents imagined the region's past and its future.

These women also made direct efforts to preserve the monuments of Texas history. The local chapter of the DRT in San Antonio quickly began making attempts to purchase the Alamo buildings. Although the city of San Antonio purchased the Alamo chapel in 1883, the Hugo Schmeltzer Company owned the convento structure. Up until this period, the Alamo housed several commercial establishments. After more than twenty years of fund-raising, the DRT purchased all the Alamo buildings in 1905.[72]

Even before the Alamo purchase, though, women helped reconfigure its plaza. In 1889, the city council allocated funds to pave the plaza and plant a garden in the center, surrounded by sixty-foot-wide streets.[73] From an open, social space, the plaza was restructured and "beautified" into a network of paths and greenery. After the flower parades, the local press noted the spectacle of the plaza, covered in flowers. The image of a site, once known for death in heroic martyrdom through battle, was now domesticated through the hundreds of flower bouquets on the plaza grounds. This process was similar to the national transformation of graveyards from spaces of simple, somber headstones into elaborately decorated parks, filled with statues and monuments, portraits of the dead and graveside flowers, and statues of weeping women. From the mid-nineteenth century onward, women domesticated death.[74] Cemeteries had also become "places of resort, suited for holiday excursion."[75] They became sites of leisure activity. Like a cemetery, the Alamo, covered in flowers, became a place for women's mourning and commemoration, as well as a place of modern leisure.

The limits of the Battle of Flowers Association's strategy became clear quite early, however. The women were putting together the parade, but gendered divisions occurred within the parade organization itself. While women created the theme and purpose of the parade, the "men formed a committee . . . to arrange financial matters and assist with the program."[76] This became a familiar pattern for subsequent parades. Women would concentrate on the educational and patriotic purposes of the parade, and men would attend to the practical matters. This division of labor had severe consequences for the Battle of Flowers Association in later years.

While San Antonio's elite women crafted roles to extend their personal power, they were hardly acts of direct transgression. Ann Douglas writes of women's intent on claiming culture as a form of "compensatory control" by which they could cross gendered divisions of power. Yet this strategy was doomed to failure. Douglas describes this phenomenon as "sentimentalism," defined as a specific type of protest against social transformation. Sentimentalism is an expression of "dragging one's heels," a practice that ambivalently rejects modernity. As Douglas writes, women "agreed to put on a convincing show, and to lose."[77] Women had reason to become ambivalent about the consequences of these rapid social transformations. Their domestic lives often isolated them from the bustling commercial life of downtown San Antonio, but their form of protest limited its effectiveness.

Over the years, as the Battle of Flowers Parade expanded to several days of events, the women also lost some control over the annual festival. One of the clearest early expressions of this ambivalence is about the changes surrounding the parade itself. As the parade became larger each year, some women sensed that the parade was losing its purpose. Friction between the Battle of Flowers members and the Businessmen's Club, who sponsored commercial ventures surrounding the parade, occurred over how to define the events.[78] As the yearly parade increased in popularity, several other festivities were added to the week's calendar. By 1904 the parade was surrounded by six days of carnival and other trades' parades. In 1906 the events were named the Spring Carnival. Many women, though, felt that the festival was losing its commemorative emphasis.

Battle of Flowers member Helen Von Phul vaguely hinted at these tensions within the organization with the note that "in some years the social feature was overshadowed by the commercial."[79] During this same period, men often assumed the presidency. In 1909, however, the association was reorganized as an exclusively female group. McGimsey diplomatically writes that

> with the beginning of the twentieth century, due to increasing population, greater business possibilities, and larger military establishments, the enlarging celebration filled the entire week. The necessity for coordination and financing became more apparent, and the ladies relinquished this task to the men, who had always shown a willingness to share these endeavors. By now there was a reason to divide the business and social features of the week.[80]

Businessmen began to take a larger role in the festival, and the Battle of Flowers ladies confined themselves to the social and patriotic aspects of the parade.

To reconcile the conflict between the patriotic and the commercial, roles were more firmly delineated along gendered lines. Men formed a separate association, the Spring Carnival Association, and the Battle of Flowers Association became more devoted to the commemorative purposes of the parade. This division was also apparent in the different parades themselves. By 1899, the Battle of Flowers was "the ladies parade" while the businessmen controlled the other parades. The program indicates this, stating that

> the first day's celebration will be in charge of the ladies and will be as heretofore—a parade of decorated bicycles, carriages, etc., to conclude with grand battle of roses . . . The second day will be under the direction of the Business Men's Club and will consist of

a grand military parade and review in the morning, a comic parade in the afternoon.

The Battle of Flowers became a spectacle devoted to sentiment and beauty, while the men's parades had military, commercial, and comical elements. The businessmen absorbed all the purposes that the ladies increasingly excluded and focused more on entertainment and developing commerce.

Using the discourse of patriotism was a way to maintain some power over what had become the city's largest event, yet this had its limitations as well. The Battle of Flowers Association women did not openly express any objections to the commercial aspects of the festival; instead, they isolated themselves. In this way, the parade that was initially a strategy for entering public life was increasingly marginalized within the festival. The gendered spheres reproduced themselves in the festival itself, and what had become the "woman's parade" was separated from the commercial life of the city.

During the next decade the imperial nostalgia of the Battle of Flowers Parade only increased, and Anglo organizers described themselves as heirs to a long line of ancestors, rather than relative newcomers to the region. At a moment when the urban environment was transforming into an American city, Anglo leaders claimed a certain legitimacy from connecting their own practices to those groups they had pushed out. An 1899 newspaper description of the parade creates a new history for the events.

The story is recorded in Old Spanish documents that when the Franciscan monks carried the cross into the wilds of Texas and founded the missions in the valley of the San Antonio river they found several tribes of Indians among whom there obtained an annual pagan celebration falling approximately about the same time as holy week. The celebration was a barbarous sacrificial festival . . . The monks, taking advantage of the coincidence in time in the pagan and the great Christian celebration became prominently identified with the Indian event. Their kind treatment of the wild tribes gave them an influence which enabled them gradually to eliminate from the festivals the brutal inflictions on man and beast and at the same time infuse into the events a crude but effective form of Christian worship. And through the flowers that grew wild on the prairie . . . the monks wrought this refinement . . . in wild floral processions . . . celebrating rough conquests . . . The long cycle of near two centuries now changed not only the man and his customs, but the land itself. The open prairie is studded with farms . . . and on the banks of the river stands a thriving city . . . there weaved yesterday another pageant of garlands and wreathes . . . the story of mankind's advancement from darkness into light . . . there are other festivals for commercial gain in the far west and in this state, commemorating no event, but San Antonio's stands out in striking contrast—women's splendid tribute to patriotism.[81]

Despite its history of battles and conquest, Fiesta was here described as a kind process by which Franciscan friars gradually influenced their Indian captives, just as women were said to refine the coarser instincts of men. This narrative connects and unifies San Antonio's long history of migrations and human conflicts as a tale of domestication. As the Spanish missionaries appropriated "savage" floral battles for their own purposes, so the Battle of Flowers Association attempted to reformulate and improve the rowdier elements of the crowd, to present an orderly procession and naturalize the history of conquest as a triumph of civilization. The passage ends with a vision of the "thriving city" itself. Like the religious who refined the wild prairie flowers into elaborate garlands and wreaths, these women hoped to weave together San Antonio's diverse communities with their appeals to patriotism. In order to assume this role, however, they had to make many sacrifices as well and may have lost control of the festival they began.

The city, like the nation, was emerging into a new era. On April 21, 1898, the same day the United States declared war on Spain, the Battle of Flowers Parade was held. Local papers made much of this coincidence. "It was a striking comparison, the two events celebrated on the same day—almost the same hour—the declaration of war and the celebration of liberty."[82] The coincidence is compelling for a number of reasons, for at this moment the discourses of war and peace, region and empire, progress and nostalgia, and public and private, merged. The army marched through the city's streets, pausing in front of the Western Union on Commerce Street for the Zouaves to wire their enlistment to President McKinley. The Excelsior Guards, the "colored" militia organization, drilled on the plaza. The bicycle club featured Uncle Sam lassoing Spanish General Sagasta and Governor Blanco announcing, "This is what we will do." Another was a palanquin carried by "two Mexicans dressed as Orientals" bearing Mr. Hilmer Guenther's children. In the same parade, a float featured a wax doll clothed in white as an emblem of peace.[83]

This procession had several of the same contradictions as the initial parade in 1891, except the "Mexicans dressed as Orientals" hinted at a mixing of the discourses of Manifest Destiny and American imperialism. Teddy Roosevelt, as he fought the Spanish-American War with his Rough Riders, named for the troupe of Buffalo Bill Cody's Wild West Show, made much of this link between the conquering of the west and the conquering of new territories. This new war was less about liberty than about expanding American power on the continent. After the war, the United States would, for the first time, hold territories whose residents would not be entitled to voting rights and several other American liberties. The "Orientals" of the Philippines would not be treated so differently from "the Mexicans" of south Texas. Like the first Battle of Flowers Parade, this parade marked the edges of a new sociopolitical order.

Both Mexicanos and elite women in the parades were the principal objects of the tourist gaze; both presented their "charms" to the booming city. The ladies paraded themselves in decorated carriages, while Mexicano vendors displayed their crafts on the plaza margins. They became spectacles for the diverse public, even as their private worlds were moved to the margins—for white women, in suburban homes, and for Mexicanos, in their west-side quarter. Before I make too much of these parallels, though, one must take into account that there were considerable differences as well. Women themselves often accomplished the changes that occurred in the Battle of Flowers parades, and the consequences of such spectacles would be very different for each group.

In 1899, the Battle of Flowers Parade found "the country virtually at peace with the world and the possessor of almost twice as much land as she claimed one year ago." At the same time, "the substitution of flowers as an emblem of peace, love and beauty is appropriate at this day—the burial of all animosities—the rejoicing over the era of good will that exists between the two great republics." Such burials would be short-lived, as the contradictions of these early parades manifested themselves more clearly in later decades. These early flower parades celebrated San Antonio's transition to modernity. The commemoration of a previous war with Mexico also took on the meanings of this new war with Spain. These Battle of Flowers parades were symbolic spaces to perform the intersections of local, regional, national, and transnational battles. A parade intended to unify the city also displayed its deepest social divisions.

· 2 ·

The Order of the Alamo

Heritage and Spring Carnival, 1900–27

IN ORDER TO UNDERSTAND HOW MUCH FIESTA HAS CHANGED IN MORE than one hundred years, one must look at a few events that have changed very little. Here is one contemporary example. Ann Elizabeth of the House of Fisher, Duchess of Imperial Jewels in the Court of African Treasures, enters San Antonio's municipal auditorium for Fiesta's 2002 coronation. As the lord high chamberlain announces her name, she begins her slow walk on the elevated runway to the main stage. She has the audience's full attention as she carefully moves forward, carrying the weight of a thirty-pound train, covered with beads and glass stones, and extending twelve feet behind her. Her arms are slightly raised at her waist, and her head moves from side to side, acknowledging the crowd. As she reaches the stage, she is met by her escort, who waits as she crosses the stage twice and pauses for her formal court bow. Modeled after the English curtsy to the British monarch, she points her right foot, then moves it in a semicircle to the back; she lowers her straight torso and bends her legs until she is sitting on them. Finally, she attempts the most difficult part of her task, a feat called the "Texas dip." As she bends forward from the waist, she lowers her head as close to the floor as possible. She momentarily loses her balance, though, and performs a more abbreviated curtsy to avoid falling sideways on the stage. Though no one calls attention to this slight mistake, Duchess Ann is clearly upset as she moves up the stairs to join the

FIGURE 3. A duchess processing in the Order of the Alamo's coronation, 1988. UTSA's Institute of Texan Cultures at San Antonio, the Zintgraff Collection.

rest of the court. Sitting on her pedestal and arranging her train, she briefly wipes tears from her eyes.

Duchess Ann is following the footsteps of her mother, grandmother, and great-grandmother before her. She is carrying her family heritage on her back.[1] Each year, as part of the city's Fiesta celebrations, the Order of the Alamo, a private men's organization, selects young women from local elite families to participate in this coronation. As duchesses, princesses, and queens of Fiesta, coronation debutantes wear elaborate gowns, attend multiple parties, and learn and perform these rituals to maintain the social position of their families in San Antonio's upper class.

Duchess Ann's severe self-critique represents the larger pressures put upon San Antonio's upper-class women. She felt that she had much to lose, as she followed a practice that has remained relatively unchanged since the coronation began in 1909. Yet if she could retrace her steps to the years before these rituals became traditions, she would find a time when much more was at stake. Two decades after Mrs. H. D. Kampmann chaired the first Battle of

FIGURE 4. Duchesses of the Order of the Alamo riding in the Battle of Flowers Parade, 1990. UTSA's Institute of Texan Cultures at San Antonio, The Zintgraff Collection.

Flowers Parade in 1891, her daughter, Miss Eda, became the first queen of the Order of the Alamo's coronation. The middle-aged women in the Battle of Flowers Parade, challenging the limits of the domestic sphere, were a symbol of the first ten years of Fiesta. Their debutante daughters, sheltered in private ballrooms, were more appropriate symbols for the Fiesta of the next twenty years. As a battle was the metaphor for the initial Fiesta parades, the Order of the Alamo was the one of this new era. The enshrined fortress became the most prominent emblem of a solidifying social order.

Patriotism and Commercial Culture

After the success of San Antonio's first Battle of Flowers Parade, elite women tried to maintain their control over the festive events that quickly grew around their famous procession. As early as 1895 the first challenge came as the city's business leaders formed an organization called the San Antonio Businessmen's Club, precursor to the Chamber of Commerce, organized to pursue investments and increase tourism in San Antonio. By the end of their first month, the club had more than four hundred members.[2] That year, they convinced the Battle of Flowers Association (BFA) to move their parade to June in order to coincide with the Traveler's Protective Association's meeting, the largest convention in the city to date. In return, the Businessmen's Club offered five hundred dollars to help stage the parade. The women agreed, with the provision that the parade would return to its April 21 date the following year.

They were not, however, as satisfied with the character of this particular parade, which honored no patriotic event and included too many commercial floats.[3] Battle of Flowers members suggested that the festival had been overtaken by commercial interests and had lost its patriotic purpose of honoring the Battle of San Jacinto.[4] The following year, they decided to assume tighter control over their event. Mrs. Elizabeth Ogden became the new president, and the women accepted only one male advisor, a local minister named Dr. G. Q. A. Rose, who served as a financial advisor. Unlike the businessmen, he did not participate in parade planning, and other male volunteers were only marshals, policemen, and the fire department.[5] Mrs. Ogden herself had long ties to the Alamo. At seventy years old, she had heard the stories of Alamo survivor Susanna Dickinson firsthand at Washington on the Brazos, the site where the Texans met to write their declaration of independence.[6] With her Texas lineage and her long involvement in charity work, Mrs. Ogden was an ideal representative of the Battle of Flowers Association. Under her leadership, their parade returned to its earlier content and patriotic purposes. The Daughters of the Republic of Texas also played an increasing role in the parade, presenting several floats and decorating the Alamo.

The men would not leave the ladies alone for long. In 1898, after witnessing the success of a similar flower parade in Waco that attracted more visitors than San Antonio's parade, the Businessmen's Club proposed to extend the parade to a two-day festival.[7] They lobbied the BFA for several weeks but were unsuccessful. Instead, other women's organizations, like the San Antonio Library and Women's Exchange, held a "paper carnival" and ball. The Daughters of the Republic of Texas sponsored a cotton ball as well. In 1899, members of the Businessmen's Club repeated their suggestion, proposing an elaborate fund-raising enterprise to finance a new festival, a Spring Carnival. They wanted to extend the parade route, invite Gov. Joseph D. Sayers, and stage their own parade the day after the Battle of Flowers.[8] Mrs. Ogden and other organizers insisted on an autonomous flower parade but allowed the businessmen to stage their own events the following day. In 1900, the businessmen decided to expand their activities even further, expanding the Spring Carnival to six days of events, with the Battle of Flowers Parade as the festival climax. Mrs. Ogden decided to surrender. She resigned as president in March. No other woman would take charge of the parade, so the Battle of Flowers was not held in 1900.[9] The men took over the festival.

The BFA reorganized to stage another flower parade in 1901, but it would no longer have the same ability to define the festival. Instead, gendered spheres of power developed within the new Spring Carnival. The flower parade stayed in the hands of its women founders; the businessmen controlled everything else. In 1905, the San Antonio Businessmen's Club formed a separate organization to stage the growing festival, the Spring Carnival Association. Four years later, the Battle of Flowers Association officially became an exclusively women's organization.[10] The boundaries solidified between men's and women's roles. The Battle of Flowers Association did not disappear, but its responsibilities narrowed. As the week's events grew beyond the initial parade, women's work for the festival as a whole decreased. Portraits of Frank Bushick and other prominent members of the Spring Carnival Association made the front pages of the local press, while the women of the BFA moved to the society pages.

San Antonio's elite women did not give up their struggle to keep patriotism at the center of this growing festival, however. In 1912, they convinced the Spring Carnival Association to change their name to the Fiesta San Jacinto Association. They hoped that replacing the carnival with a reference to the Texan battle would remind the public of the festival's purpose. Their successful efforts also hinted at a growing division among the businessmen themselves over the character of the week's events. Some men, like attorney William H. Aubrey, organized the first Spring Carnivals to draw as many visitors and residents as possible. To do this, they borrowed elements from many other national festivals, including the Midway of Chicago's 1893 Columbian Exposition and New Orleans's Mardi Gras. They envisioned a festival that was "part San Antonio International Fair, part honky-tonk carnival, part extended convention, and part Mardi Gras pageant and social event."[11] With this eclectic set of events, the Spring Carnival Association hoped to make San Antonio into one of the centers of a growing national commercial culture.

Like the BFA women, though, some men began to feel that the carnival needed a greater emphasis on genteel pageantry. The most prominent man to express these concerns was John Carrington. As a member of the Chamber of Commerce, Carrington worked with the Spring Carnival Association to promote the week's events, but he felt that a sense of gentility was missing from the carnival. In order to foster this sensibility, Carrington, along with friends Franz Groos and J. H. Frost, founded the Order of the Alamo in 1909.[12] Though this organization was composed of the city's economic elite, it defined itself as "a distinctly social organization in which no commercial interest of any sort would be felt."[13] Like the women of the Battle of Flowers Association, these elite Anglo men wished to create a separate social sphere within the city's public culture to oppose the growing commercial culture and emphasize an elite form of patriotic pageantry. Despite their stated intentions, this organization did further their economic interests, using their club to enhance their social status. Although these men emphasized heritage, they did not have the same goals as elite women's organizations of the time. While the BFA transgressed the boundaries of domesticity through their historic pageantry, the Order of the Alamo tried to reinforce the divisions between gendered spheres.

Queens and Cavaliers

The main goal of Carrington's Order of the Alamo was to select a queen for the festival, though they were not the first organization to have this responsibility. Before the Order of the Alamo, the Battle of Flowers Association selected parade queens. One of the most well known was Clara Driscoll, who was crowned Queen of the Carnival from 1904 through 1906. Staying true to their patriotic mission, the BFA chose her for her role in "saving" the Alamo from demolition. Driscoll donated the funds needed to purchase the Alamo building for the Daughters of the Republic of Texas. Her activities exemplify elite white women's voluntary activity of the period. Her selection as carnival queen further elevated her status as Alamo savior.

When the Order of the Alamo took over the responsibility in 1909, their new reigning queen represented the end of the Battle of Flowers Association's role in this process. The order formalized the queen's selection, creating rules and voting processes. The Order of the Alamo also isolated this royal role from the public space the BFA had created. The BFA queens were prominent society women who often, like Driscoll, demonstrated their dedication to public service and patriotism. The Order of the Alamo queens did not necessarily have this history of voluntarism. As young debutantes, they were just entering adult society, and their primary purpose was to elevate the social status of their families, not advertise their individual service. While the BFA queens were presented in the public Alamo Plaza, these new queens were revealed in Beethoven Hall to a more limited audience.

As part of a festival honoring U.S. patriotism and Texan independence, it may seem ironic that festival organizers would select queens for their annual commemoration. San Antonio's practice of crowning temporary queens was a ritual that licensed behavior outside of egalitarian norms and a reference to medieval carnival practices. As in other such rituals, these queens had no political or official power.[14] Instead, as was common in the pageantry movement at the turn of the century, they represented a romantic departure from everyday social order, promising to banish sadness and bring happiness to their kingdoms during carnival week.[15]

Yet they also reflected a solidifying social order in San Antonio. The Order of the Alamo selected young women of the city's most prominent families for the queen's court, and their presentation in the coronation was part of the long series of balls and receptions that introduced these women to San Antonio elite society. The Order of the Alamo was part of a continuing (and growing) tradition in American debutante culture. In cites ranging from Philadelphia to Charleston, elite gentlemen of the community selected the young debutantes who would become part of their social circle. Staging balls and cotillions, these men would become the gatekeepers for local elite culture.[16]

In the late nineteenth and early twentieth century, debutante rituals became more expensive and elaborate. The carnival queens of New Orleans's Mardi Gras became the most well-known national symbols of these new rituals. Appearing in publications across the country, New Orleans's carnival queens attracted the attention of many civic boosters, who sought to emulate their rituals.[17] By the late nineteenth century, New Orleans's Mardi Gras parades were becoming well-known spectacles, attracting up to a hundred thousand tourists in 1900.[18] Organized by krewes, male carnival societies, these parades became models for other civic pageantry. These krewes staged elaborate coming-out parties for their debutante daughters, passing out jeweled favors and making themselves local and national celebrities.[19]

The Order of the Alamo, like the BFA, used their heritage to "serve the public." Though their efforts were made in the name of public interest, like much of the historical pageantry movement of the time, they maintained a very narrow view of history, one that gave a sense of legitimacy to their private organizations but was relatively inaccessible to those outside their social circle. The pageantry movement presented a version of the past that emphasized consensus rather than social change and conflict.[20] They presented a simplified, narrow view of history in the name of, but not controlled by, the larger public.

Abner Cohen was one of the first anthropologists to describe the ways that elites construct distinct cultural rituals, developing a set of beliefs and practices to differentiate themselves from the rest of society. San Antonio's coronation, like so many other elite rituals, was designed as a performative language meant to distinguish elite culture. At the same time, though, the elite must convince the public that their social rituals serve a larger social goal. Often elites do this through dramatic performance, "by claiming to possess rare and exclusive qualities essential to society at large." These qualities are often communicated through vague, mysterious symbols and rituals in order to create a sense of "mystique of excellence."[21] The coronation had all these traits. By creating elaborately themed pageants each year, San Antonio's elite could create a distinct set of rituals to define themselves in the name of the public good.

The Order of the Alamo was not unique in this sense; the coronation was one among many similar pageants across the United States created for a distinct American historical moment. In the context of urbanization, increased immigration, and improved communications technologies, residents of the same locale were less likely to share the same cultural background and experiences. In response, many civic officials sought to redefine community identity and social cohesion.[22] These officials used the past as a source of traditions that could "offer emotional respite from the consequences of modern progress."[23] Thus, many local pageants merged Progressive concerns of urban reform with antimodernist nostalgia. For members of patriotic and hereditary societies, this pageantry was a way to reinforce their own social position as well. They sought to educate the public with their notions of "civic identity, social order, and the moral principles they associated with the past—to preserve Anglo-American supremacy in public life."[24] The Order of the Alamo's coronation, with its elaborate ceremonies and royal robes, was a marker of Pierre Bourdieu's concept of "social distinction," practices that legitimate social differences.[25] This type of distinction was particularly popular in the late nineteenth and early twentieth centuries.

In all these pageants, a veiled elite organized their events in private, secretive rituals. The Order of the Alamo was no different. The queen's identity was kept from the public until the coronation itself, and members voted for their choice of queen through secret ballot. Beginning in 1921, order meetings were held within the Alamo chapel, including the selection of the queen. Thus the queen was symbolically "born" within the Alamo walls.[26] She was selected from the oldest family line, having the most female royal relatives and the father who was active in the order.[27] In such a way, the Alamo became symbolically intertwined with the maintenance and social reproduction of San Antonio's heritage elite.

In order to further integrate this elite practice with the festival's stated purpose, the Order of the Alamo maintained the teaching of Texas history as one of its primary goals. Yet one would be hard pressed to find other local history in coronation rituals. In fact, while John Carrington had some interest in Texas history, he was more engaged in recreating traditions from England.[28] Perhaps his interest in the English had to do with his family heritage or the fact that the pageant form itself derived from the arts and crafts movement in Britain.[29] Carrington's interest in English pageantry was part of a larger "American Renaissance" at the turn of the century, as artists, writers, and city planners used medieval and Renaissance traditions to enrich what they believed were "the thin artistic currents of the New World."[30] Though the Order of the Alamo, through its name and use of the building, connected itself to Texan independence, during the first decade of San Antonio's coronation, organizers had little interest in displaying Texas history. San Antonio's early coronation themes made almost no reference to regional events. Carrington's vision was indeed nostalgic, calling forth the codes of medieval England, but he expressed little interest in the local. The worlds created on early coronation stages were entirely magical and fanciful. The first Court of Flowers was followed by the Court of Roses and then the Court of Spring. These were themes of romance and make-believe.[31] The coronation placed women in flights of fantasy, into a world of timeless motifs.

Beginning in the 1920s, and increasingly after 1930, more historic themes emerged. These later courts of "Empire," "Imperial Russia," "Italian Renaissance," "Eternal India," and "Heraldic Britain" were often broad, mythicized empires, but they represented a larger shift toward history. Although this happened throughout the country, it had particular meaning in the South. Sectionalism merged with Old World nostalgia, as southerners asserted the South's distinct contributions to national culture.[32] In some parts of the South a romanticized portrayal of antebellum history and congenial race relations characterized their pageantry. This nostalgia had existed since the Civil War, when the defense of southern women became a focus for resisting racial equality.[33] Southern pageant organizers made renewed efforts to portray a proud Confederate past. Grace Elizabeth Hale demonstrates how white southerners constructed their identity in the midst of modernization. By "attaching identities to physical and geographical spaces and places" southerners made sense of an urbanized, industrialized modern world of strangers, and racial identity became the focal point for such organization. Such new constructions of whiteness converged with a growing consumer culture and its emphasis upon visual materials and the spectacle.[34]

Portraying this vision of the antebellum south was a bit more difficult to accomplish in Texas, though, particularly in San Antonio, with no local history of a planter elite to idealize (and distort). The Texans' experience demonstrated quite clearly that there were many southern histories. In order to reconcile a form of antebellum nostalgia with the local environment of San Antonio, pageant organizers took a different path. For the Texas Centennial in 1936, the pageant script for the Court of Adventure describes "alien peoples . . . imbued with the spirit of adventure and love of freedom have appeared from the east to claim the land . . . the hour of departure of the Indian has arrived." These "alien" white settlers, after struggling in the western wilderness, bring forth "a new race . . . whose character will be composed of the finer qualities and attributes of the peoples of their forefathers' countries."[35] Such a description of hardy white settlers should be familiar to any student of western history and the ideology of Manifest Destiny. Combined with such distinctly "English" rituals, though, this account takes a new meaning. Just as so many families of San Antonio's heritage elite moved westward from both the upper and deep southern states, so did this elite ritual of the first families of Virginia merge with a tale of western pioneers. Such descriptions also clearly defined coronation participants as worthy of their dominant position in San Antonio's contemporary society.[36] In a segregated social world, these southern transplants, in their sojourn to Texas, described themselves as an improved, robust white race.

While trying to contain threats from outside the elite social body, the coronation ritual also attempted to control the power of young women.[37] As the queen and her duchesses were introduced to San Antonio society, they became vessels for something outside themselves, bodily representatives of their family heritage, race, and class.[38] The walk to the coronation stage was a precise exercise in self-control and thus social control of the female body.[39] After a time when many elite white men were anxious about the rise of the "New Woman" who challenged Victorian norms, they created rituals to reinforce distinct gendered roles for these young debutantes.[40]

It is easy to find this emphasis on control of the female body in the coronation rituals: the careful walk, the precise bows and curtsies, the shining dresses and trains that overwhelm individual bodies. The spectacle of dozens of San Antonio's elite women, arranged on stage with their symbols of family heritage, became an important component of the coronation very early. In 1913, the *San Antonio Express* asked the bachelors of the Order of the Alamo for their requirements in Fiesta royalty. In this poll, the most important quality was "beauty," the next was their family's social status. As the article noted, "not one mentions brains."[41] Of course, the coronation was not entirely a beauty pageant; women did not compete against each other openly, and despite the newspaper poll, their positions were determined more by family heritage than personal beauty.

Beauty and heritage were closely intertwined terms in elite ritual, though, particularly in the American South. While the presentation of young debutante beauties was quite common throughout the country, this ritual had a distinct meaning for male southerners as well. The Order of the Alamo's coronation was a presentation of the ideals of southern beauty. As Elizabeth Boyd writes in her analysis of the creation of this mythical ideal, the southern beauty was a construct designed to protect the boundaries of white upper-class manhood.[42] Southern chivalry depended upon the myth of the southern beauty, who was defined as physically weak, submissive, and deferential to her husband. She was innocent and took no interest in intellectual pursuits or life outside the interior space of her home. Thus, she depended upon male protection.[43] The spectacle of these young debutantes dutifully carrying their trains certainly communicates a certain amount of submission and deference.

The myth of the southern beauty, however, obscures the perceptions that these women may have had about their own performances. These young women were also interested in more independent pursuits. Miss Eda Kampmann, the first Order of the Alamo queen who later married her "prince," Joseph Frost, not only favored woman suffrage but also became an active member of the Equal Franchise Society. She also reported her interest in outdoor sports. Like many of the other debutantes whose lives were reported in the local social directories, Miss Eda was part of a generation of women who were open advocates of women's legal equality. Of those socialites surveyed in 1917, 90 percent were in favor of suffrage.[44] Many of them also proudly reported their interest in travel and driving their own cars. While there is no record of their precise feelings about the coronation rituals, it should be safe to suggest that they saw themselves differently than the bachelors interviewed in the local newspaper. In fact, some may have enjoyed the coronation for the publicity and sense of personal power, not as a limitation.[45] What is certainly clear is that many coronation queens and duchesses would later become members of the Battle of Flowers Association. Although they entered Fiesta celebrations in different ways than the BFA founders, many found little contradiction between their roles as duchesses and later as parade organizers.

Defending the myth of the southern beauty, though, would continue to be important to the men of the Order of the Alamo, particularly to John Carrington himself. Seventeen years after founding the Order of the Alamo, he decided to form another organization. In 1926, he founded the Texas Cavaliers, another men's social club designed to elect the king of Fiesta. Carrington drew from the southern mythology of the cavalier—a country gentleman who has the characteristics of leadership, bravery in war, horsemanship, and chivalric loyalty to his mother and wife.[46] Since the early nineteenth century, southern writers cultivated the heroic qualities of the cavalier as the defining expression of genteel life in the South's planter society. After the Civil War, the cavalier became a symbol of the lost cause, a "figment of a utopian social world."[47] This nostalgia had a powerful effect upon Carrington as he sought to translate these ideals into his Texas landscape.

As he had done with the queen's coronation, Carrington wanted to create an organization that would reliably and systematically elect a king for the week's festivities. Before this, the Chamber of Commerce, the Spring Carnival Association, and then the Fiesta San Jacinto Association had selected the king, but this process was inconsistent and rather disorganized. The year after the cavaliers formed, they elected King Antonio to reign over Fiesta, and they have been in charge of the role to this day.[48] Carrington had even more ambitious goals for the cavaliers, including sponsoring the Pilgrimage to the Alamo, to facilitate social relations between the military and civilian populations, and "preserve the Texas tradition of horsemanship in this age of automobiles."[49] For the first few years, the cavaliers held a Tournament of Roses complete with jousts and knights in armor. Reviving a tradition popular in his native Virginia, Carrington created another form of southern chivalry.

Some of his goals did not survive. The tournament was discontinued after a few years. The cavaliers could never wrest the Alamo pilgrimage from the hands of the DRT, and horse riding never achieved the popularity Carrington had hoped. In fact, Carrington himself never rode a horse, though he loved the "horseman idea."[50] Many other cavaliers had difficulty with their horsemanship as well, abandoning their riding activities after their stables burned down. They were not fond of their uniforms either. After the first year most cavaliers refused to wear the tights and armor outside of the tournament itself and wore red military-style jackets and blue riding breeches instead. Carrington did not like to see the armor go and never wore the new uniform.[51]

Unlike Carrington, many of his fellow cavaliers were not interested in jousting. For them, it seems, Carrington took the nostalgia for medieval knighthood a bit too seriously. They were more interested in the other cavalier rituals, though. During their induction of new members, the cavaliers had exclusive use of the Alamo chapel. A few rare photographs capture the militaristic ceremony where initiates pass underneath the uplifted swords of current members. Cavaliers are symbolically born within the Alamo walls, and the Texas shrine once again represents their elevated status in the city's public culture.

So the most important function of the cavaliers did survive. This organization, like the Order of the Alamo, provided an exclusive space for San Antonio's Anglo elite men to fraternize and solidify the social bonds that would help maintain their dominance in the city's socioeconomic affairs. Outside the Alamo walls and the closed worlds of elite coronations, San Antonio's business leaders demonstrated the connections between the Order of the Alamo and the social order of the Texas Modern, and John Carrington would be right in the middle of it all.

Race, Space, and Flies

In the almost twenty years between 1891 and 1909, San Antonio transformed into a modern city. In the first decade of the twentieth century, San Antonio's building activity rose by 600 percent, street improvements rose 900 percent, and hotel and office facilities rose 500 percent. By the 1920s, San Antonio had become the state's leading city in population.[52] The city had a broad agricultural economy, a complex array of military facilities, and an extensive railroad system. This modernization transformed the city's downtown plazas into an Americanized central business district. San Antonio also became a center for unskilled and semiskilled labor.[53] The city needed this labor for its rapid growth, and Mexicanos, both native-born and immigrant, continued to built San Antonio and the Southwest.[54]

Like other southern cities, San Antonio also became increasingly stratified by race and class. As a city with great ethnic diversity, San Antonio continued to develop into many separate ethnic "towns," each with their distinct social realities.[55] Some communities were relatively integrated with the Anglo elite. In the early twentieth century, German American families lived around the King William neighborhood just southeast of the central business district. They were well represented in social clubs like the Texas Cavaliers and the Order of the Alamo. Legal and physical boundaries proliferated, however,

FIGURE 5. King Antonio reception before Fiesta, 1934, within the Alamo chapel. San Antonio Light Collection, UTSA's Institute of Texan Cultures at San Antonio, Courtesy of the Hearst Corporation.

THE ORDER OF THE ALAMO

between the central district and the west and east sides with their "nonwhite" populations; they were separate communities within the growing city.[56] Mexicanos lived predominantly in the "Latin Quarter" on the west side, and African Americans were restricted to the east side.

Communication between these distinct towns within the town was complex. In many ways the social lives of those on the east side and west side were separate from the life of the rest of the city. As the city grew, though, there were a number of spaces and opportunities for interactions across the lines of race and social class as well, particularly in the central business district. As the New South became more urban, rapidly growing cities like San Antonio became cities of strangers, cities of impersonal social relations and mass culture. Jim Crow laws were, in part, a backlash to these changes, an effort to assert racial boundaries and white supremacy in the context of modernization. [57] At the same time, the central business district, as the center for labor, commerce, consumption, and public spectacle, was a gathering space for everyone in the city. Regulating behavior in these places was more difficult than in residential neighborhoods.

In a larger American context, white racial order was connected to civic order. Order and efficiency became "the watchwords of progressive America."[58] Renewed concerns about everything from housing conditions to political corruption characterized a broad social movement at the beginning of the twentieth century. Part of this movement focused on improved sanitation and a national program of public health. Normalizing the social body also meant new regimens for personal hygiene.[59] By 1910, cleanliness was part of being a good American, and public health officers transformed urban spaces with this new emphasis.

In San Antonio, this preoccupation with personal hygiene took the form of a curiously intense hunt for flies. John Carrington himself, as secretary of the city's Chamber of Commerce, sponsored a fly-swatting contest to improve public health. On July 4, 1911, the *San Antonio Express* announced the results of their first annual contest. Among the top five boys who won, more than one million flies were killed. The contest was the largest of its kind in the nation. In an effort to clean the city, the newspaper reporters encouraged boys to kill as many flies as possible, as they were believed to carry many diseases, including typhoid, dysentery, and tuberculosis.[60] A few girls participated in the hunt as well; their results were counted but not considered in the contest. This was specifically a contest for young boys.

Looking back at John Carrington's childhood, his personal concern with hygiene is understandable. As a younger man, he was told he was threatened with tuberculosis. As a result, his family moved to central Texas, settling in the German town of Comfort, which was said to have a beneficial climate for respiratory problems. San Antonio was well known as a resort for consumptives, so great concern was given to the cleanliness of its hotels, railroad cars, and restaurants. After marrying a young woman from this town, Carrington moved to San Antonio and involved himself in real estate and other business enterprises.[61]

By the beginning of the twentieth century, though, treatment of those suffering from tuberculosis had changed dramatically with the acceptance of germ theory. Once pampered in the most luxurious resorts and spas, the "contagious consumptive" was now "a marked entity, politicized and racialized."[62] San Antonio, a city that welcomed consumptives in the finest downtown hotels in the 1890s, passed several laws banning tuberculosis facilities inside city limits in 1909.[63] Carrington, who had guarded his body from contamination when young, later created tests of manhood in cleaning urban space. The fly-swatting contest was part of training young men to police their environment, to guard it from contamination. Looking to Carrington's other role, as head of the Order of the Alamo and the Texas Cavaliers, one can also see his concern with guarding the social body of San Antonio's elite from the threats of a rapidly changing, growing city. As Carrington helped to clean the dirty city streets, he also maintained the pure, elite bodies of Fiesta monarchy.

As Mary Douglas observed, fear of dirt is often deeply connected to fears of social disorder.[64] Closely connected to this new concern with public cleanliness was the fear of new immigrants, "the unwashed."[65] Though germ theory had existed for almost twenty years, it did not gain wide acceptance in the United States until after 1900, during the same era as thousands of new immigrants entered the country.[66] Many "native" whites had long considered these new immigrants from eastern Europe as unclean and thus more susceptible to disease. While previous theories about preventing diseases like tuberculosis emphasized keeping a clean environment, however, the discovery of microscopic organisms escalated fears of contagion. Fears about germs merged with fears about immigrants. "Rapidly reproducing germs threatened American bodies in the same way that hordes of new immigrants threatened the national body." Germs were often portrayed as an invading force, and consumptives were increasingly stigmatized and racialized.[67]

In San Antonio, many Anglos' greatest fears were about the city's Mexicano population and the disorder that they might bring. From 1900 to 1930, the city's Mexicano population increased from 13,722 to 82,373 residents. Though many ethnic groups came to San Antonio in greater numbers, Mexicanos arrived at the highest rates. In 1900 Mexicanos made up 25.7 percent of the population; in 1930 they were 35.7 percent.[68] As the city's Mexicano population became a greater part of the city, negative stereotypes of their culture shifted. Nineteenth-century Anglo settlers emphasized the idea of Mexicanos as a conquered people, the losing side in the battle for Texan independence and U.S. annexation. These ideas did not disappear in the twentieth century. Yet newer ideas about Mexicano inferiority focused on the idea of dirtiness. Mexicanos were increasingly marginalized by the specter of contamination and were controlled and segregated to defend the Anglo social order.[69] The local press described these fears clearly.

If you go down there into those filthy hovels and see men and women and children, ragged, uncombed, unwashed, sitting about dirty tables . . . you might begin to realize that those people who live in such degradation might come in close touch with you. For how do you know that the big pecans in your nut cake . . . your salad or ice cream have not been handled by those same dirty fingers.[70]

"Dirtiness" became the rationale for segregating Mexicanos. A University of Texas bulletin issued in 1923 called for separate schooling on the basis of differences in cleanliness.[71] Other public spaces were segregated as well. Anglo south Texans defined both African Americans and Mexicanos as separate, inferior races whose movements in public spaces were controlled through spatial segregation.[72]

As the city was booming economically, segregation increased. Beginning in the late nineteenth century, light-rail lines improved transportation services and encouraged a boom in real-estate sales on the outskirts of the central business district. Anglo San Antonians moved to these developments north of downtown. These new subdivisions refused to sell to African Americans or Mexicanos. As Anglos moved north, African Americans occupied segregated ghettos on the east side.[73] By 1930, most Mexicanos lived on the west side. This "Latin Quarter" had become characterized by poverty, dilapidated housing, ill health, and few sanitary facilities.[74] While developers on the north side built parks and neighborhood centers, the west side had almost no city services or new construction. Most housing consisted of floorless shacks, crowded together without plumbing or electricity. With such living conditions, tuberculosis did become a severe problem for the Mexicano population, one of the major causes of death.[75]

While the city used Mexicano labor, many Anglos resented their presence and expressed this sentiment in continued neglect of west side development. Anglos also promoted strategies of separation and control. This segregation affected all modes of public life. The first segregated Mexican school was established in Texas in 1902; by 1930, 90 percent of the schools were segregated.[76] As Mexicanos entered the state in greater numbers, predominantly as agricultural labor, their relations with Anglos were increasingly marked by anonymity, and segregation functioned to organize and discipline these new Mexicano "strangers."

These boundaries had to be vigilantly guarded, though. In south Texas, the rapid increase of Mexicano immigration also led to calls for a closed border. In 1921, Rep. James Slayden, husband of the first Battle of Flowers Parade organizer Ellen Maury Slayden, argued that the new immigrants brought high social costs and embarrassment. Farmers and urban workers joined him in his call for repatriation of Mexicano laborers. In contrast to these restrictionists, growers and their business allies wanted an open border to continue the influx of cheap labor. Through the 1920s, national policy supported the growers. While national legislation in 1917, 1921, and 1924 severely limited immigration from Asia and certain parts of Europe, Mexico was excluded from these restrictions. In 1928, however, President Hoover sided with the restrictionists and closed the U.S.-Mexican Border by executive order. In 1929, politicians reached a compromise between the two factions that restrained the movement of Mexican laborers to state borders.[77] Through the first three decades of the twentieth century, these immigration debates reveal the contradiction Mexicano immigrants faced when they entered south Texas. Welcomed for their labor, they were reviled for their presence in the city's social life.

Revolution in Mexico

As these restrictionist debates demonstrated, the efforts to mark boundaries were always tenuous, and as Anglos tried to regulate Mexicano mobility within the city's public space, political borders were threatened as well. The war that Fiesta organizers did not officially honor was even more crucial to its performance of social order. Mexico was in the middle of a long revolution, and San Antonio would play a major role in the ensuing events. For several decades south Texas was a site for Mexican political refugees to organize for various new regimes, and the struggles for Mexican independence were closely intertwined with calls against Anglo discrimination north of the border. As early as 1891, Catarino Garza led a rebellion against the Porfirio

Díaz regime.[78] His revolt also became a protest against the oppression of Mexicanos in south Texas. Garza, a newspaperman who was active in mutualistas, mutual-benefit associations throughout the region, connected the struggles of Mexicanos against abuse and discrimination on both sides of the border. He managed to gather more than a thousand men and clashed with both the Mexican and U.S. armies for the next year. Eventually he escaped to Colombia, where he died three years later fighting in a Liberal army.[79] His rebellion quickly became a legend and would be joined by another figure, Gregorio Cortez. In 1901, a sheriff came to Cortez's farm in central Texas to arrest him for horse theft. In the ensuing conflict, the sheriff wounded Cortez's brother, and Cortez killed the sheriff. A long manhunt followed, but Cortez was eventually captured and sentenced to life in prison for the murder of a second sheriff during his flight. Cortez claimed his innocence in the original horse theft, and local Mexicanos managed to gather enough support to secure his pardon in 1913. After his release, Cortez briefly fought in the Mexican Revolution.[80] Though Garza's political rebellion and Cortez's individual defiance of gringo justice were different in many ways, both Garza and Cortez became folk heroes to Mexicanos throughout the region, and their struggles demonstrated the connections between Anglo oppression and the political corruption of the Díaz regime.

The border region continued as a site for political refugees to organize against Díaz. In 1904 Enrique and Ricardo Flores Magón, brothers from Oaxaca, fled to Laredo and soon made their way to San Antonio, where they resumed the anti-Porfirian newspaper *Regeneración*. Continually harassed, they moved to St. Louis, Missouri, and became part of U.S. anarchist circles and eventually relocated to Los Angeles, publishing the paper when possible.[81] By 1906, the paper had nearly twenty thousand paid subscriptions across both nations. The same year, the Flores Magóns founded the Partido Liberal Mexicano (PLM), which called for liberal reforms such as a single four-year presidential term, limited workdays, and an end to child labor. The brothers also made radical calls for redistribution of property in order to create a more egalitarian society in Mexico. At the same time, a column in their newspaper documented the experiences of Mexicanos living in the United States, the authors complaining bitterly of discrimination, racism, and exploitation.[82] Again, the popularity of *Regeneración* was the result not only of the ways it articulated an alternative political vision for Mexico but also for the ways it linked this vision to the daily struggles of Mexicanos living in south Texas.

In 1908, a hacendado from the Mexican state of Coahuila, Francisco Madero, began a presidential campaign against Porfirio Díaz. More moderate than the Flores Magóns, he nonetheless fervently criticized the corruption of the Porfiriato and called for free elections and an uncensored press, along with many other liberal reforms. The campaign itself was a failure, and Madero himself was jailed and charged with sedition the day of the election in 1910. He managed to escape and fled across the border to San Antonio, where he issued a manifesto declaring himself provisional president. He called on all Mexicans to revolt and stayed in San Antonio to set up his revolutionary headquarters. Though Díaz's *federales* crushed many of Madero's planned uprisings, other more popular revolts came in their place, led by leaders such as Emiliano Zapata in the southern state of Morelos and Pancho Villa in the northern state of Chihuahua. By April 1911, these popular rebellions had taken most of the countryside, and on May 21, Díaz agreed to resign.

The overthrow was the result of several forces. Díaz's regime stripped millions of peasant families of their lands and excluded much of the nation's middle class from political power as well. Madero's struggle united many disparate protests against Díaz's rule. Once the dictator's rule was over, however, Madero found the forces he unleashed difficult to control. In 1913, Gen. Victoriano Huerta, commander of the federal army, had Madero assassinated and dismissed the congress as well. A new Coahuila hacendado, Venustiano Carranza, emerged to oppose Huerta and restore Madero's moderate form of government. Pancho Villa and other revolutionary groups soon joined him. Zapata, by contrast, fought alone. For the next decade Mexico would be embroiled in civil war, between both Huerta and revolutionaries and then among revolutionary factions themselves.[83]

The U.S. military played a role in this conflict as well. President Taft formed a Maneuver Division at San Antonio's Fort Sam Houston, and Texas Governor Colquitt used the Texas Rangers and the Texas National Guard to try to contain uprisings.[84] In 1912 Taft threatened to send U.S. troops into Mexico to protect U.S. residents, but the new President Wilson did not intervene, though Colquitt urged a large-scale U.S. invasion.

Colquitt left office in 1915, the beginning of the most violent period of the Mexican Revolution in south Texas. Though northern Mexico had long been the center of revolutionary activities, during the next two years the border region became a full-scale war zone.[85] In this same year, the Plan de San Diego was created, a manifesto that called for a redrawing of national boundaries and taking back the territory Mexico lost in the Texas Revolution.[86] In quite a radical proposal, the authors of the Plan de San Diego used the Mexican Revolution as an opportunity to call for an even greater independence from Yankee tyranny. The plan called for an armed uprising against the

United States to commence in little more than a month. Texas, New Mexico, Arizona, Colorado, and California would be liberated and would, it was hoped, join Mexico when its revolution was complete. Blacks would be aided in "obtaining six other states of the American Union," and ancestral lands would be returned to the Apache and other Indian groups of the region.[87] The messenger, a man named Basilio Ramos, was captured, released, and fled to Mexico, and some considered the plan a joke. Yet in subsequent months it may have inspired a series of raids across the borderlands. Ramos's arrest, the discovery of the plan, and the subsequent raids increased the fears of many Anglos in south Texas.[88] In the following months, groups of men organized companies that burned railroad bridges and cut telegraph lines. They also seemed to attack farmers who were local segregationists, and Mexicanos who were part of local political machines. Attacking these instruments of modernity, Jim Crow segregation, and displacement, these *sediciosos* fought wars abroad and at home.[89]

Though many ambiguities remain in the story of the origins of the Plan de San Diego, Benjamin Johnson makes a strong case for its connection to local conditions in south Texas, especially in its interracial appeal and its emphasis on discrimination in the United States.[90] Perhaps the clearest connection, though, is in the plan's critical (albeit somewhat utopian) nostalgia for a reunified greater Mexico, unbroken by the political and economic boundaries of the modernization. In the most radical alternative social vision of the Plan de San Diego, the peoples segregated by Jim Crow here make their own place—they carve their territories out of the American republic. They assert their independence rather than live in subservience to Anglo tyranny.

Clearly the authors of the plan did not achieve these ends, but their ability to imagine such goals reflected a heightened awareness of cultural identity. Throughout the U.S. Southwest, thousands of political refugees came to the United States during the Mexican Revolution, along with thousands of other laborers. The rapid acceleration of Mexican immigration may have raised the anxieties of Anglos, but it also revitalized local Mexicanos' cultural ties to Mexico. In San Antonio, Mexicanos' geographical and cultural segregation on the west side also contributed to a greater sense of their ethnic identity. Along with African Americans, Mexicanos developed separate social, legal, and cultural institutions within a segregated social order. On the east side, African American churches like Bethel African Methodist Episcopal and Mount Zion Baptist nurtured a sense of community through social celebrations and financial assistance. Fraternal organizations like the Black Masons also provided other secular services to the African American community, like funds for health care and low-interest loans. The community organized to build homes for the elderly and orphanages, while bars and lounges provided separate leisure-time activities.[91]

Mexicanos also developed a cohesive cultural community, a separate town with its own language, customs, and traditions.[92] The exiled *ricos*, former loyalists to the Díaz regime, promoted Mexican culture in San Antonio through distribution of books, magazines, and records, including establishing the Spanish-language newspaper *La Prensa* in 1913. While the ricos focused on politics in Mexico, others focused on local concerns. Mexicanos formed many mutualistas, self-help societies that served as sources of social support and financial assistance.[93] In 1911, La Agrupación Protectora Mexicana (the Mexican Protective Association) formed in San Antonio, a group of farm renters and laborers, both native- and foreign-born, who organized for changes in working conditions. And in that same year representatives of the mutualistas, newspapers, and other leaders gathered in Laredo, Texas, for the Primer Congreso Mexicanista (the First Mexicanist Congress). During this meeting, they proclaimed the need for unity and denounced inferior schooling, lynchings, labor exploitation, and land loss. While individual organizations differed in their strategies for community improvement, Mexicanos in Texas organized throughout south Texas to work for the interests of this growing ethnic community. In the 1920s, a new generation of Mexicanos established societies like the Orden de Caballeros de América, founded in 1927, which encouraged citizens to assimilate to given conditions, pay poll taxes, become bilingual, and become more politically active. In 1929 leaders of the Order Sons of America in Corpus Christi, the Orden de Caballeros de América of San Antonio, and the League of Latin American Citizens of South Texas came together in Corpus Christi to form the League of United Latin American Citizens (LULAC).[94] Eventually, LULAC became the largest Mexican American voluntary association in the United States.

These social movements occurred outside of Fiesta's boundaries, yet many of them, LULAC in particular, later played a major role in the festival. While not officially recognized by Anglo elites, these new organizations performed their own critical nostalgia. The name Orden de Caballeros recalled Spanish horsemanship and genteel culture. They articulated a "gentleman's club" parallel to the Order of the Alamo and the Texas Cavaliers. Like the Texas Cavaliers, some Mexicanos developed their own code of chivalric masculinity. Decades later their vision became a part of Fiesta as well. For this moment, though, these developing orders created community within the context of segregation.

The leisure-time activities of San Antonio's Mexicanos and African American activities were "out of place" in the rituals of the Anglo heritage elite. One Fiesta space, however, demonstrated the instability in the social order of the Texas Modern. As the commercial spectacles of the Spring Carnival took over San Antonio's streets, San Antonians of all ethnic backgrounds mingled with a greater amount of mobility than at other times in the city's public space. These carnivals were not utopian moments of interracial harmony, but they opened a symbolic and geographic space for expressing the complexities and contradictions of modernity.

In the Lugar Festivo

While some of San Antonio's elite focused on the rituals of the coronation and the Texas Cavaliers, other city boosters developed an elaborate Spring Carnival of commercial amusements. Trades' Day parades and burlesques competed with the more austere Battle of Flowers Parade. Traveling carnival shows occupied the public plazas every night of the week, and midway shows drew great crowds. These events were part of a national rise in a shared leisure culture. In a rapidly urbanized society, immigrants and native-born residents, men and women, and various social classes participated together in these new commercial spectacles. These amusements, in turn, presented more varied, complex versions of contemporary events, and of history, than the hereditary organizations envisioned.

Like the circus and the world's fairs, San Antonio's Spring Carnival offered new spectacles, including "human diversity, gender difference, and bodily variety."[95] Carnival organizers closed part of Commerce Street to traffic and set up booths for any business that would rent them for the week. Garlanded and illuminated arches covered each intersection. At the north end of Main Plaza and the west end of Alamo Plaza, the organizers designed *lugares festivos* by temporarily enclosing these spaces for attractions and charging a fee. The shows on Main Plaza were for men only, featuring attractions like a "wargraph with moving war pictures" and "Happy Holmes' dancing girls."[96] Alamo Plaza was reserved for less risqué amusements, including "an electric fountain and theater, an ossified man, baby incubators, and a man who bites off the heads of rattlesnakes."[97] As the new social Order of the Alamo formed among the elite, San Antonio's streets became a new Coney Island. While the language of the coronation was refined, ordered, carefully articulated, and racially purified, carnival language was multivocal and riddled with contradiction. The discourse of the early Battle of Flowers parades was splitting in two—the elite coronation expressed the firm borders of modernity, while the carnival expressed its ambivalence.

These ambivalent gestures were also part of making race. San Antonio Anglos, like whites across the United States, "made modern racial meaning not just by creating boundaries but by crossing them."[98] In these carnival transgressions, San Antonio Anglos played with "other" identities, and the other they fixated on was the Mexican. When the Spring Carnival Association became the Fiesta San Jacinto Association in 1912, the BFA hoped this change would bring San Antonians' thoughts back to the Texan battle for independence. This new Fiesta, however, also articulated a continuing paradox of the festival—the commemoration of the battle to sever Texas's ties with Mexico would always depend on the symbols and practices of Mexicanness. The burlesque parades and carnival participants would frequently "play Mexican" in an ambivalent performance of racist prejudice and desire. Through the

FIGURE 6. Nighttime view of San Fernando Cathedral decorated for Spring Carnival. In the background are city hall and city market, ca. 1904. UTSA's Institute of Texan Cultures at San Antonio, Courtesy Virginia Essington.

carnival, white San Antonians superficially celebrated Mexicanness, yet their parody often served to reinforce normative ideologies of racial and gendered difference. In this way, the carnival was often complicit with the coronation in promoting the Texas Modern.

When Spring Carnival opened on April 17, 1900, King Alegría and his royal court arrived via the railroad to Alamo Plaza. Twenty miles south of the city, this king boarded the car of the International and Great Northern Railroad and was greeted at San Antonio's Sunset Station. By taking the train, he signaled his ties to an instrument of Texas modernization, but this king spoke a more riddled tongue. He had an "imperfect knowledge of the great English's tongue," and thus had to speak through a translator.[99] His country of origin was unclear, as his messenger, "refused to tell" for unspoken reasons. The mayor of San Antonio, speaking to the royal, noted that he lived "in a land where the sweet, soft Spanish is the native tongue" and that whether this land be Mexico or Spain, he was welcome here. Clearly, King Alegría spoke with a carnivalized tongue, a sound shrouded in ambiguity. Yet his language was also strangely familiar. This local Anglo San Antonian king performed his role as a foreigner, arriving from a mysterious land of the most familiar "exotic" in the city. His arrival signaled that this festival would be both modern and Mexican.

Until the Texas Cavaliers came onto the scene in the 1920s, this carnival king was at the center of San Antonio's Spring Carnival and Fiesta. Based on Mardi Gras's King Rex, he used a mocking language. In 1905 King Selamat (tamales spelled backward) and his Knights of Omala (Alamo backward) opened the week with a blazing spectacle of electric lights and fire. As he arrived at the plaza, the monarch raised his mask and revealed his identity to the crowd.[100] Secrecy was an important component of the king's role, but the context of his appearance, and the revelry that followed through to midnight, created a more jubilant tone than the king of the Texas Cavaliers would create twenty years later. King Selamat differed from the cavaliers' King Antonio in many ways. The King Selamat of 1905 wore a long satin robe and wide sash around his very broad girth. He wore a large gaudy crown and several tin or metal decorations on his robes. He looked every bit the part of a robust medieval king. The cavaliers' first King Antonio also wore long, velvet royal robes, but by the following year, 1928, these were abandoned for the more military-style jacket and breeches described earlier. While both kings called for merriment and an end to the troubles of daily life, the new King Antonio provided a more sober display of the new social order.

Though Fiesta's royal roles sobered through the decades, the daily carnival continued to provide a space for San Antonians to represent multiple histories and imagine alternative social orders. And though the city's "Latin Quarter" was increasingly marginalized in daily life, Mexicanness saturated these carnivalesque performances. All the parodies, the burlesque parades that mocked the royal court, took on the vestige of Mexican cultural life. As Mexicanos became more segregated from public life, they became more symbolically central to San Antonio's public culture.[101] However, these new representations were unlike the early Battle of Flowers parades that portrayed the Mexican with a form of imperialist nostalgia. During three decades of high Mexican immigration, Anglos could be sure this was no vanishing race. Instead, new carnival practices attempted both to degrade and to emulate Mexican culture. Carnival space could present the most repressive aspects of social life. The mocking laughter of carnival often served as "hegemonic humor," containing transgressive rituals and behavior.[102]

In the process of parody, Mexicanness was performed and openly expressed, though distorted. The heretical behavior allowed during carnival time had the potential to persist as challenging images of difference, to materialize impossible possibilities that could affect social order in the future.[103] Through the midway shows on Alamo Plaza, people were allowed both to laugh mockingly and sometimes fear the dangers of "primitive" cultural displays but were also introduced to a baffling array of alternative possibilities. A quote from the *Daily Express* describes this well.

> At times the scene was one that the spectator would instantly think had been taken from Dante's "Inferno" magnified a thousand times and suddenly dropped into the heart of the city. At another . . . one really imagined ones' self mysteriously transformed into a character in the "Arabian nights" where weird, opalescent many shaded, inconceivable views unfolded themselves before ones' startled vision.[104]

Significant here is that the displays are said to "transform the self" through these visual displays. The thrill of electricity, the orientalist visions of difference, were experiences that took one "out of place" in order to share these "inconceivable views." At the same time that the city's Mexicano population was marginalized and made radically other by the modernizing project, Mexicanness became a symbolic repository for oppositional practices and views, as well as the object of parody.

Like the coronation, Fiesta's commercial displays took flights of fantasy, taking spectators out of their social world through the wonders of electricity and imaginative displays. Ironically, though, this allowed a space to express multiple contemporary concerns. Some spectacles commented directly about current events and struggles, particularly the trades' parades and the burlesque performances. Others provided visibility for San Antonio's diverse population. The days after the first coronation, a trades' parade presented floats from the city's industries. One, by the A. B. Frank Company, carried women who worked in the factory where Alamo overalls were made. The women, dressed in white with fancy yellow hats, were in front of a sign that read "We are the girls who make them."[105] African American teamsters also drove two dozen wagons from the Carr Wood and Coal Company. Such parades offered a limited visibility of the diverse communities that made up San Antonio.

Other parades presented a history filled with conflict. In 1915, the Pageant of Caliph presided over San Antonio streets. Gendered and racial cross-dressing abounded as the Duchess of Chili Con Carni and her court of men in gowns presided.[106] The Bingville Police Department carried a wagon loaded with black-faced "Negroes" and chickens. The parade portrayed the worst stereotypes along with political satire. A float of the presidents of Mexico and the Dogs of War commented on the numerous leadership changes. Díaz, Madero, Huerta, and others occupied different sections of the float, surrounded by the gates of hell and wolfish dogs. Another float of the "happy family" alluded to the war in Europe, as "the Kaiser, the Czar, a Japanese, a Frenchman and an Austrian carried on a continuous battle royale along the line of march of the parade." A shepherd and his wandering flock symbolized the victims of the stock exchange, and the "Suffer-Yets" in hoop skirts blew instruments of "flamboyant discord" through the crowd. These floats portrayed a social world of conflict and struggle.

The coronation did not escape their satire. In 1917 a mock coronation, sponsored by the Rotary Club, entertained the crowd at Alamo Plaza. Her majesty, Queen Loco, and her two-hundred-pound flower children tossed vegetables around the stage. After falling down several times and boxing the ears of some flower children, the queen later dragged the king to center stage and forcibly crowned him.[107] In a reversal of coronation ritual, the queen's court members were heavy, clumsy men who dominated their escorts. They were the symbolic inversion of the southern beauty, performing dominance rather than passivity and weakness. These were no feminists, though. Instead, this ritual portrayed the dangers of empowered women. As it parodied the coronation, this mock performance also reified the feminine sphere. Presenting monstrous, overpowering women, this spectacle of men's play served to reinforce the gendered social order.

On the same day as the mock coronation, another newspaper article bemoaned the changes to Alamo Plaza. "Right in front of the sacred Alamo, a snake charmer had his artistic sign," indicating a low state of civic pride. The Alamo, as it stood, was "relegated to the background" of the festival. Yet the article was only partially correct. Though the solemn ceremonies of the Pilgrimage to the Alamo, the coronation, and the Texas Cavaliers moved to the background during carnival festivities, the two types of events were closely entangled as well. As the name Fiesta San Jacinto itself suggests, festival organizers continued to define themselves through the language of the other. The festive King Alegría performed Mexicanness as a way to maintain the boundaries of whiteness. Positioning this foreign king as an exotic outsider temporarily relieved white men from their daily modern lives. Yet this temporary expression of Mexicanness served as a way to normalize whiteness.

At a time when carnival rides, burlesque shows, and street vendors encouraged large crowds, Fiesta organizers made increased efforts to control crowd behavior as well. As the Spring Carnival expanded, organizers created new regulations for public behavior. An article in the *San Antonio Daily Express* in 1906 posted a list of the "ethics of the carnival," declaring a list of rules for the crowd and parade participants. The crowd was told not to blow horns while the parade was passing and not to bring whips, return balls, or slapsticks.[108] No confetti throwing was allowed on the sidewalks, only in the streets. Secondhand confetti picked up from the street was also not permitted, probably for hygienic reasons. Three years later, confetti was banned entirely from the parades.[109]

The line between participant and spectator was firmly set. As the article states, "The streets are for the maskers and revelers, who have the right of way. The sidewalks are for the spectators and those who do not desire to take part in the revelry."[110] The line between sidewalk and street also represented the distinction between passive spectator and active participant. The means by which the sidewalk crowd would participate in the parade, through horns, balls, and confetti, was increasingly regulated or eliminated. Along with the rise in visual culture so predominant in the early twentieth century came the increasing delineation of those who acted and those who merely watched. Carnival parades, which brought particular anxiety, often blurred this line by the close proximity of audience and participant.

Perhaps only this juxtaposition of the ordered rituals of the heritage elite with the chaotic displays of the Spring Carnival could capture the complexities of modernity in San Antonio. If, as Baudelaire wrote, modernity is both "the transient, the fleeting" and "the eternal and immutable," Fiesta's dual spectacles captured it well.[111] While the coronation queens carefully walked within the framework of elite, timeless motifs and reproduced the dominant social order, the Texas Cavaliers guarded them. At the same time, the Spring Carnival Association and its King Alegría celebrated an ephemeral, fragmented world. These two visions were not entirely separate—the coronations referenced exotic flights of fantasy, and public regulations and anxieties circumscribed carnival goers' festive behavior. Seen together, these dual performances presented the "paradoxical unity" of modernity—presenting a social reality of "perpetual disintegration and renewal, of struggle and contradiction, of ambiguity and anguish."[112] At a time of rapid economic transformations, the heritage elite tried to maintain the oppressive structures of their social worlds, while other San Antonians played with these boundaries.

The coronations continue, remarkably unchanged, to the present day, yet they are no longer the center of Fiesta San Antonio. As Fiesta grew through the twentieth century, the order of the Texas Modern began to unravel. The heritage elite maintained their rituals, but they eventually became less effective in assuring their dominant place in the city's civic culture.

· 3 ·

Night in Old San Antonio

The San Antonio Conservation Society, 1924–48

TODAY, STRUGGLING THROUGH THE CROWDS AT FIESTA'S
Night in Old San Antonio (NIOSA), it is difficult to imagine this event as a
romantic retreat to the "San Antonio of yore." The festival seems just like many
other urban street fairs, with its emphasis on music, fried foods, and overpriced
beer. In 2002, the number of attendants during the four days of NIOSA was
estimated at 46,551, and the amount of tax dollars generated for the city was
about $77,008.[1] Yet in some ways NIOSA does mark a return to the bustling
street life of nineteenth- and early twentieth-century San Antonio. In these
four days, San Antonians return to the streets of one of the city's oldest neighborhoods, La Villita. They walk past more than 240 booths representing many
of the city's ethnic communities and historical eras—French, German, Spanish,
Mexican, Chinese, and Anglo pioneers. Understanding NIOSA's place in San
Antonio's public culture involves understanding the hostesses of one of Fiesta's
biggest parties, the San Antonio Conservation Society (SACS). Much of the
following history of the organization is not directly tied to Fiesta, at least not
until the 1940s. The SACS, however, played a vital role in defining the city in
a way that future Fiesta organizers would later emulate and expand.

In 1936, one of the casualties of San Antonio's health reforms was the banning
of the famous chili stands. For more than a century, Mexicano families set up

outdoor chili stands on the city's downtown plazas, and many well-known travelers had commented on their distinctive role in San Antonio's night life. O. Henry wrote of the delights of chili con carne in "The Enchanted Kiss" when he came to town in 1895. That same year, Stephen Crane visited the stands as well.[2] In the nineteenth century, these open-air booths filled Military Plaza, offering tamales, enchiladas, chili con carne, tortillas, and coffee. In 1889, when the new city hall was built on the plaza, most of these stands moved further west to Haymarket Plaza. They gained enough national recognition to secure a place in the Chicago Columbian Exposition of 1893, which featured a booth with a sign reading "The San Antonio Chili Stand."[3]

In the Depression era, though, sanitation regulations mandated the end of this distinctive feature of the city's nightlife. In response, a concerned group of city boosters, women cultural conservationists and an emerging Mexican American middle class, in one of their few coordinated efforts tried to save the chili stands. For them, this regulation represented both the loss of heritage and a harmful blow to a burgeoning tourist industry. They were unsuccessful, but they invented a powerful mythology of the reign of the "chili queens" in San Antonio guidebooks.[4] In 1934, Frank Bushick, onetime president of the Fiesta San Jacinto Association and later city commissioner, wrote of the old chili stands in *Glamorous Days*, his book of San Antonio tales.

> But the chief attraction which made Military Plaza a show place at night were the chili con carne stands . . . little hollow squares formed of wobbly tables covered with greasy oil-cloth and surrounded by benches on the outside for the customers. . . . All classes patronized them, some attracted by the novelty of it, some by the cheapness. A big plate of chili and frijoles, with a tortilla on the side, cost but a dime, ten cents. A Mexican bootblack and a silk hatted tourist would line up and eat side by side. Cowboys, merchants and hack drivers touched elbows. It was a genuine democracy of Bohemia. All were free and equal at the chili stands.[5]

Bushick describes these stands as the meeting place for downtown's diverse population of natives, tourists, Anglos, Germans, and Mexicanos of all classes. With romantic rhetoric, he described these stands as part of life at the "frontier" of American civilization. Although men often worked at the chili stands, Bushick focused on the chili queens, the women who ran these all-night booths, as the reigning "monarchs" and hosts of San Antonio's exuberant nightlife. Bushick's elaborate descriptions of these queens, with their "bewitching black eyes" and "rich olive skin" evoked plenty of desire for an older social order.[6] The longing of this "democracy" of cowboys, bootblacks, and hack drivers represented a subtle challenge to Texan modernity.[7] Such nostalgia for the egalitarian world of the chili queens would seem particularly understandable as San Antonians experienced the hardships of the Depression, which led many to question the benefits of American capitalism.

Yet Bushick was not primarily interested in returning to the preindustrial days of the chili stands. He was not a cowboy but a well-known businessman who was invested in recreating the "atmosphere" of the open-air chili stands, and he was appealing to many American tourists who were looking for greater authenticity in the southwestern United States, America's "Orient."[8] For a rising Mexican American middle class, by contrast, the chili stands represented a continuation of Mexicano cultural practices and a viable business. As members of this middle class fought to preserve the chili stands, they also fought against their increased spatial marginalization on the city's west side and the "unsanitary" depictions of both Mexicanos and their cultural productions.

The most vocal group in the effort to restore the chili stands, though, were the mostly Anglo, middle- and upper-class women who called themselves the San Antonio Conservation Society (SACS). For these women, saving the chili stands was part of a larger process of reinventing the city and themselves. Bushick wrote about desiring the chili queens, but the SACS had a powerful longing as well. As they tried to re-create the chili stands, they performed a distinct nostalgia. Though they could not restore the booths permanently to downtown public life, they did invent a modern chili stand for tourist consumption. For the 1936 Texas Centennial, they won a temporary reprieve from the ban. Joined by the Centennial Association's Arts and Atmosphere Committee and LULAC, SACS gained permission for the chili stands to remain at Haymarket Plaza to create "a typical Mexican atmosphere project of chili stands, arts and crafts shops and a flower mart."[9] In order to accommodate city officials, SACS promised to retain safe and sanitary measures. They suggested "screening begin at home, that food sold at chili stands be prepared in sanitary homes and brought to the stands where it would be kept warm and served under sanitary conditions."[10] These "sanitary homes" were the residences of SACS members themselves.

In the process of this temporary restoration of the chili stands, SACS literally removed them from their social context, the homes and neighborhoods of the Mexican section of the city, and placed them in their own upper-middle-class homes. Such a project brought about the intrusion of the local Anglo elite to supervise Mexican culture itself.[11] SACS took cultural custodianship of the "Mexicanness" of the city and appropriated the role of defining San Antonio's "atmosphere." Eventually, in 1948, it would incorporate its own fundraiser into Fiesta. This street fair, eventually called a Night in Old San Antonio, transformed one of the city's oldest neighborhoods into SACS's romantic vision of San Antonio's nineteenth-century plazas. Here, they reconstructed the gas-lanterned chili stands. During Fiesta, the members of SACS made themselves into the city's new chili queens—hostesses of San Antonio's biggest party.

During this time, Fiesta took a decidedly westward turn in its imagery and symbols. Encouraged by a Spanish revival across California and New Mexico, better relations with the Mexican government on both a local and national level, and changing gender relations, some of San Antonio's elite women turned away from the southern pageantry of Fiesta's royal courts to restore the missions, sponsor a Mexican Christmas pageant, and dress in indigenous costumes of Mexican "peasants." In the process, they demonstrated a growing fissure in the social order of the Texas Modern. SACS's interest in things Mexican was part of a gradual shift toward the political and cultural integration of Mexicanos in San Antonio.

The Mexican Vogue

The San Antonio Conservation Society participated in new ways of thinking about culture and cultural difference. In the late nineteenth century, their predecessors defined culture as the best of what was thought and produced, especially from Europe. The Battle of Flowers Association emulated Mexico City's elaborate flower parades (which themselves emulated the French flower parades of Nice and Cannes); like Mexican elites, the organizers of the parades were interested in what they viewed as "high" forms of cultural display. Three decades later, SACS articulated a more relational concept of culture and a new tolerance and affirmation of cultural difference. SACS became interested in the arts and crafts of the folk. Like other Americans at the time, the members were attempting to "reposition themselves in the map of the world and to redraw the boundaries between themselves and others."[12] During this period, anthropologists emphasized the notion of separate and integral cultures, a way of identifying groups and setting up distinct value systems within each culture, rather than judging them on an evolutionary scale of progress.[13]

Part of this effort was to reevaluate American identity not as the poor relation of Europe, but as having a distinct culture worth preserving and studying. In response to the displacements of modernity, many Americans looked for a rooted, authentic social identity.[14] Molly Mullin notes that some intellectuals found this authenticity in the Indians and Mexicans of the southwestern United States, affirming the value of those who had long been undervalued in the rhetoric of civilization and progress.[15] For many Americans, the Southwest became a place to find a preindustrial simplicity that the modern city could not offer.[16] SACS did not view Mexicano cultural practices as continually changing and adaptive.[17] Instead, they encouraged a static Mexicano culture that, with its unchanging nature, was an antidote to their own modern lives.

Before the mid-1920s, American awareness of Mexicano culture was limited. They admired Mexico's picturesque qualities, but racism distorted their perceptions of the people.[18] During the Díaz era of the late nineteenth century, travelers noted what they considered positive changes in terms of how they conformed to American standards, and U.S popular culture promoted negative stereotypes of Mexicans as bandits or insurgents—the greaser in many early American motion pictures.[19] Important political and economic developments also stirred a greater international awareness among Americans, however. The United States became a major economic and military power after 1900, which accelerated after World War I, and this new international role brought increased attention to the cultures of other peoples, including a greater interest in Latin America. U.S. hegemony in the Caribbean after the Spanish American War, along with expanded investment, encouraged this trend.

As American individuals and corporations made more financial investments in Latin America, some intellectuals also began to assert that peoples of the Western Hemisphere had a shared history and experience.[20] Americans used this sense of commonality to emphasize ties to Latin America as well as distinguish American culture from European. These intellectuals had an increased interest in cultural nationalism—recovering the material traces of an American past and promoting distinctive American art, literature, and music.[21] Connected to this concern was a sense of antimodernism and romantic primitivism. Critics of industrialization found an appealing antidote in the cultures of seemingly simpler and more authentic communities.

The stabler and more peaceful situation in Mexico after 1920 also contributed to this new interest. Álvaro Obregón's administration sought to decrease the power of the military, enact a program of land redistribution, and improve the conditions of industrial workers, as well as other programs of educational and social reform, while also protecting private property and foreign investment. He had a moderate, pragmatic program of reform. He encouraged a period of cultural renaissance for Mexico, as the country's indigenous traditions became fashionable.[22] In 1921, the Obregón administration celebrated the hundredth anniversary of Mexican independence with a series of events highlighting Mexico's national traditions, including folk art, dances, and music. Diego Rivera and other muralists painted the themes of Mexican history on the countries' public walls.

From the late 1920s until World War II, Mexico became a mecca for North American travelers, while Mexican artists and performers found a warmer welcome in the United States than ever before, even as their compatriot laborers found a closed border after 1930.[23] The U.S. government, partly to counter the activities of fascist governments and the Soviet Union, also approved treaties providing for the exchange of publications, students, and professors among all American republics. In 1940 the Office of Coordinator of Inter-American Affairs was established under Nelson Rockefeller, exhibiting an anti-European orientation and an intense interest in Pan-Americanism.[24]

The interest of these Americans in Mexico was twofold. On the one hand, government officials and intellectuals fostered a sense of commonality, a Pan-Americanist sameness. On the other, artists and cultural critics sought Mexico as a site of difference. For SACS members, this dual movement characterized their ideas of Mexican others within San Antonio as well. Through their efforts to preserve the material traces of a Spanish-Mexican past, these women linked the Spanish era to the American present. Yet by promoting Mexicano expressive culture as a static relic of a simpler, primitive time, SACS also participated in orientalizing the Southwest.

Mexicanos and the City

While SACS members restored Spanish missions, most Mexicanos in San Antonio were living in poverty with high rates of tuberculosis, virtually no public facilities, and a death rate ranked second highest among the five largest cities in Texas.[25] During this period Mexicanos did most of the menial work in the city and provided the vast pool of surplus labor. Despite these conditions, the late 1920s to the early 1940s marked a time when the Mexicano community became a greater part of the city's economy and its political life. Class differentiation accelerated during this period. After three decades of high immigration, San Antonio's Mexicano community in 1930 was made up of a very small upper class of exiled ricos, who came after the Mexican Revolution, a middle class of professionals, and a large laboring class.[26]

By 1941 this middle class had achieved some success in altering the political climate of San Antonio. The Mexican American middle class had greater power as well as a new sense of identity and culture that encouraged a degree of integration and political recognition in the city.[27] A new organization, the League of United Latin American Citizens, entered into the cultural debates. LULAC was created in 1929 in Corpus Christi, Texas, and its members were primarily part of this middle class.[28] Their entry into local politics signaled the first time a Mexican American organization had exerted significant influence on city affairs since the Civil War.

World War I was one catalyst for this change. Returning veterans had greater access to education and began to believe that their future was in the United States, not Mexico. These veterans had a renewed determination to fight injustices against Mexican Americans.[29] LULAC articulated a growing Mexican American consciousness. This new identity contrasted with the ricos, political exiles who sought to maintain allegiance to Mexico.[30] Instead, this new middle class expressed a dual consciousness and a program for integrating and functioning in American society. They sought political integration but also nurtured Mexican cultural pride.[31]

This new middle class sought the full benefits of American citizenship and participation in local political life. Unfortunately, the Great Depression hindered their efforts. Many new immigrants, unable to find jobs, became destitute. This period also marked the greatest deportation movement in U.S. history, with the "voluntary" return of hundreds of thousands of people to Mexico.[32] The exiled ricos had new opportunities to return to their original homes, as the Mexican government urged them to come home to help rebuild the country. Those who remained in the United States experienced a dual oppression, discriminated against in the job market and treated as a racialized, inferior cultural group.[33] In 1930, Mexicans' racial status in the census was changed from "white" to "other races," demonstrating this increased racial discrimination.[34] As a result, members of the rising Mexican American middle class distanced themselves from the laboring class. They tended to call themselves Latin Americans rather than Mexicans and emphasized their American patriotism.

Geographical discrimination also contributed. In home and housing contracts, Mexicanos (like African Americans) were not allowed to buy houses or land outside the west side, unless they claimed to be Spanish instead of Mexican.[35] This effort was very similar to Hispanos' efforts in Santa Fe, New Mexico, where the designation Spanish American was used to define themselves as civilized heirs of brave conquistadors. Unfortunately, this effort often reified, rather than challenged, Anglo racism and political control.[36]

Richard García delineates four views Anglos held about Mexicanos during the 1930s in San Antonio: indifference, a wish for their repatriation and deportation, the belief that Mexicans were criminal, and the hope for more of an interrelation between the communities.[37] The last two were the most prominent. Many Anglos still regarded the Mexican other as the treacherous greaser. Racism and prejudice still dominated Anglo views. Yet some Anglos also recognized that the impoverished conditions of this community hindered the city's overall economic growth. At the same time as Mexicanos were scapegoated for taking "native" jobs during the Depression, some city leaders began to call on the business sector to help the city provide better housing, financial rehabilitation programs, an improved school system, employment benefits, and civic beautification programs. City government advised that plans for the 1936 Texas Centennial celebration employ Mexican and African American workers. García summarizes that

> by the mid-1930s the city's elite finally began to recognize that San Antonio had developed as a city with various ethnic communities that had never been integrated fully and saw the city's recovery programs as a possible means of strengthening social and cultural life as well as integrating the city's body politic.[38]

The Mexican American middle class enthusiastically advocated this political integration.[39] Organizations like the Mexican Businessmen's Association, the Latin American Department of the San Antonio Chamber of Commerce, and the West Side Improvement League had some political influence, though minor.[40]

Maury Maverick, a Rooseveltian liberal from a well-established San Antonio family, was the first politician to fight the city machine by focusing on the west side. As a U.S. congressional representative in 1935, he became the "Mexican's friend," targeting his campaign on the west side and to low-income Anglos in the suburbs of Harlandale and South San Antonio. He had supported the Congress of Industrial Organizations (CIO) and the pecan-shellers' protest in 1938, when twelve thousand Mexicanas began a strike that lasted several months.[41] Conservative Paul Kilday defeated him that year. Immediately after his defeat, he joined the San Antonio mayoral race. His support on the west side showed when he won the race.[42] Through Maverick's congressional and mayoral campaigns, urban politicians were forced to address the issue of ethnicity. Maverick was elected mayor in 1939 in an election marked by heavy voting, the result of the Mexicano community's turnout and Anglo dissatisfaction with the political machine. This election also showed the political interdependence of Anglo and Mexicano communities and revealed the rise of a strong but diversified Mexican American middle class.[43]

Maverick was also popular among some members of the Mexican American middle class because he addressed them as Americans. Unlike other candidates, who tried to speak to the Mexican community in Spanish, he spoke to them in English and acknowledged their role as full-fledged citizens.[44] He fought for better wages and supported unionism, which gave him the backing of many working-class Mexicanos. As mayor, he also brought about the census reclassification of Mexicans as "white." Thus, he participated in efforts not only to give Mexicanos full citizenship, but also the benefits of a white racial identity. He restored the chili queens to downtown plazas, though he required vendors to follow new sanitation regulations.[45] Maverick, more than any previous mayor (or any subsequent mayor for several decades) advocated for Mexicanos' full social and political inclusion. Though he was defeated in his attempt at a second mayoral term in 1941, his politics brought about a new philosophy among the city's governing elite.

SACS did not make public statements embracing the political inclusion of Mexicanos in the city, but its efforts were part of a larger recognition among many of the city's Anglos. In 1940, the San Antonio business community, the religious community, and the political elite appointed a fact-finding committee on social welfare to evaluate the changes of the 1930s. They found that there was an "awakening in San Antonio of the élan vital" with the following political purposes:

a determination to make San Antonio the modern city it has the position and the power to be; an awareness that the welfare of its citizens is of basic importance to its economic health; a growing consciousness of the people in power that discrimination against a strong segment of its population [the Mexicans] is not wise . . . in fact that it is not healthy politically, educationally, economically or socially to discriminate. Political recognitions [must be extended to] its Latin American population.[46]

Anglo politicians and businessmen needed to integrate Mexicanos as American citizens in order to facilitate citywide growth and prosperity. City leaders were not interested in complete cultural assimilation, however. As SACS and other organizations realized, promoting San Antonio's

Mexicano culture was also the key to its modern identity. For different reasons, both Anglo urban politicians and Mexican American middle-class leaders embraced a dual approach—Mexicanos would be politically integrated as Americans but culturally defined as Mexican. In order to both industrialize the city and preserve its special "atmosphere," the Anglo elite now took this dual approach to inventing the city. It shaped the city's interethnic relations and its tourism industry for decades to come.

Construction and Restoration

While SACS often spoke in the language of antimodernist nostalgia, its appropriation of Mexicano cultural practices was decidedly modern. Its efforts at cultural preservation were more constructive than restorative, as traditional practices were taken out of their original context and reinvented for modern San Antonio.[47] As SACS members removed chili from the Mexican section and remade it in their own upper-class homes, they displaced other cultural practices from the producers as well. The women saw themselves as the sole guardians of a disappearing culture and atmosphere. The San Antonio Conservation Society took the lead in revitalizing San Antonio's tourist industry. Through a combination of campaigns to both preserve historic buildings and construct new tourist landscapes, SACS encouraged and financed a number of preservation projects that put the city at the head of a national historic preservation movement. It initiated or greatly contributed to the efforts to enlarge the grounds of the Alamo, restore the San José mission and the Spanish Governors' Palace, and construct La Villita and the Riverwalk.[48] Charles B. Hosmer notes of SACS that "it was a woman's world with a pleasant admixture of Latin culture."[49]

One of SACS's main influences was Charles Lummis and his Landmarks Club of California. Lummis combined an interest in local history and tradition with a belief that art could profoundly influence society through moral uplift.[50] He published five books about his travels throughout the Southwest and tales of Spanish pioneers. From 1894 to 1909, he served as editor of *The Land of Sunshine*, the magazine of the Los Angeles Chamber of Commerce. Through this magazine, Lummis combined boosterism with regional art, literature, and ethnography. He also campaigned against American imperialism, ethnocentrism, and racism and for the restoration of the California missions.[51] For Lummis, the Spanish past offered an example of manly courage. The conquistadors and Fransciscan fathers preceded Anglo pioneers in their zeal to civilize the West.[52]

Several of his followers articulated a more feminized version of the Spanish revival, however. In 1924, Lummis advised Rena Maverick Green, one of SACS founders, on how to purchase and restore San Antonio's missions. Green followed his guidance, reporting to other SACS members that Lummis viewed the missions as both art and as historical relic, "as the expression of the artist's vision and the embodiment of a great spiritual idea."[53] SACS meetings also featured speakers from California. One speaker, Miss Gail Harrison of Santa Barbara, spoke about Santa Barbara's support for its "Spanish atmosphere" in the preservation of the mission and "a street in Spain," where adobe houses of tea rooms, gift shops, and other shops were housed, along with a community arts center. This also influenced new architecture, as a new bank, library, and hotel were built in this Spanish mission style. Harrison argued that San Antonio had even more buildings and artifacts to preserve and thus could capitalize on the Spanish mission style as much as, or more than, Santa Barbara.[54] Harvey Smith, an architect who worked on the restoration of the Spanish Governors' Palace, also wrote an article emphasizing the importance of drawing tourists to San Antonio. He argued that tourists from the East and North are not interested in modern skyscrapers and factories, as they had plenty in their own towns. Instead, they looked for the "picturesque" assets.[55]

Rena Maverick Green hoped to influence local philanthropists and civic boosters with these stories of California's success. "San Antonio has all the qualities as to physical beauty, racial peculiarities, and old architecture that sends hundreds of people to Europe each year," she stated. She suggested preservation of homes, parks, establishing farmers markets in each section of the city, and constructing a public laundry of Spanish design on the west side.[56] In March 1929 SACS sponsored a historic tour of the city, called Vuelta de la Ciudad de San Antonio, to benefit their annual competition for who had the best city plan that promoted growth and also kept the city's individuality by conservation of its quaint, historic buildings. The tour was conducted by SACS and featured several speakers who detailed their experiences in several historic houses. They also visited the chili stands and ended the tour with a dinner at El Fénix.[57]

Green was clearly influenced by the Spanish revival movement in California and New Mexico as well. In Santa Fe's historical pageantry and fiestas of the time, a local Hispano population set themselves apart from Mexicans of the Southwest. Because these New Mexicans still enjoyed more political power than Spanish-speaking populations in either California or Texas, and because New Mexico did not have as many new immigrants from

Mexico, they were able to maintain this self-definition. For Santa Fe Anglos, embracing a Spanish American community offered a way to attract more American settlers and avoid dealing with the region's racial inequalities.[58]

SACS did not make as many efforts to rigidly separate Spanish from Mexican practices. In San Antonio, Green's comment about the city's "racial peculiarity" demonstrated that San Antonio's tourist industry relied on things Mexican. Though the city had promoted the allure of its Mexican section since the mid nineteenth century, this activity accelerated in the late 1920s and 1930s. City boosters sold San Antonio as a site of difference within the nation's borders and an escape from daily modern life. In this process, Mexicano people themselves became part of the tourist spectacle. Their behavior, dress, and cultural productions became tourist attractions themselves.[59] Many visitors came to San Antonio to observe the perceived authenticity of things Mexican.

There was, though, a tension with the Anglo population of San Antonio between acceptance of the Spanish fantasy and their rejection of the reality of Mexicanos in the twentieth century.[60] SACS, more interested in Spanish buildings of the past, neglected Mexicano residents in the present. During the great influx of Mexican immigration from 1900 to 1930 San Antonio Anglos welcomed the labor, but many were clearly anxious about the dramatic increase in Mexican population. Politicians, professors, ministers, and eugenicists warned about the negative consequences of this immigration.[61] The Reverend Robert McLean compared the influx of Mexicans to a bad case of heartburn: "This chili con carne!! Always it seems to give Uncle Sam the heart-burn; and the older he gets, the less he seems to be able to assimilate it!"[62] Though many San Antonians wanted a taste of the exotic, they also feared the effect that overindulgence of this new carne would have on their civic (and national) public.

For SACS, this tension was particularly complex. The members did not express much direct concern for Mexicano city residents. They concentrated on preserving buildings, not people. Yet they did not entirely retreat to the fantasy of Spanish heritage either. As they embraced the chili stands and other Mexicano cultural practices, SACS recognized Mexicano residents' place in the city's public life. They did not express anxieties about the growing population of Mexicanos in the city, but they did not seek their cultural empowerment either. SACS operated within a space between the Spanish fantasy and Mexican reality. To some extent they embraced Mexicano culture and Mexicanos' presence but wanted to supervise their role in the city's public culture.

Cultural Conservation

The San Antonio Conservation Society articulated its relationship to both Mexicanos and Mexicanness through its distinct concept of cultural conservation. In their first meeting, the women defined themselves broadly as "interested in the preservation of all things characteristic of San Antonio, things of historic as well as aesthetic value—losing which, San Antonio loses local color and atmosphere."[63] Their goal was to preserve buildings, documents, and "anything admirably distinctive of San Antonio."[64] They found the term preservation too narrow for their ambitions, and so they chose the term cultural conservation.[65] In doing so, they hoped to not only preserve buildings, but also save the natural environment. SACS also showed an interest in maintaining cultural practices, which set them apart from other women's organizations in the city.

Thirteen women attended the first meeting on March 22, 1924. Many of these middle-class women were artists, and many were also active in numerous other voluntary organizations. The cause that united the organization's founders was the potential demolition of the Market House for street widening. Though their campaign was unsuccessful, their effort was unlike any previous preservation campaign in the country because they targeted a purely commercial building. The Market House was less than a hundred years old and was not connected to any prominent historical event or family. Unlike most preservation organizations that focused on buildings' roles in well-known historic events, SACS was interested in aesthetic appeal as well. The Conservation Society argued that the building's Greek Revival style made it one of the few examples of classic architecture in the city.

SACS members wanted to conserve the historic landmarks, but they articulated a broader definition of saving the city's heritage. The Market House was their first concern, but they quickly took on a number of new causes as well. Within that first year, they began their effort to obtain temporary leases from the Roman Catholic Church to make parks on the lands around San Antonio's four missions, with the exception of the Alamo. The following year, they joined with the DRT Alamo chapter to purchase the remaining private property around the Alamo church. In 1926, they supported the opening of San Antonio's first public museum, the Witte. In 1929, they headed a restoration committee for the Spanish Governors' Palace. By 1936, they had completed restoration of the San José mission, and held their first Indian Harvest Festival on the grounds, an event that later became NIOSA. From 1939 to 1941, they aided in the creation of San Antonio's Riverwalk.[66]

These multiple projects demonstrate that SACS was concerned with both historic preservation, contemporary beautification, and promoting a distinct atmosphere. In 1931 the women created their official seal. They included the tower of the San José mission church that represented their concern with historic buildings. Underneath, a wild olive branch symbolized their interest in the natural environment. Above, an "all-seeing eye" watched over these two elements.[67] This seal shows their presumed guardianship of San Antonio's heritage. Though they did not focus exclusively on San Antonio's Spanish colonial landmarks, their extensive work on the missions and the governors' palace fostered a particular interest in this era of the city's history.

The Conservation Society's two founders highly influenced its distinct sense of purpose. The first cofounder, Rena Maverick Green, was an artist as well as an established civic activist. As the granddaughter of Mary Adams Maverick and the widow of Robert B. Green, who had served as county judge and in the Texas senate, she had long-standing political connections in the state. She was one of the first women elected to the San Antonio board of education. She also worked to get women appointed to the San Antonio police department and campaigned for woman suffrage through her position as state chairman of the National Woman's Party.

Green was also a watercolorist and sculptress who had studied art in Provincetown, Massachusetts, and San Francisco. In 1924, Green was already chairperson of the missions committee of the Daughters of the Republic of Texas. Later that year, when she joined with Emily Edwards to form the Conservation Society, Green was fifty years old. As a widow, she could sign legal documents without her husband's cosignature, which gave her greater ability to lead SACS projects.[68]

Emily Edwards was also an artist and had a similar interest in civic service. Edwards, however, showed this interest through social work and teaching. Born in 1889, Emily Edwards was raised in San Antonio. When she was nine, her mother died, and her father enrolled her in the Ursuline Academy, a convent and boarding school in the center of downtown. Edwards later commented that when she and her two sisters moved into the convent, "we had gone away from home into the heart of the city."[69] From this early age onward, Edwards lived in spaces that merged private homes with public service. As a teenager, she left San Antonio to stay with her aunt in Jane Addams's Hull House, where she taught and attended the Chicago Art Institute. She then taught art in Chicago. When she returned to San Antonio, at the age of thirty-five, she became an art teacher at San Antonio's Brackenridge high school.[70] She was highly influenced by Mexican muralist Diego Rivera. After a few years in the Conservation Society, she left to study under Rivera in Mexico City, returning to San Antonio for frequent visits.

FIGURE 7. Joyce Boothe and Joanna Hull in costumes for
the San Antonio Conservation Society's Indian Harvest Festival,
1939. San Antonio Light Collection, UTSA's Institute of Texan
Cultures at San Antonio, Courtesy the Hearst Corporation.

Green used her previous political experience while Edwards used her artistic skills to organize their first challenge to city government. In September 1924 Edwards, elected the first president of SACS, staged a puppet show for city commissioners in an effort to encourage preservation of the "uniqueness of the city." Edwards made the puppets herself, based on sketches she and Green had previously made while sitting in the back row of a city commissioners' meeting.[71] The puppet show succinctly dramatized both the purpose of this newly formed group as well as how issues of gender and race were intertwined in this society's construction of San Antonio's public history. Entitled *The Goose with the Golden Eggs*, the play represented the city as a goose whose eggs were its unique characteristics. The eggs were named the Heart of Texas, Missions, History, Tourists and Beauty. The actors (or puppets) were Mr. and Mrs. San Antonio, an unnamed Stage Manager, and five current city commissioners. The Stage Manager introduced himself as the Spirit of Yesterday. His brown skin and long mustache marked him as Mexican, distinct from the other puppets. Mr. and Mrs. San Antonio were a white, middle-class couple, from their dress and skin color. As this demonstrated, a Mexicano man embodied the Spirit of Yesterday, while the actors of today were Anglo San Antonians. The stage manager introduced Mr. and Mrs. San Antonio standing with the goose, and Mrs. San Antonio held up each of her eggs admiringly. After she described each of the city's fine characteristics, however, Mr. San Antonio impatiently declared that "income is too slow, I want more Prosperity."[72] The couple struggled as Mr. San Antonio went for his knife to kill the goose, but Mrs. San Antonio begged the city fathers to decide the goose's fate.

In scene two, the mayor and city commissioners discussed the incoming Texas governor, Ma Ferguson, and Commissioner Lambert declared, "Boys can you beat it, a petticoat seated!" Commissioner Wright replied, "But now we'll have the surprise of our lives, if we find we have to listen to our wives." Afterward, Mr. and Mrs. San Antonio entered and spoke before the commissioners. Mr. San Antonio complained about the crooked, narrow streets, noting that "now, I'd have only Broadways, and cut her lanes and make this speedway." He mentioned that his wife has different tastes, since "her home is old buildings that simply won't fall down . . . she has her own customs . . . She even eats chili not served in Duluth." At the end of the play, Mrs. San Antonio pleaded, "Ah, spare this goose for future use; the voice of culture begs. Your reward will come, for this precious goose will lay more golden eggs." The mayor put the question to the audience, who, filled with Conservation Society members, shouted, "No!" The curtain fell with Mrs.

FIGURE 8. Reproductions of the puppets from the Conservation Society's puppet show, originally used in 1924. On the left are the mayor and city managers. On the right are Mr. and Mrs. San Antonio, the Stage Manager, and the goose that represents San Antonio. Courtesy of the San Antonio Conservation Society Foundation, Lewis F. Fisher photographer.

San Antonio clutching the goose. The Stage Manager stood before the curtain with a shiny new egg, saying "See, the egg laid on the way . . . Save Old San Antonio, ere she die."

The contrasting roles of Mr. and Mrs. San Antonio clearly illustrate a gendered vision of the conflicts between the forces of progress and nostalgia. While the men, represented by business interests, developers, and some city officials, were interested in profits and industrialization, their wives fulfilled the role of preservers of culture.[73] This dichotomy reflected nationwide preservation movements of the time, yet the Conservation Society's mission was distinct in its emphasis upon combining preservation with a concern for future tourism. These women did not see their cause in opposition to progress but as a way to market the city more successfully to tourists, through preserving its distinctive characteristics. They played the roles of keepers of the past but also fully wished to participate in the modern industry of tourism. Further, they echoed other efforts during this period to market the city not only as a center for commerce and industry, but also a commodity itself, sold to visitors for the experience it offered. SACS's first effort to save the Greek Revival market demonstrated that this organization, from its beginning, was keenly invested in the marketplace. The women of SACS used their position in the cultural marketplace as a source of racial and gendered power. As members of an Anglo social elite, society members used their political influence to adopt Spanish and Mexican buildings, performances, and practices and reformulate them into commodities for tourist consumption.

Sentimental Restoration

In Emily Edwards's puppet show, the Stage Manager was presented, literally, as an apparition. In the Conservation Society's version of history, living Mexicano actors for the most part were displaced. The Stage Manager created the scene for the actors of today and then bowed out of the story. In doing so, he gave guardianship of San Antonio's history to the women of the Conservation Society. The Spirit of Yesterday, as embodied by a Mexicano man, set the stage, but white women would make San Antonio's golden eggs into the commodities to sell the goose.

Their cultural custodianship did not go unchallenged by the social actors of the early twentieth century. Soon after news of the founding of SACS spread, Adina De Zavala, head of the Texas Historical and Landmarks Association (THLA), contacted Emily Edwards. Many years later, Edwards recalled that "Miss De Zavala called me up and told me that that was her field . . . there was just room for nobody else. She was furious." Edwards tried to reassure De Zavala that SACS did not see itself as a historical society. "When we went to incorporate there was no category except the historic society in which we could enter without a great deal of trouble," Edwards explained. The category they desired, cultural conservation, did not exist.[74] Edwards's efforts to soothe De Zavala failed. In response to SACS's founding, De Zavala's THLA increased its activity, doubling its production of historic tablets and hosting a number of dedication ceremonies.[75]

De Zavala's concerns reflected her long, embattled position as defender of San Antonio's landmarks. By the time of SACS's founding, she was already one of the most active preservationist in the city's history. Her most well known efforts are those to restore the Alamo and how her vision conflicted with another Alamo preservationist, Clara Driscoll. De Zavala was the granddaughter of the first vice president of the Texas Republic, Lorenzo De Zavala. For many years she had been one of the most active and vocal members of the DRT and led the organization's efforts to purchase the Alamo grounds. Although the state had taken control of the Alamo chapel in 1883, the Hugo Schmeltzer Company owned the convento walls of the mission and used them for commercial interests. For several years, the DRT worked at restoring the mission chapel and lobbied for custodianship of the Hugo Schmeltzer building. Eventually, De Zavala secured an agreement with Gustav Schmeltzer that he would not sell the property before giving the DRT members the opportunity to acquire it, but they needed funding. De Zavala knew of Clara Driscoll, the daughter of a wealthy railroad and ranching entrepreneur, as a prominent young woman who might have some interest in helping her efforts.[76] She approached Driscoll about the Alamo in 1903, and afterward the two worked to purchase the site. In 1904, Driscoll personally donated $17,812.02 to complete the $25,000 needed for the purchase. For this, she became known as the "savior of the Alamo," and in 1905 the state of Texas gave her custodianship of all the Alamo grounds. De Zavala and Driscoll had serious conflicts over what to do with the newly purchased building, however.

From her research, De Zavala believed that the walls of the Hugo Schmeltzer building were originally part of the convento structure of the Alamo mission. She wanted to restore this piece of Alamo property. Driscoll, by contrast, believed that the chapel was the only structure of importance to the battle and therefore the only building worth preserving. She claimed the monastery had fallen to pieces long ago anyway and advocated the demolition of the Hugo Schmeltzer building in order to highlight the Alamo chapel and beautify the site. The state DRT, and many San Antonians, became deeply divided over the issue, between De Zavalans and Driscollites. In 1908, De Zavala actually barricaded herself in the building in order to save the walls from destruction, in an event that is often called the "second battle of the Alamo." The fight eventually split the DRT, as Driscoll and her supporters created a separate Alamo Mission Chapter of the DRT and forced De Zavala's chapter out of the DRT in 1910.[77]

Ultimately, a portion of the walls remained, as the Texas governor, Oscar Colquitt, in a special meeting in December 1911, decided there was enough evidence that the walls were part of the original convento and thus should not be destroyed. De Zavala, though ousted from the DRT, had partially won her fight to preserve the walls. In 1913, however, funds were exhausted before the restoration was complete, and the lieutenant governor, who seemed to side with Driscoll, ordered the upper story wall demolished while Governor Colquitt was out of state.

Richard Flores argues that this disagreement over the Alamo restoration reflected a difference in Driscoll and De Zavala's private visions of the Alamo. For De Zavala, restoring the mission was part of a "poetics of restoration," an effort to place the Alamo within its wider historical context, chronicling its long history of Indian, Spanish, Mexican, Texan, and U.S. presence. In this process, the restored Alamo would also symbolically address the socio-economic displacement of Mexicanos in the Texas Modern.[78] Driscoll was more interested in legitimizing the prominence of Anglos. Thus, her private vision followed a "poetics of sentimentality" that presents the Alamo story focused solely on Anglo martyrdom at the 1836 battle and isolates this fight from its complex social and historical grounding. Her sentimental narrative separated the Anglo heroes of the battle from their wider context and served to show Anglo Texans' superiority to the Mexican other.[79]

After she left the DRT, De Zavala continued her preservation work through her new organization, the Texas Historical Landmarks Association, begun in 1912 with the purpose of preserving San Antonio's other mission buildings and establishing a Texas Hall of Fame in the Alamo's long barracks (previously the Schmeltzer property). She was unsuccessful for the time in this latter goal, but she did begin to preserve the other four missions and placed plaques on several other historic buildings of the Spanish colonial era, including the governors' palace. Her vision of social restoration of the Alamo itself, however, would be overshadowed by Driscoll's sentimental goals.

After struggling with Driscoll for so many years, De Zavala was probably wary of yet another preservation group competing for custodianship of the city's landmarks. Rena Maverick Green was also chairing the mission chapter of the DRT, the very same chapter that had replaced De Zavala's chapter. The Conservation Society, with its interest in the missions and the governors' palace, threatened De Zavala's specific projects as well. In terms of saving the city's historic landmarks, though, SACS had much in common with De Zavala and also agreed with her vision of Alamo restoration. In 1929, the DRT, the THLA, and the Conservation Society joined forces to ask the city to provide funds to purchase the remaining private property surrounding the Alamo in order to create a park.[80] Their unity quickly dissolved over specific park proposals. Seven years later for the Texas Centennial, these organizations were divided over the DRT's new plans to once again tear down all the adjacent buildings in order to clear the view of the Alamo chapel. The Conservation Society, like De Zavala, felt that many of these buildings were of historical significance, and together they petitioned the Junior Chamber of Commerce to oppose the DRT's plans.

The DRT ignored their protests. One member of the DRT offered in its defense that "it was the purpose of the centennial celebrations to observe the one-hundredth anniversary of the independence of Texas, not the Spanish period, the Civil War period or any other era."[81] The different philosophies of the two organizations were very clear. The DRT pushed historical considerations aside and was solely interested in a memorial to the defenders of the Alamo. It participated in a preservation movement that served to justify the members' own social and ethnoracial positions; as descendents of the Anglo Texan defenders they were honoring, members of the DRT made themselves guardians of the Alamo as symbol of the racial stratification of the Texas Modern.

The Conservation Society, like the THLA, was more interested in accurate rebuilding of structures from the Spanish colonial period. In this case, SACS followed a poetics of restoration. Like De Zavala, they were interested in maintaining links to the city's Spanish and Mexican past through historic preservation. Conserving historic buildings and opposing mass culture and industrialization, SACS seemed to long for a restoration of a Spanish and Mexican past. Colonial buildings were part of this process, but contemporary Mexican American customs became cultural property as well. SACS also claimed cultural custodianship of the city's past, yet it took charge of recreating its Mexicanness. This eclectic mix of causes reflected a restorative concern with incorporating all elements of San Antonio's diverse architecture, cultures, and historical periods.

Unlike De Zavala, though, SACS did not act out of a repressed concern for the social displacement of Mexicanos by the forces of modernity.[82] Instead, its efforts worked toward growth of a modern tourist industry. The society's efforts were part of the displacement of buildings, cultural practices like the chili stands, and the natural environment, and it reconstructed them into the context of selling the experience of the city. SACS did not make a clear distinction between conserving the past and selling that past for public consumption. As its puppet show makes clear, its interests also reinvigorated efforts to market the city to modern tourists.

SACS articulated its sentimental restorative purpose through several projects, spanning a period from the mid-1920s until World War II. During this time, SACS was aiding a modern social order, but this was not the order of the Texas Modern. Instead, SACS's efforts contributed to a slow unraveling of the racial stratification of the Texas Modern. Through its various campaigns to maintain Spanish architecture and Mexican cultural practices, SACS participated in larger, citywide efforts to incorporate Mexicanness, and Mexicanos themselves, into the city's life. Unlike the DRT, SACS did not represent the Mexican other as the greaser, or a corrupt defeated enemy. In SACS's vision, the Mexican other became quaint, a vestige of a vanishing social world, but also a vital component of a new tourist economy.

Usually SACS expressed these concerns in terms of the city's landscape. Early on, it began to fight efforts to change San Antonio's downtown streets. In December 1929 some San Antonio Anglo residents petitioned the city to change the name of Zarzamora Street to Aviation Boulevard. The petitioners stated that Zarzamora was not of historical significance and difficult to spell. SACS counterpetitioned, noting the beauty and rhythmical sound of the original name. The name Zarzamora was an example of the Spanish colonists' "adaptation of [their] language to a new environment... It literally means brambled, or thorny mulberry and was the name applied to the dewberry the Spanish found growing around San Antonio."[83] Two weeks later the society used the same strategy to defend Losoya Street, which some businessmen wanted to rename Broadway. A society committee further argued that every city had its Broadway, but none had a Losoya Street. The name should be retained for its reference to Jesús Losoya, an early Spanish settler, and for the name's musical cadence.[84] SACS combined historical preservation with aesthetic concerns but also had a particular interest in cultural adaptation. Like the Spanish colonists, who created the word *zarzamora* to respond to their new environment, SACS used romantic language to adapt to changing social conditions. The society's keen interest in how San Antonio's multiple communities conformed to their environment in the past was also a concern about how the city's preindustrial past could be reconciled with its modern present.

La Villita

One of the most notable examples of the way SACS and other civic organizations struggled to construct a new social order was in the restoration of one of the city's oldest neighborhoods, La Villita. Originally a Coahuiltecan Indian village in the early eighteenth century, Spanish soldiers had moved to the area by the end of the century. After a great flood in 1819, many of San Antonio's Spanish residents also moved to its high ground. German immigrants arrived in the 1840s, followed by immigrants from France, Switzerland, and Mexico. By the Depression, the area had deteriorated and was housing some of San Antonio's poorest Mexican residents.[85] In 1935, the chairman of the Conservation Society's planning committee recommended that this neighborhood be targeted for renovation, as it was also the site of the Mexican General Cos's surrender to the Texans in 1835. In 1938, the society held its first meeting in La Villita, and the speaker proposed a restoration modeled after Los Angeles's Olvera Street, remade into a center for Mexican handicrafts and activities and "of great interest to tourists and lovers of the quaint and picturesque."[86]

San Antonio's new mayor, Maury Maverick, quickly took up the cause. A cousin of Rena Maverick Green, Maury Maverick had previously helped SACS in its efforts to restore the San José mission when he was a U.S. congressman. Through Maverick's friendship with Franklin D. Roosevelt, the National Youth Administration began the cleanup. Typical of the New Deal era politics, Maverick proposed that the restoration of La Villita would also provide jobs for the unemployed and unite the Western Hemisphere in an act of Pan-American friendship. On October 12, the Villita Ordinance was passed. Maverick envisioned La Villita as a "project that would ennoble the lower-class Mexican American barrio" as well as establish a link to Latin America and San Antonio's Mexican past.[87] Maverick quickly acquired the land and began the cleanup.

In part, La Villita's restoration was also modeled after the nationally known re-creation of Williamsburg, Virginia. Similar efforts were also made in New Orleans, Charleston, and Cape Cod. Yet the architect of the Villita project, O'Neill Ford, proposed that this neighborhood had styles "infinitely more varied and original" than those other projects. After several meetings with the mayor and SACS, he proposed "a sensitive and carefully restored group of little houses that show clearly that our own culture has produced, from a varied source, an architecture not based on any 'style' but definitely establishing a character that is native."[88]

Such comments reflect a cultural nationalist concern with defending American architectural traditions. Yet his goals also reveal an emphasis upon atmosphere. Ford wanted La Villita to "create a mood rather than be a museum-style restoration to a specific period of time."[89] This was partly the result of confusion of houses rebuilt several times. The architecture of La Villita, therefore, would be done to show how various styles were adapted over time, by different cultural groups, to yield a unique style. The result would be "one general atmosphere . . . [with] no sharp separation of things that make houses and grounds and furniture one fine whole."[90] SACS heartily endorsed Ford's plan. By the end of Maverick's mayoral term in 1941, La Villita was completed.

The mayor and SACS considered La Villita a great success. For each of the projects' backers, La Villita's restoration represented a new civic unity, one that restored the fragments of the city's diverse ethnic communities into a coherent social whole. The one group left out of this new unity, however, was the residents of La Villita who were relocated during the cleanup. The families of this "slum" were picked up, relocated, and written out of the history of the neighborhood. La Villita became "less a neighborhood and more a commercial marketplace, a decontextualized collection of artifacts."[91] A few testimonies from La Villita's relocated residents remain. For example, Connie Peña Solís recalled memories of her childhood in La Villita. Despite the poor living conditions, Solís described the neighborhood as a cohesive community, while progress reports on the cleanup described the removal of "human wreckage."[92]

Though Ford attempted to show a continuous history of varied architectural adaptations, he and other preservationists did not recognize the radical rupture their own work made in the social worlds of La Villita's contemporary residents. Maverick's utopian language of hemispheric unity and barrio ennoblement masked a careless disregard for this community. The cultural landscape of La Villita was now peculiarly disembodied, devoid of its numerous former residents or sparsely populated with Mexicano craftsmen and tourists.

The Canary Island Fantasy

Like Maverick, the Conservation Society showed a glaring disregard for contemporary Mexicano social actors. Instead, as the society took custodianship of Mexicano spaces and practices, its members tried to embody these cultural attributes themselves. At their meetings and fundraisers, SACS members often wore dresses from various Mexican states. They sold Mexican crafts at the San José mission and hosted innumerable Mexican suppers. In 1931 the Conservation Society celebrated the restoration of the Spanish Governors' Palace. The members also wanted to honor the two-hundred-year anniversary of the arrival of Canary Islanders, the original Spanish colonists of San Antonio, so they sponsored a historic pageant with society members playing the roles of these early colonists. Rena Maverick Green was baffled, though, when the descendents of these Canary Islanders insisted that they play the parts themselves. Eventually, Green worked out a compromise so that society members would still play certain roles in the production.[93] SACS did have one member who was actually a Canary Island descendent, Esther Carvajal, who helped organize the pageant. Green's surprised response to the Canary Island descendents, however, also reveals the degree to which many SACS members absorbed this sense of cultural custodianship.

Their appropriation of the Canary Islanders' dress was a form of mimetic play, connected to the performance of other ethnic identities throughout the country. Phil Deloria defines mimesis as a particularly modern performance. In his study of "playing Indian" throughout U.S. history, Deloria describes white performances in the early and mid-twentieth century as distinctively concerned with cultural authenticity. Mimetic play of Indianness was part of the modern quest for an authentic identity. These performers viscerally appropriated otherness through their bodies, which gave their performance a "powerful material reality."[94] For SACS members, performing the roles of Canary Islanders offered them an opportunity to "become" the city founders. Their performances gave them the symbolic heritage of San Antonio. As they took the place of the Canary Island descendents themselves, they also legitimized their role as cultural custodians.

SACS members did not insist on performing in all the pageants they sponsored, though. In 1928, when they began to sponsor the Spanish-language play *Los Pastores*, they hired the group of Mexicano actors who had been performing the play for many years on the city's west side. Mrs. Carvajal also organized the society's sponsorship of the *Los Pastores* play. This shepherds' play was based on a Spanish medieval practice but had continued within San Antonio's Mexicano community each Christmas season. The performance could last from three to five hours and consisted of a reenactment of the hazards confronting the shepherds who were making their way to see Jesus Christ in the manger.

The society sponsored a performance at Mission San José for two years and resumed sponsorship in the mid-1940s. They hired Mexicano players from the Guadalupe Church, who performed the play in their own community as well. The performances at the mission differed from its Guadalupe counterpart, however.[95] At the mission performance, the society hired a translator to provide summaries of the play's scenes. The translator spoke at the same time as the Spanish-speaking players, often drowning them out. At the Guadalupe Church there was no translator; the audience was socially and culturally similar to the actors, and the performance was in a small church.[96] At the mission, the socioeconomic and cultural differences between most of the audience members and the players encouraged little interaction between the actors and the crowd. Although some SACS members were fluent in Spanish, they often failed to understand the meaning of the play. One translator commented that the play was so confusing that very few people understood what it was all about.[97] A newspaper review of the 1928 mission performance described the play: "Forty scenes in loose or far fetched sequence followed each other through the weird religious performance."[98] SACS sponsored this "confusing" production to invest in the spectacle of the Mexicano performers, not in the meaning of the play itself. The English translator, instead of bridging between the social spaces of the performers and the audience, reified their separation by speaking over the actors' voices.

SACS decided to perform themselves in the Canary Island pageant and not in *Los Pastores*. They offered no explanations for this distinction, but I suggest that they were not willing to cross the social space and the perceived racial boundary between their Anglo selves and these Mexican others. By the twentieth century, the descendents of the Canary Islanders were integrated into San Antonio's "white" society, rather than the Mexican one.[99] Their Spanish ancestry distinguished them from the contemporary Mexican. By portraying themselves as Canary Islanders, the members of SACS could link themselves to the city's Spanish past.

The limits to this mimetic contact are clear as well, however. While embodying the presence of a Spanish past, SACS members also distanced themselves from the Mexican of the present. They distinguished between Spanish ancestors and Mexican contemporaries as a way of confirming the social distance between themselves and the Mexicano actors. The women of the San Antonio Conservation Society played the Canary Island fantasy in order to reinvent themselves, yet they also participated in continuing racial divisions.

NIOSA

Unlike many of the female cultural preservationists in New Mexico and California, many of whom were transplanted northeasterners, the women of SACS were primarily San Antonio natives from established families of late nineteenth-century San Antonio. They looked to San Antonio's Spanish and Mexican past to establish a public voice, but they were also embedded in the racial order of the New South. Like the Battle of Flowers Association, SACS articulated a public role for them that differed from the myth of the passive, domestic southern lady. As they took custodianship of San Antonio's Mexicanness, they also found new ways to redefine southern womanhood. Yet the public roles of SACS members largely depended upon the private labor of Mexicanas. Most of SACS's "Mexican dinners" were cooked by their Mexicana maids. Mexicanas also performed most of the labor for one of SACS's biggest events, the Night in Old San Antonio (NIOSA). During this street fair, SACS members' activities showed a continuing tension between their public custodianship of Mexicanness and their reliance on Mexicana labor. This fair also demonstrated the continuing gap between the romantic rhetoric of restoration and the reality of a racially stratified society.

This street fair began as the Indian Harvest Festival in 1936 and was held in the newly restored San José mission. It portrayed the imagined life of the Indians at the missions, including live farm animals and an elaborate pageant featuring the matachin dance. The event continued for several years, bringing profits from the candy-selling booths and gypsy numerology readings. In 1940, the festival evolved into the River Jubilee in order to celebrate the San Antonio River Beautification Project and featured a parade of boats. In 1946, the Fiesta San Jacinto Association encouraged the Conservation Society to stage their festival during Fiesta week and promised to underwrite the event. In 1947, this River Festival moved up to the restored La Villita and boasted sidewalks lined with concession stands. In 1948, the festival assumed its current name, A Night in Old San Antonio.

The events grew, and volunteers increased. Attendance rose above one thousand in 1942. Elizabeth Graham, a society member, created donkey carts for children to ride down the streets, reminiscent of the carts that had carried produce and other supplies around San Antonio's nineteenth-century plazas. In another feature, a flock of geese was herded down the street. In 1947, Mrs. Ed Leighton, who had run the Indian Harvest Festivals at San José, announced she would put replicas of the old-time chili stands on Juárez Plaza to serve Mexican food.[100] SACS would now have a more permanent construction of the chili stands and offer a wide variety of other ethnic foods as well. Organizers divided NIOSA into several sections representing different historic periods like Villa España, the Mexican Market, and Frontier Town.[101] For children, SACS designed Clown Alley. During NIOSA, SACS created a more family-oriented version of the Spring Carnival attractions. It presented vestiges from the city's diverse cultural history but displaced these practices from their earlier context and reconstructed them as tourist commodities.

Some of the booths featured society members' own home-baked cookies and pies, but the most famous food maker, and the namesake of one of NIOSA's most crowded stands, was María Luisa Ochoa, the housekeeper for society member and onetime president Ethel Harris. For many of the festival's early years, Harris pressed Ochoa to make tortillas for the event. Apparently, this was not always the easiest relationship. Another SACS member, Esther MacMillan, recalls that

every year, Ethel [Harris] would call me and say, "Esther, you've got to come out and talk to Maria. She's not going to do it." And I would say "Why don't you do it? She works for you. She's living in your house." "You've got to come out and talk to her," she'd say. I would go out and talk to Maria. And every year we gave her workers just a little more money . . . And I watched . . . what she did. She ordered the maize . . . And she mixed them and the lime water until she could *feel* [my emphasis] when it was right. And, somehow or other, those were the best tortillas that ever were.[102]

Unfortunately, SACS members recorded little else about their personal relationships to María Luis Ochoa, but this negotiation reveals several interesting possibilities. First, Ochoa's unwillingness to make the annual tortillas demonstrated her ability to bargain for better pay. She seemed well aware of the profits that SACS gained from their annual festival and wanted to negotiate for higher wages for her work.

Second, the tension shows a deeper conflict. Hiring Mexicana housekeepers like Ochoa relieved Harris, like other white, upper-class women,

FIGURE 9. María, the famous tortilla maker for the Conservation Society's first NIOSAs. UTSA's Institute of Texan Cultures at San Antonio, Courtesy of Frank J. Wallace Collection.

from the burdens of private domestic duties. As Ochoa labored, Harris could do the public work of cultural conservation. Grace Elizabeth Hale argues that in the South, white women constructed the mammy image of black women "to ease the constrictions of southern white womanhood." Black women's physical labor mattered, but their symbolic labor mattered even more.[103] As self-sacrificing mother figures, more devoted to their white owners than their own families, the mythical mammy provided a mother figure and a source of inspiration. Often, women who had public roles as activists praised their mammies as their liberators. The mammy "let them out of their home in the unnamed liberation of their whiteness to be temperance organizers, suffragists, artists, and writers." [104]

In San Antonio, this racial stratification also played out in Anglo-Mexican social relations. Mexicana housekeepers served many of the same functions as mammies. They also revealed the deepest contradiction within southern womanhood. White women physically and symbolically depended on nonwhite women for their own independence, even as they denied their participation as social equals.[105] For SACS members, this symbolic dependence was particularly acute. These white women spent much of their public lives constructing and representing ideas of Mexicanness, yet their presentation depended upon Mexicana labor.

Esther MacMillan, in her account of María Luisa Ochoa's preparation of the tortillas, was fascinated by the way she seems to "feel" the appropriate mixture of ingredients. For MacMillan, Ochoa's method was almost magical. She watched María make the tortillas, but she could not imagine accomplishing the same feat herself. MacMillan naturalizes Ochoa's work while separating herself from this kind of labor as well. At times, SACS members would make some of the food for NIOSA, yet their accounts of these efforts are riddled with trial and error. For example, Jane Maverick McMillan and her husband tried to modify a Peruvian *anticucho* recipe for more than a year. "One set we made tasted like vinegar sticks," she recalled. By the time they found a good recipe, their efforts had "ruined all the family iceboxes."[106] While they romanticized the cooking of their housekeepers, SACS members became more aware of their anxious, modern selves. Furthermore, their attempts to reformulate southern womanhood, to reinvent themselves as public custodians, were also dependent upon modern racial segregation.

As SACS members made themselves the new chili queens and became the hosts of one of Fiesta's biggest events, they transformed both the festival and the city. They worked to integrate San Antonio's Spanish colonial architecture and Mexicano practices and performances into the city's tourist industry. They were not as interested in lessening the social distance between themselves and the Mexicano actors in the present. Instead, like the Battle of Flowers Association, they wanted to create new public roles for themselves in San Antonio's civic culture. They celebrated the city's Spanish ancestors rather than its Anglo pioneers, but they acted as other members of the heritage elite—taking cultural custodianship of the past to affirm their own social power in the present. As they embraced Mexicanness, though, they complicated the Anglo-Mexican binary of the Texas Modern. SACS's nostalgic vision in NIOSA came at a time when Mexicanos became a more integrated part of the city. Segregation and discrimination certainly continued, but these performances showed the cracks in San Antonio's racial order.

. 4 .

Juan Q. Public

Reynolds Andricks and the
Fiesta San Jacinto Association, 1950–70

IN APRIL 1956, THE EDITORIAL PAGE OF THE *SAN ANTONIO EXPRESS NEWS*
featured an illustration inviting the city's public to its annual Fiesta celebration. In the drawing, a mailman delivers a letter to a man at 123 Everystreet.
The man smiles as he opens his Fiesta Fun invitation, which is addressed
to Mr. and Mrs. Juan Q. Public.[1] This image represented a constellation of
changes during the postwar period. First, the cartoon reflected a continuing
association between Mexicanness and festivity. Yet there are important shifts
in emphasis as well. For much of Fiesta's early history, many San Antonians
were excluded from the private balls and pageantry that made up the festival.
This cartoon represented an increasing emphasis on Fiesta as a mainstream,
inclusive festival, a party for Everyman. Finally, the cartoon revealed that
in San Antonio, the rhetoric of inclusion would take on a Spanish accent.
Efforts to create a more egalitarian festival would become enmeshed with
Mexicanizing the city for the week. Fiesta represented a week when John
became Juan, and San Antonio dressed Mexican. While Fiesta celebrated
civic unity, the festival also embodied difference in its emphasis on Mexican
culture. This Everyman discourse was targeted toward the Anglo middle
class, while making only tenuous gestures toward San Antonio's Mexican
American community.

Before World War II, Fiesta was divided into two types of celebrations. The city's heritage elite, those in organizations like the Texas Cavaliers and the Order of the Alamo, had a series of private parties and charity balls. The rest of San Antonio's public watched the Battle of Flowers Parade and went to the Carnival. When the Fiesta Association invited the San Antonio Conservation Society to include their Night in Old San Antonio as part of Fiesta week, however, they signaled the beginning of many new events during the festival. By the late 1950s, the annual celebration had grown to ten days of events, including two new parades. Many of these new events celebrated the modern commercial attractions of the city and contributed to an ever-growing tourist industry. Most of these new events were either free or charged a modest admission price. The Fiesta Association wanted to encourage more Fiesta participation, particularly from the city's Anglo middle-class residents. In the 1940s, San Antonio experienced rapid growth, almost doubling in population and, like other Sunbelt cities, basing much of this growth on the developing industries of defense and tourism. As these new residents moved to the suburbs of the north side, Fiesta organizers tried to bring them back downtown for the festival. In order to do this, festival boosters would rely on the rhetoric of democracy and inclusion, so prevalent in other realms of postwar discourse. This rhetoric of inclusion affected Fiesta's political organization, its reigning monarchs, and its promotional materials.

Challenging the Heritage Elite

When the ladies of the Battle of Flowers Association organized the first parade in 1891, the primary purpose was a patriotic celebration of Texas's victory at San Jacinto. The Battle of Flowers Association was a space for elite white women to take custodianship of public space. In a gendered division of labor, commercial promotions became a male sphere while women reserved the loftier goals of patriotism as their distinct domain.[2] As the festival grew beyond the parade, though, the Battle of Flowers Association lost its power to control the festival. Civic boosters, often upper- and middle-class businessmen, made the parade and its surrounding events into a larger commercial spectacle. The charter of the Fiesta San Jacinto Association (FSJA), adopted in 1905, reflected a compromise between the commercial purposes of the festival and patriotism.

This Association is a non-profit, benevolent, educational organization, created and existing to honor the heroes of the Alamo and San

Jacinto, to commemorate their sacrifice and victory, and to keep alive among the people, near and far, at home and abroad, the history and traditions of the great and glorious past of San Antonio and Texas. To this end, and to further the recognition of San Antonio as the historic and cultural, as well as commercial, center of the Southwest, this Association shall act as the planning and coordinating agency to assure the appropriate and credible series of parades, pageants and other events staged by this and other agencies and organizations of the community.[3]

Such a flexible constitution maintained a space for remembering historic battles, but the ways in which San Antonio could be promoted as "the historic and cultural, as well as commercial, center of the Southwest" was open to multiple interpretations. Although membership in the association was limited to "reputable citizens, firms or corporations of metropolitan San Antonio" and had to be elected by the board of directors, such requirements were far less stringent than San Antonio's more elite social clubs, where family lineage or sponsorship was necessary to enter. Within FSJA's membership, a few member organizations had privileged positions. The Battle of Flowers Association, the Texas Cavaliers, the Order of the Alamo, the San Antonio Conservation Society, the San Antonio Woman's Club, the San Antonio German Club, the San Antonio Pioneers Association, the Junior Chamber of Commerce, and the Daughters of the Republic of Texas were all excluded from membership dues and were guaranteed positions on the board of directors. Most of these organizations had restrictive membership requirements.[4] Thus, the heritage elite, who ushered in the Texas Modern in the late nineteenth century, enjoyed a privileged place in Fiesta.

At its inception, the membership of the FSJA was almost identical to the constituency of its most prominent participant organizations listed above. After World War II, though, FSJA's membership changed significantly. Although these organizations continued to be represented on the board of directors, the executive committee became the group responsible for most FSJA decisions. Significantly, none of the participating organizations had a representative on this committee from 1948 to 1959. Instead, the San Antonio businessmen on the committee, who held the positions of president and executive secretary, were not necessarily part of the board. The executive secretary, in particular, could not be a board member. As a result, the organizations on the board had no direct control over FSJA decisions during this period. The conflicts between the goals of the organizations on the board of directors and the goals of the executive committee would lead to the eventual collapse of the FSJA.

These two groups, the board of directors and the executive committee, maintained fundamentally different concepts of Fiesta. The board of directors, represented most consistently by the Battle of Flowers Association, wanted to emphasize the commemorative intentions of the festival and thus relied on a discourse of heritage, education, and patriotism. As members of San Antonio's heritage elite, the directors conceptualized their role in terms of civic duty to the larger public. Most of these organizations used family lineage to justify their prominence in San Antonio's public culture. The Daughters of the Republic of Texas traced their ancestry to the Texas Revolution, the Texas Pioneers to nineteenth-century Anglo settlers who arrived in Texas before statehood. The Battle of Flowers Association, the Texas Cavaliers, and the Order of the Alamo traced their familial roots to the origins of Fiesta itself.[5] As Fiesta heirs, these groups justified their leading role in the festival.

The executive committee members, by contrast, hailed from the city's new business class, upper- and middle-class men who did not have family ties to the Texas Republic or to Fiesta's origins. In order to increase their role in Fiesta, they spoke the language of democracy and inclusion to widen the scope of Fiesta celebrations. The executive committee also took greater interest in Fiesta's potential role in promoting San Antonio's commercial growth, particularly its tourism industry. They wanted to expand the variety and number of Fiesta events to encourage participation from more diverse segments of the city's population. While the executive committee did not evenly represent San Antonio's diverse middle class, the calls for inclusion struck a responsive chord. Many residents, particularly from the suburban Anglo middle class, embraced their crusade to open up Fiesta's ranks.

Two Cities

For these newly settled residents, Fiesta, like the city itself, needed to incorporate this wider public. In the two decades following World War II, San Antonio faced a crisis of urban growth. During the Great Depression, New Deal growth policies and powerful southern congressional delegations had directed great amounts of public capital to the region, providing the foundation for postwar growth. The availability of cheap land and labor, coupled with the city's lack of unions, also encouraged private investment. Like other Sunbelt cities, San Antonio invested in new postwar industries to spur economic growth as well, especially defense and tourism.[6] These two industries became the core of the city's postwar development. Local boosters promoted San Antonio as a city of military labor and tourist leisure.

Fiesta literature of the time expressed this sense of San Antonio's dual identities. A 1953 Fiesta Invitation stated that "we have always had two cities—one of peace, the other of conflict." Local boosters developed a downtown landscape of a peaceful Riverwalk for tourists, while building military bases on the outskirts of the city. San Antonio had become the location of nearly all Air Corps training during World War II. These bases attracted thousands of civilian jobs such that the population increased during the 1940s from 253,854 to 406,442.[7] Postwar growth encouraged another sense of dual identity—the modern verses the antiquated city. For many decades, boosters had promoted this juxtaposition of the ancient and modern city, and now this vision spread past the highways. As middle-class families moved out into the modern suburbs, downtown restoration and development emphasized San Antonio's history as a Spanish colonial outpost. The city of peace and war was also the San Antonio of yore and a modern city, a city of traditional Mexican markets with military bombers flying overhead.

The great contradiction in this historic-modern city was continual racial segregation. The most marked contrast between the two cities of San Antonio was the difference between the growing Anglo city to the north and the neglected Mexican town of the west side. City growth exacerbated the problems of providing adequate services to both the city's older central neighborhoods and new, unincorporated suburbs. San Antonio was already well known for poor public services.[8] Many of the new suburbs suffered from inadequate planning as well. Because Anglo residents sought to maintain racial segregation, some wealthy suburbs moved to incorporate during the 1940s, which threatened the city's tax base. Along with other Sunbelt cities, San Antonio's political and economic elite sought municipal reform.[9]

In 1946, the Council-Manager Association was formed in order to challenge the machine that had dominated city politics during the 1930s. The group accused the city's representatives of hindering progress and inefficiency in handling service problems. Their goal was to gain greater political stability and orderly urban development to attract developers and investors.[10] In 1948, Jack White, one of the leading reformers, became mayor, and in 1951 a full slate of reform candidates won the city commission from the machine. This new council quickly moved to expand city services and annexed enough territory to double the municipality's total area. By 1953, however, this council was beginning to resemble the machine it had replaced, as White attempted to increase mayoral power. To counter his efforts and ensure a longer lasting political change, reformers created the Good Government League (GGL) in 1954, a political organization whose aim was to defend a nonpartisan council-manager government while limiting the power of the mayor.[11]

The conflicts over city government's uneven spending for neighborhood improvements also demonstrated a less-than-peaceful relationship between the city of yore and the rapidly developing north side. The GGL increased its membership efficiently, winning the majority in the council in 1955. Many members came from the city's wealthy neighborhoods of Olmos Park, Alamo Heights, and Terrill Hills, but the league directed much of its public monies to newly annexed areas on the north side. The league passed bonds for highway building and sewer and water infrastructure in the expanding suburbs. This growth-oriented strategy presumed that these expenditures would benefit the entire city; however, the GGL paid little attention to the older neighborhoods in the west, east, and south sides of the city, which were also the ones in greatest need of basic improvements.[12]

In the process of consolidating power into one reform league, the GGL eliminated smaller organizations that had served low-income communities through jobs, favors, and public projects.[13] Because most of San Antonio's Mexican American and African American populations lived in these older areas, the GGL benefited the city's Anglo population at the expense of other constituencies. Although Anglo dominance was already firmly entrenched in the city's political and economic structures, the Mexican American and African American communities' neighborhoods had actually fared better under San Antonio's earlier political machine. Through a system of patronage, a variety of neighborhood improvements were guaranteed. Thus, Mexican Americans in the city were consistently against the GGL and displayed this antipathy in their support of anti-GGL candidates and in low percentages of voter registration and turnout rates.[14] In fact, Mexican Americans were more likely to support Anglo independent reformers than Mexican American GGL candidates. Frequently, the GGL would attempt to lure west side voters by promising drainage projects and other service improvements. These projects were approved, but the council and city administration would never build them.

Although the city's growth was uneven, important national and regional conditions also led to the development of a more empowered Mexican American community. Along with the growing middle-class organizations that had developed in the late 1920s and 1930s, returning World War II veterans increased their civic activity. They protested against segregation, launched voting registration campaigns, and fought for educational reform. These returning veterans, recipients of the GI Bill and college degrees, expanded the base for the middle and skilled working classes throughout south Texas. Such developments also led to the growth of a Mexicano consumer market. In order to accommodate this new market, Anglo businesses began to promote an atmosphere of tolerance and cooperation. In 1954, San Antonio passed a desegregation ordinance for city facilities. While these middle-class organizations were unable to acquire much more than symbolic rewards, especially for working-class Mexicanos, the political activity of this community and Anglo accommodations of the period signaled an important change in the city's interethnic relations.[15]

The GGL also attempted to incorporate Mexican American and African American candidates on their slates. Among other candidates selected over its history, 78 percent were Anglo. In 1955, however, the league selected one Mexican American candidate and subsequently two Mexican Americans for each election. From 1964 on, it also endorsed one African American. With such token membership, the GGL hoped to discourage much protest. Other organizations attempted to challenge the league's candidates, but few met with any success. The GGL maintained its power by at-large elections.[16] It was also consistently able to select members of the Mexican American middle class in an initial step to incorporate them into city government.[17] Mexican American participation in GGL politics did provide a consistent source of conservative leadership within the Mexican American community. As Rodolfo Rosales points out, this approach was based on the idea that direct confrontation would undermine political inclusion; these conservative leaders used these new inside positions to gain entry into municipal decision-making and join forces with the business communities' reform agenda.[18] Alfred Vásquez, a stockbroker from El Paso, was the most visible leader of this conservative middle class. He and others formed the Committee for Community Progress, also known as the "west side GGL," an informal organization dedicated to this goal of political inclusion.[19]

Not all Mexican American middle-class leaders followed this political agenda; liberal middle-class leaders actively organized in Democratic state politics, though they were shut out of municipal government. It is important to note, though, that for those who chose the conservative route into the GGL, a price was paid. In order to accommodate the growth interests of the GGL reformers, which they believed would eventually extend to Mexicano barrios as well, they eschewed their role as spokespersons for the Mexicano community within the city. For municipal government of the time, political inclusion also meant the erasure of ethnic- or class-based partisanship.

In addition, other state and national policies threatened the political gains Mexican Americans had made during the previous decade. The forced repatriations that had broken up many families during initiatives like Operation Wetback in 1954, in which citizens and noncitizens were often equally at risk of deportation, were continual reminders that although Mexican Americans had American citizenship, they were often vulnerable to harassment and discrimination.[20]

Heritage and Democracy

Like the GGL, Fiesta's postwar leaders emphasized a festival dedicated to political inclusion, rather than elite patronage. As occurred in municipal politics, this shift came after a long battle for reform. The first public discussion of FSJA's internal conflicts came in the *San Antonio Express News*, in a letter columnist Paul Thompson wrote on March 14, 1959. Thompson commented that "the battle for control of the FSJA . . . could wreck Fiesta as presently organized."[21] He claimed that Reynolds Andricks, FSJA executive secretary, caused most of the conflict, and in a sense, he was correct. Andricks was the most active representative of postwar FSJA membership, and he created most of the recent changes to the festival. In 1948, Andricks, a civil engineer, was elected to the board of the FSJA. Between 1950 and 1960, he served as president or as executive secretary of the association. His name appears on almost all association letters and publicity materials. Andricks's defense for expanding Fiesta was an interesting mix of boosterism and populism, and his main goal was to open up the ranks of Fiesta organizations to the Anglo middle class. He was also interested in making Fiesta a more nationally known event, thus attracting greater tourism to the area.[22] He complained that up to this point, Fiesta had been more like a private party for the city's social clubs than a citywide celebration.[23] In order to encourage greater participation from other sectors of the city, he spearheaded the creation of several events, either free or open to the public.

Part of the reason for Andrick's success was his tight control over the association. As executive secretary, he controlled all the financial records. Under his leadership, the executive committee began to make most of the decisions about how the association's funds were allocated to the various groups who sponsored Fiesta events. At the time, this committee did not, however, include any representatives from the Junior Chamber of Commerce, the Order of the Alamo, or the Texas Cavaliers—a few of the organizations responsible for many of Fiesta's older events. Thompson's column voiced the protest of these groups against Andricks's "one man rule."[24] Under his leadership, these organizations stated that their own events, including the Battle of Flowers Parade, the queen's coronation, King Antonio, and the River Parade had been overshadowed by the new Fiesta Flambeau.

Over the previous ten years the association's promotional materials had devoted greater attention to the FSJA's new parade, the Fiesta Flambeau, which Andricks founded in 1948. The Flambeau parade was a reference to the torches once carried along the nighttime parades in New Orleans carnival, though San Antonio's parade used flares like those used by the police.[25] This new parade attracted greater crowds than the Battle of Flowers, as many enjoyed the cooler temperatures of a night parade. Andricks found parade participants by calling the military bases in the city, which did not have floats in the Battle of Flowers Parade. He also recruited the Shriners, along with other commercial firms and social groups that had been overlooked by the Battle of Flowers organization.[26] In doing so, he was including much of the city's new middle class. Andricks also began to make arrangements to exchange floats with festivals in other Texas towns and even nationwide. Within the first two years, there were as many as twenty-five out-of-town floats in the parade. Eventually, the Flambeau appeared in Washington, D.C.'s, Cherry Blossom Festival, the Minneapolis Aquatennial, the St. Paul Winter Carnival, and the Tournament of Roses in Pasadena.

Andricks made the parade's success his personal mission. One year, he signed Mickey Dolenz (then a child star of the TV series *Circus Boy*) to ride an elephant in the parade. When Dolenz and his mother failed to arrive at the assembly point for the parade, Andricks hailed a police car to drive him to their hotel and retrieve the child star. As they were heading back to the parade, Andricks could not find his police escort, so he jumped in the police car and drove it back to the parade himself. He later learned that he had "stolen" the wrong police car, but the parade began on time.[27] As the preceding story indicates, Andricks insisted on tight control of the parade. In the process of creating it, the FSJA also channeled more money to the Flambeau and to goodwill trips to other national parades but failed to also increase spending for other Fiesta events.

On top of all this, the association was at a deficit. In a meeting in May 1958, the FSJA was sixteen thousand dollars in debt. State Rep. Raymond Russell called for an independent audit, but Andricks blocked his efforts. The protesting groups also discovered that the association was running most of the festival on advance payments made by the Fiesta Carnival, which was controlled by a private contractor. Any changes in Carnival ownership, or refusals by city councilmen to issue permits for public-land use, would threaten the entire festival. Thompson also claimed that Parker Southern, the president of the FSJA, and Prospero Zottarelli, another member of the committee, had decided to run for city council that year. These decisions, the organizational leadership claimed, "plunged the association into politics."[28] They believed that the Fiesta Association, as a nonprofit civic association, should not have its representatives participate in city government. Ironically, many members of the FSJA had held positions in the city. The FSJA's first president, Frank Bushick, later became city commissioner. Frequently, participation in the FSJA provided an opportunity for visibility that encouraged many members to seek public office.

Andricks, however, was also interested in maintaining the fiction of Fiesta's nonpolitical purposes. Never one to keep silent in these matters, Andricks sent a letter of response to FSJA members two weeks after Thompson's column was published. Andricks emphasized the nonpolitical purposes of the association, in that it "exists solely to coordinate and stage events of the Fiesta." He also refuted Thompson's claim that his position in the association was dictatorial.[29] Unfortunately, much of Andricks's response did more to encourage his opponents. He attempted to show that each of the objecting organizations had positions on the board and that their approval was necessary for all spending decisions. At the same time, he revealed that the executive committee, which was responsible for all actions between the board meetings, did not have representatives from these groups. He also gave inadequate explanations for the association's deficit spending (attributing most of it to "recession" and "rain") and failed to give full access to the financial records.

More important, the language of his rebuttal reveals that the source for much of these conflicts had much more to do with politics than either side would recognize. While defending the FSJA's practices, Andricks argued that the institution of new events during the last decade had

> increased the scope of the celebration in order to include people from all walks of life who previously had had no part in Fiesta. These people were not members of certain social groups and had been virtually left out.[30]

In case this very thinly veiled attack on the protesting organizations was not already clear, Andricks included that when the executive committee attempted to address the aforementioned conflicts and sought advice from the board, "it did not receive any recommendations from the participating organizations, including the strictly social groups to which the complaining parties belonged." Andricks also claimed that those who were criticizing his policies were simply jealous and "do not understand the purposes and proper operation of a festival and the part it plays in directing nationwide attention to the city."[31] A fundamentally different conception of Fiesta was embedded in Andricks's remarks, a distinct philosophy that worked well with the growth-oriented political climate of the city.

Don't Reign on My Parade

As the FSJA fought this internal battle, new practices that critiqued the traditional Fiesta royalty emerged as well. The first overt parody of the queen's elaborate coronation, the Cornyation, began within NIOSA. The coronation was and is a space for demonstrating the superiority of the city's oldest and wealthiest families.[32] In the context of Fiesta's new democratic ethos, this public spectacle quickly became the target of criticism. Beginning in 1951, NIOSA sponsored their lighthearted spoof of the event to benefit San Antonio's Little Theatre. This new parody featured the Court of the Cracked

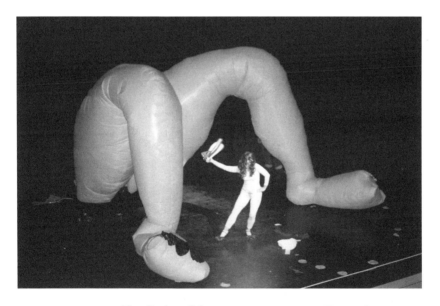

FIGURE 10. The display of the grotesque at a recent Cornyation. Photographed by Sarah Ehrisman, Courtesy of the author.

JUAN Q. PUBLIC

Salad Bowl with King Anchovy presiding over the Duchesses of Scallions, Radishes, and Parsley.[33] Even as the Cornyation turned to local political satire at the end of the 1950s, though, very little direct criticism was aimed at the coronation participants themselves. In the mid-1960s, SACS discontinued their sponsorship of the event, perhaps because of its increasing political satire.[34] The Cornyation featured grotesque displays of bodies and cheap fabrics and was a direct inversion of the coronation, much like the burlesque parades of the early twentieth century. The bodies on display at the Cornyation were oversized and erotic, featuring bulging breasts and buttocks, a direct inversion of the demure bodies on display at the coronation.[35] For its sponsors, though, these carnivalesque inversions were not wholly embraced in its early years.

The more successful pageant of this period was the creation of Miss Fiesta. While John Carrington wanted to bring a greater sense of gentility to Fiesta's events with his queen's coronation, Reynolds Andricks wanted a more democratic representative with his Miss Fiesta. The coronation queens were always taken from the names of the San Antonio Country Club, and many families had long uninterrupted dynasties. Because membership in these clubs was so limited, Andricks decided to create a rival role in 1950. Instead of having the aristocratic title of queen, though, this new representative would simply be named Miss Fiesta. Andricks also emphasized that Miss Fiesta would also be democratically elected. Each subsequent year, the association sponsored a contest in which candidates were nominated from three of the city's colleges—Our Lady of the Lake College, Incarnate Word College, and San Antonio College. Each school selected thirty young women based on academic standing, personality and charm, and appearance in evening dresses. Then, a panel of judges from the FSJA would select the twelve finalists, four from each school. These twelve women would participate in the pageant in the Municipal Auditorium, and the winner would be chosen by the audience and a panel of five judges.[36]

As multiple Fiesta queens pass spectators in the Fiesta parades, one of the most frequent shouts is for them to "show us your shoes." They may then lift their skirts to reveal tennis shoes or fuzzy slippers. This demonstration is certainly mild compared to the women who respond to different catcalls by taking off their tops during Mardi Gras. Perhaps, however, the growing popularity of such foot-baring practices is a social comment as well. The elevated, spiritual bodies of the pageant queens are asked to reveal their feet of clay. Both the queens of the Order of the Alamo and these new Fiesta beauties provided idealized feminine forms to be consumed by the male observer. Yet Miss

Fiesta not only presented an inviting image to consume, her role was also created as an alternative to the queen's court. Miss Fiesta imitated the more modern beauty pageant form with values and symbols specific to the middle class and challenged the aristocratic and Eurocentric classical bodies of the queen and her court. Robert Lavenda describes similar small-town queen pageants in Minnesota as hybrids between the debutante ball and the beauty pageant. Lavenda argues that these towns, with an egalitarian ideology, reject the elitism of the debutante form.[37] Instead, they use the popular democratic form of the beauty pageant, because it purportedly values talent and community service as well as physical beauty. The beauty pageant is "fundamentally a bourgeois play form: the winners get material goods in the form of money, trips, cars, scholarships, modeling contracts, and so on."[38] Festival organizers seek a community representative whose election is based on achievement, though, not beauty. Thus, physical attractiveness is not as important as embodying the character of the middle class. The pageant celebrates upward mobility and tutors them in the social mores of the middle class.[39]

Like the Order of the Alamo queens, Miss Fiesta pageant members represent a larger civic body. The debutantes reproduce elite status in the coronation, however, while the Miss Fiesta pageant espouses middle-class community ideals of democratic achievement through the form of the beauty pageant. Miss Fiesta reached her position through a contest in which she demonstrated her particular oratorical skills and past accomplishments. Her initiation was a representation of individual achievement, rather than a presentation of family lineage. Much of the structure of the competition was modeled on the Miss America Pageant. Promotions of Miss Fiesta did not emphasize physical attractiveness, however. Instead, special attention was focused on the historical essay each Miss Fiesta finalist wrote and presented as part of the contest.

The Miss Fiesta role does not parody the coronation queen; it offers a more subtle critique. By imitating the classical ideals of the queen's court, Miss Fiesta seeks to become part of the high culture of Fiesta's royal ranks. At the same time, her role transgresses discourses of class distinctions. Although seeking to legitimate their high positions in official Fiesta events, the incorporation of this new role also shifted the terms of inclusion and exclusion in Fiesta representations. The classical pose of the queen was now open to a wider number of women.[40]

The differences between the queen and Miss Fiesta are also demonstrated on the body. Instead of wearing gowns and long trains reminiscent of the English monarchy, where the queen literally carried her family lineage on her back, Miss Fiesta wore a much simpler formal dress. Her outfit has not changed significantly, usually reflecting contemporary prom dresses. The outfits have no trains and are not connected to any particular theme. The wearer selects her own wardrobe as well. The difference in costume not only made the position more economically feasible for most San Antonians; the dress also communicated a distinctly middle-class sensibility. Miss Fiesta chose her own dress, rather than fitting into a previously designed corona-tion gown and train.[41] Miss Fiesta's humbler attire made her appearance in the Flambeau Parade less dazzling but less socially removed as well. While Miss Fiesta's appearance was more individuated, cut off from family lineage, she also diminished the boundaries between herself and the audience. She was placed on a pedestal, riding atop an elevated flat, and yet she also represented the middle-class myth of a classless society. While Miss Fiesta embodied many of the familiar classical values of privatization and elevation, she also demon-strated an emphasis on mobility and process. While set apart from the crowd, Miss Fiesta simultaneously communicated that her role was accessible to all.

As the new reigning monarch of Andricks's Fiesta Flambeau, Miss Fiesta became the symbol for Fiesta's new democratic ethos. In one of the main promotional photos of 1957's Fiesta, Miss Fiesta sits on top of her float, the Alamo in the background. During the 1950s, the Fiesta Association made her not only the reigning monarch of the Flambeau Parade, but of Fiesta entirely, diminishing the roles of the Queen of the Order of the Alamo and King Antonio. For the first time, middle-class San Antonio residents had new opportunities for attention during Fiesta. Bettsie Guerra Heis, Miss Fiesta of 1954, expressed this sentiment well.

> I was from the East Side of San Antonio and that was a big deal, and I was so proud. My dad had a service station on the East Side. I remember one day riding by with a police escort in a convertible. And daddy was standing out in front of the station and he had a handkerchief in his hand and he was waving it. He was so proud. I'll never forget it.[42]

For Heis, a Mexican American from a less affluent part of the city, her par-ticipation in Fiesta was a unique opportunity for public visibility. Unlike the queen, she also had a more expansive public role. While the queen's duties were largely limited to appearing at private parties and decorating parade floats, Miss Fiesta often traveled to other cities to promote the parade and partici-pate in the FSJA's publicity campaigns. In many of the early years, Miss Fiesta would attend the Tournament of Roses Parade on her own float. Because her title was named before Fiesta week, she also had prefestival publicity. The queen, nominated in secret and not revealed to the public until her coronation, had fewer opportunities to talk to the press. While the coronation's rituals fall into the private-domestic sphere of young women as units of familial reproduction, Miss Fiesta transgressed some of the limits of this domain.

Miss Fiesta did not act as an independent public representative, however. Reynolds Andricks closely monitored her behavior. Diane Thiel Bozorgi, Miss Fiesta of 1965, had mixed feelings about her year in the role. Though she has many positive memories of going to the Rose Bowl and other festivals, she also felt that she was their advertisement piece, an unpaid representative who had to agree that this role came first.[43] She felt overwhelmed, missing trips home for Thanksgiving and most of Christmas break. Often, she would be called for an appearance the night before an event and had to miss classes and final exams. The pressure of the schedule eventually led her to drop out of school for a time. For the full year that she was Miss Fiesta, she was at Andricks's beck and call. These requirements were written into Miss Fiesta's code of conduct. In this code, she was instructed that she should be available for activities that are "planned on a split-second timing." Miss Fiesta was also to keep to a rigid protocol with regard to her media appearances.

> In speaking in public or to news media, when authorized by the Director of the Fiesta Flambeau, a furnished written text will be followed. No statements shall be made to anyone in private or in public which may be, or may be construed to be, unfavorable to her college, the Festival San Jacinto Association and its events, or to any individual connected with these organizations.[44]

Not only was she to speak from a prepared text, but she was also not permitted to change her hair or dress, drink or smoke in public, or have unofficial escorts at any activity. Bozorgi's parents were not even allowed to attend events with her.

While Diane Thiel Bozorgi and other Miss Fiestas had a highly visible role in civic events, they often found themselves to be just as limited by gendered constraints on their performance. These young women were not independent spokespersons for Fiesta, but vessels for Reynolds Andricks's vision. It seems that part of Andricks's desire to closely control Miss Fiesta was his personal grudge with the heritage elite. Bozorgi commented that he gave the impression that "he was fighting with something." He had a strong

FIGURE 11. Miss Fiesta crowned by Rudolph Richter,
with Reynolds Andricks holding her wand on the right, 1956.
San Antonio Express-News, UTSA's Institute of Texan Cultures
at San Antonio, Courtesy of the Hearst Corporation.

personality and intimidated several Miss Fiestas.[45] Aside from Andricks's
personality, though, the limits of the role itself often isolated these women.
Strictly chaperoned and displayed, Miss Fiesta was not so different from the
Queen of the Order of the Alamo. She was a representative of Fiesta's new
democratic vision, but in other ways her duties separated her from the larger
world. Bozorgi explains that in the turbulent years of the late 1960s, she felt
she had "one foot in a satin pump and another in a Birkenstock."[46] She was
an eighteen-year-old college student, becoming an adult and witnessing dramatic social change. At the same time, during her role as Miss Fiesta, she
was cordoned off from these events, attending luncheons, and parading on
fantastical floats.

Losing the Battle

For Andricks, Miss Fiesta was the ultimate symbol of a democratic Fiesta. The heritage elite, though, would no longer tolerate his continuing monopoly of the festival. Although Andricks and the FSJA president, Parker Southern, made several attempts to reconcile the rift, including organizing a planning committee to discuss the problems, the protesting organizations decided to withdraw from the FSJA. On April 28, 1959, the leaders of the Battle of Flowers Association, Texas Cavaliers, Order of the Alamo, German Club, and Junior Chamber of Commerce wrote to the Fiesta San Jacinto Association to announce their resignations. Henceforth, they decided that they would continue to stage their own Fiesta events independently. Shortly after their letter to the FSJA, the groups also sent a letter to the press, explaining their reasons. In a draft of this public announcement, the groups responded to Andricks's March letter. Many of their comments simply restated previous concerns about finances and unequal treatment for their own events, yet the main sore point seemed to be Andricks's dismissal of the social clubs. In the group's letter, Mrs. William H. Spice, Jr., president of the Battle of Flowers Association, refuted Andricks's claims:

> A look to the history of these organizations fails to document that they came into being to promote social aspirations. The Battle of Flowers started Fiesta in 1891 by staging a parade to commemorate patriotic ideals. The Fiesta Association itself came into being about 1906 because the business men of the city were asked by the Chamber of Commerce to form an organization that could give these ladies some help . . . To add to the color and festive mood deemed proper in memorializing the winning of our freedom at the San Jacinto Battlefield, the Cavaliers were asked to organize and take over the furnishing of a king . . . and the Order of the Alamo to add to the celebrations a beautiful Coronation spectacle and the furnishing of a Queen, all for the purpose of emphasizing the patriotic aspects of the San Jacinto victory.[47]

This response redefines Andricks's attack on the social clubs. These organizations were not created to promote social aspirations, the letter claims, but promote patriotic ideals and public service. Thus, such lofty goals serve to legitimize the organizations. Andricks, however, was not criticizing these groups' purpose so much as their membership policies. What the organizations' response fails to address are issues of access. Becoming a Texas Cavalier or a member of the Battle of Flowers Association is not an easy task. In both these cases, potential new members have to be recommended and sponsored by an existing member, as well as voted in by the organization as a whole. In addition, the number of members is severely limited. Thus, becoming a member involves long-standing ties to San Antonio's social elite. By shifting the social club debate to issues of purpose, these social clubs could more effectively deal with Andricks's claims.

The letter also emphasizes organizational histories to remind the public of where Fiesta had its origins. The Fiesta Association itself is defined as coming into existence in order to "help the ladies." Thus, the association originally served to assist the Battle of Flowers Association, not direct them. Furthermore, the Battle of Flowers was the original event of Fiesta. Mrs. Spice was putting Andricks in his place and asserting her organization's role as the primary caretaker for the festival. She ignored the reality that several men's organizations had already diminished the Battle of Flowers Association's prominence. She portrayed the Texas Cavaliers and the Order of the Alamo as those men who answered the women's call to help, without acknowledging that they now controlled most of the pageantry for the festival.

Yet Mrs. Spice's assertions were lost on Andricks. He was not concerned with respecting elite women's volunteerism. Reynolds Andricks's attacks were directed at the ghost of John Carrington. When Carrington formed the Texas Cavaliers in 1927, one of his motivations was to provide "better management" of Fiesta itself.[48] Carrington felt that the elite, and particularly a male elite, should establish control over Fiesta. Carrington believed the festival was an extension of the country club roster's role as the guardians of tradition. Andricks, by contrast, was searching for ways to incorporate middle-class Anglos into San Antonio's civic activities. A coalition of those organizations that followed Carrington's philosophy led the revolution of 1959. Andricks was not alone in his criticism of the social clubs, however; several other San Antonians echoed his comments.

While Paul Thompson supported the elite protesters, San Antonio's other citywide paper, the *San Antonio Light*, defended Andricks. *Light* columnist Don Político provided a background to the conflict that was very similar to Andricks's claims. When Fiesta began, the columnist wrote, San Antonio was a small town that did not need a big festival, yet after World War II the city had grown "from a one-horse town to one of the great metropolitan areas of the country." Fiesta, however, had not matched the city's development. "The Fiesta wasn't big enough for the town—not to mention visitors—and it was based on too narrow a segment of the city's growing population." As the FSJA, under the leadership of Andricks, made Fiesta big enough to accommodate the new city, "the old social organizations were left behind, but didn't realize it."[49] By incorporating many new events that were mostly free and open to the public, Don Político argued, Fiesta had broadened the festival to include all. New events such as the Flambeau Parade have become equal to, if not more popular than, the older ones. The columnist largely dismissed the financial disputes and claimed that "the real rub" was the diminished power of the social organizations.

The battle continued in the press long after the association's membership divided. On May 4, 1959, Mrs. Spice wrote two more letters to the city's papers. One letter was to Paul Thompson and the *San Antonio Express News* newspaper, praising his "straightforward and factual reporting" of the participating organizations' reasons for withdrawing from the FSJA. Her second letter was to Col. Dwight Allison of the *San Antonio Light*, as a response to the Don Político column. She began her letter with a refusal to be quoted by the *Light* in the future, stating that her words have been misrepresented. Her most important refutation, however, was once again the accusation that the Battle of Flowers Association is "purely a social group." In fact, she ended her letter with a manifesto of the BFA's mission, which is worth quoting at length.

> I strongly refute the suggestion that the work we do to commemorate the ideals of the men who won our freedom at the Alamo is a decadent work … We hold to the undisputable fact that these events are sponsored as a part of our responsibility to the youth of the community and to help them to live up to the great heritage our past has given them. While most of the world struggles against oppression, regimentation and tyranny, we maintain that the spirit of the Alamo is one which we wish to commemorate as an example to our youth, this country's most valuable asset. We believe that in these days when a questionable set of values is being made attractive to them on all sides, such as the dope peddlers around the corner, the rock-and-roll type places of entertainment, the glorification of the mobster and gang rule, the philosophy of the beatnik, we believe it necessary to honor some plain old-fashioned virtues such as bravery, courage, honor, self-sacrifice, the courage of one's convictions and the faith in the right … The parade is not entirely chicken wire and crepe paper, but in the development and building of the floats, long hours were spent in historical research and they are executed by groups learning

to work and live thru [*sic*] cooperation with each other, and sharing in the pride of group accomplishment. The "importance of the traditional Fiesta events" HAS NOT [her emphasis] "declined" and will never decline regardless of the size of this city . . . We are acting as a small beacon shining in a confused world.[50]

Mrs. Spice's depiction of contemporary San Antonio does not quite match Don Político's. For her, the modern city is filled with corrupting influences. Of course, Spice's combination of cultural conservatism and cold war anticommunism was quite familiar at the time, yet her battle with urban growth and consumer culture is particularly revealing. For San Antonio's elite women, commemorating Alamo heroes was a refuge and a source of power. The women who spent all year building crepe paper floats fostered and maintained an exclusive community that was expressed through the language of heritage. These women attempted to secure a place for themselves in the future by an emphasis on education. Teaching the youth offered a role for the social clubs of the present. San Antonio's elite maintained a private culture within the public culture of Fiesta. Through a series of private balls and fundraisers, this group set itself apart from the wider city public. They justified their social position through their service to the larger community.[51]

Eventually, Spice and her heritage-based coalition achieved a partial victory. Andricks could not successfully run Fiesta without these organizations' participation. A new organization formed called the Fiesta San Antonio Commission (FSAC). Like the previous organization, this new commission relied on a board of many participating member organizations (PMOs). The new commission did not have an executive committee, so each PMO had a stronger voice in Fiesta changes. The FSAC had a president, but this role was not as powerful as the executive secretary.[52] The city's heritage elite would regain its prominence in Fiesta, but this new commission also had many new PMOs, including Andricks's San Jacinto Association.

Many of these new PMOs represented a wide variety of middle-class civic organizations. These previously warring factions found a compromise where the heritage groups could retain their prominence yet would also share their power. This new arrangement allowed each group to maintain its own event, but elite women had the most to lose in this compromise. The Battle of Flowers Association, the Daughters of the Republic of Texas, and the San Antonio Conservation Society would maintain their custodianship of particular events, but Fiesta would definitively move outside their distinct public domain.

Andricks lost his personal battle for control of Fiesta, but subsequent Fiesta organizers had to accommodate the sentiments he represented. Fiesta would now be organized under the egalitarian rhetoric of inclusion. While the newly formed Fiesta San Antonio Commission represented a return of the old guard, this reinstatement included a rhetorical distancing from the commemoration of the Texan independence battle. The prevailing language of inclusion had simultaneously become a language of forgetting.

Forgetting the Alamo

In order to understand this shift, one must understand the centrality of Alamo memory for San Antonio's heritage elite. As the self-appointed guardians of tradition, the Battle of Flowers, the DRT, the Order of the Alamo, and the Texas Cavaliers all used the Alamo as their symbolic inheritance. As a commemoration of Texan independence, Fiesta celebrated these organizations' social and political prominence. This elite also merged the Texans' cause with wars in the twentieth century. In 1918, when the Fiesta Association decided to suspend the festival during World War I, the DRT sponsored a pilgrimage to Alamo Plaza. Various patriotic and military organizations laid wreaths in front of the Alamo chapel and the names of the 189 Texans who died in the battle were read. The ceremony became an annual Fiesta event, further tying commemoration of the Alamo battle with U.S. patriotism.

This focus on commemoration was not so important to those who could not exploit these ancestral ties. For those who were not part of the heritage elite, the Alamo was not central to constructing their legitimacy in the city. These San Antonians did not simply forget the Alamo, however. Instead, they renegotiated its meaning within a growing consumer economy. The process of Alamo refashioning came at a time when the Alamo was a widely known symbol of patriotism and the principal tourist site in the city. This would have profound consequences for the custodians of the Alamo, the Daughters of the Republic of Texas. The heritage-minded Daughters of the Republic of Texas wanted to maintain their exclusive role in Alamo custodianship. For them, the Alamo was a shrine of Texas nationalism, while other members of the city reformulated the Alamo as a space to celebrate a larger, diverse public.

By 1958, the Fiesta San Jacinto Association's official festival invitation included the familiar Alamo inscription, stating that "at this shrine the people of Texas promise 'We Shall Not Forget.'" Yet by this time, many San

Antonians did not focus on the Alamo remembrance, at least during Fiesta. In the decades after World War II, Fiesta organizers increasingly promoted the festival as a celebration of the city's history and development, not as a commemoration of Texas independence.

The diminishing role of the Alamo corresponded to a new negotiation of its place in the city's economy. After World War II, additions to the Alamo grounds and the creation of the Riverwalk began to restructure the city's downtown environment. For city boosters, the Alamo was a resource to market commodities for tourist consumption.[53] The DRT maintained official custodianship, but these business interests controlled the public image of the Alamo. The DRT's vision was inconsistent with Anglo consumer culture, which stressed the "canonization of commodities, not shrines, as the primary ingredient of cultural identity."[54] Yet the DRT had more to lose than whether coonskin caps would be sold on Alamo grounds. Their custodianship of the center of San Antonio's public culture depended, in part, on their definition of the Alamo as a space apart from the commercial activity of the city. Like the Battle of Flowers Association, the DRT had refashioned the Alamo into their particular public space. As they lost the ability to define this space, they also lost much of their distinctive role in the city's public culture. The DRT would maintain its control over the Alamo grounds, but they did not control the place it would occupy in the local or regional imagination.

As Fiesta grew, solemn commemoration was less important than festive leisure. In 1948, Davis's description of the Alamo pilgrimage disappears from the invitations. While subsequent invitations continued to include information on the pilgrimage, these later narratives were simplified and reduced. To replace them, more stories about Fiesta as a whole emerged. These new stories emphasized a peaceful landscape. In 1949, the first cohesive history of Fiesta supplanted the pilgrimage.

> The Fiesta has grown up as naturally as any flower that grows out of the rich earth. In the atmosphere of old San Antonio, with its soft, semi-tropical air, its dramatic history, its blend of mellow traditions from Spain and Mexico with many other, different ways of life, a Fiesta of some kind was as inevitable as the blossoming of the huisache or the bluebonnet.[55]

In this description, Fiesta emerges out of nature and the mellow traditions of Spain and Mexico. Rather than a commemoration of a historic event, Fiesta's creation seems inevitable, the product of the mixing of cultures; the only mention of history in this passage is to say that it is dramatic. Later in the narrative, the anonymous author writes, "Wherever you go in the city during Fiesta week, there is something colorful to see, and there is music and laughter in the air." Instead of honoring a battle site, Fiesta grew out of this local color. Alamo remembrance was not central to the vision. A short time is set aside for Alamo memory, but this was increasingly circumscribed.

> Because Texas will be recalling once more a proud page from the Lone Star state's most patriotic past, the week-long fete will be fraught with overtones of the utmost solemnity, although for the most part, gaiety will be unrestrained.[56]

During the Alamo pilgrimage, the DRT maintained the solemn tones of commemoration, while civic boosters emphasized a festive atmosphere.

At this time, Fiesta was presented as feminine and Mexican, closer to nature than to civilization.[57] To develop an atmosphere of peaceful leisure, Fiesta boosters employed popular stereotypes of both women and people of color as passive and self-indulgent. A 1958 newspaper cartoon promoting Fiesta depicts NIOSA as a woman in Mexican costume. She cries, "Afuera!" as she kicks a man out the door of the festival's gate, which is surrounded by signs for tamales, fun, street dancing, and cascarones. The ousted man represents the current economic and political troubles. He has "gloom, recession, taxes and cold war" written on his jacket.[58] The NIOSA representative crying, "Afuera!" is a woman. NIOSA is shown as a feminine space where one can escape the modern world, a place for laziness, indulgence, and consumption.

How NIOSA was to be presented was also the dominating discourse of the city's tourism.[59] This also explains how the Alamo became less central to Fiesta. Perceived as the site of masculine heroism and a battle marking the Anglicization of Texas, it was a sharp contrast to the romanticized, Mexicanized tourist landscape celebrated during Fiesta. This tourist landscape, however, does not account for the meanings that San Antonians performed when they went to Fiesta. Embedded in these festive tones was a new hybrid identity for the city's Anglos. For middle-class Anglos in particular, celebrating Fiesta was also a way to establish their own place in San Antonio's public culture. Unable to demonstrate family lineage from Alamo heroes, many Anglos found a powerful performative language for expressing this new sense of civic equality and unity through the process of "playing Mexican."

Embodying Difference

As the discourse of inclusion dominated Fiesta invitations and newspaper debates, more and more images of Mexicanness appeared in the promotional materials and in popular dress. This phenomenon was not new to Fiesta. Carnival participants of the early twentieth century reaffirmed racial boundaries when they played Mexican, and the women of the Conservation Society wore Mexican dresses as they searched for a new identity for themselves within the parameters of southern womanhood. This ethnic cross-dressing had a different meaning for San Antonio's postwar Anglo public, however. When the Mr. and Mrs. Juan Q. Public were invited to attend Fiesta in the 1950s and 1960s, they found a way to perform a doubled, hybrid civic identity.

In 1946 the Fiesta San Jacinto Association began a drive to encourage city residents to wear costumes during Fiesta week. In honor of the centennial anniversary of Texas's annexation, the FSJA wanted celebrants to wear clothes typical of the nineteenth century, either "frontier, colonial or Mexican costumes."[60] In addition to a huge publicity campaign, FSJA members suggested encouraging girls' sewing classes in public schools to make costumes and meeting with major retail stores to have their employees in costume.[61] According to the papers, the campaign was a success. City councilmen, county commissioners, and Chamber of Commerce members were photographed in costume. The FSJA promoted the idea as a way everyone could participate in Fiesta. Wearing costumes will also "achieve the objective of making San Antonio known as the most colorful city in Texas" by reminding visitors of San Antonio's romantic past as a cattle-raising center and frontier city.[62]

This new democratic form of dress was also meant to be easily accessible to the city's populace as a whole. Press statements frequently mentioned that any small gesture would be sufficient for a costume, a belt, vest, or hat would do. The most popular costumes divided into two categories, the Western and the Mexican. Racial divisions were encoded in this division. Western was clearly the Anglo cowboy, including boots, a fringed vest, jeans, and a cowboy hat. As Mexicans, men would wear a sarape over their shoulders, plain white cotton shirts and pants, sandals, and a sombrero, while women would wear brightly colored full skirts and off-the-shoulder peasant blouses.

Some public figures made clear distinctions between the two styles. City Comm. R. W. Stappenbeck claimed he would not wear a sarape because he represented "Texas, not Mexico. I will wear an old cowboy outfit like my forefathers who pioneered here."[63] Stappenbeck repeated a common idea of the Anglo cowboy, but of course this outfit itself is derivative of the Mexican

FIGURE 12. Peterie Guerra, a Miss Fiesta in the 1950s, in her "western wear."
UTSA's Institute of Texan Cultures at San Antonio, Courtesy of Carol Canty.

JUAN Q. PUBLIC

vaquero tradition. Though Stappenbeck, like many others, made clear divisions between the Anglo and the Mexican dress, these categories were more entangled than he suggested. Both costume styles were removed from modern life. The gringo cowboys and Mexican peasants were romanticized images of a premodern West, unlike the world of contemporary Anglos and Mexican Americans. In addition, the cowboy represented a nostalgic version of rural, working-class whiteness.[64]

During this time a range of new ideas suggested that social boundary crossing was a question of behavior. Carey McWilliams identified closely with California Latinos, and Norman Mailer "sang the black virtues of the hip" in the "white Negro." In a time of the "lonely crowd," of shallow conformism, some San Antonio Anglos found escape by performing a time and a race apart.[65] Unlike the tourists who visited New Mexico to find redemption in the authentic vision of otherness, or the white-middle-class hobbyists who sought this same authenticity in replicating Native American ritual, Anglos during Fiesta performed sameness while they performed difference. These gringos were hybrid creatures, incorporating a remote, nineteenth-century, cattle-ranching town into a modern industrializing city. Their metaphorical cross-dressing allowed them a space between these ethnic groups. Anglo Mexicans were performing a double identity; they imagined themselves as both Anglo citizens of a growing modern city and part of an ethnically diverse public with a long history.

Thus, Mexican play became the performative metaphor for this new democratic language of inclusion. City boosters thought one of the keys to invigorating their modern city was to sell its diverse past, and many recognized Mexicanness as part of the city's present and future. Yet Anglos were more ambivalent about the place of Mexicanos themselves in the city's public life. They continued to segregate public facilities and ignored the development of the city's west and east sides. They also kept distinct ethnoracial boundaries. Negotiating the social relationships between Anglos and people of color was a contradictory process. Like other Americans, San Antonians made efforts to reconcile the difference between the city's inclusive rhetoric and the city's history of racial segregation.[66] For San Antonio's Anglos, Mexicans were on a contradictory axis, "so close as to be part of a slowly forming multicultural society; so distant as to be racially distinct."[67] In order to address their contradictory feelings, white San Antonians tried to forget history during Fiesta, yet this was not easy to do.[68] While negotiating new relationships among an ethnically diverse population, Fiesta promoters turned, once again, to the Alamo.

Re-membering the Alamo

In Fiesta, one of the first hints at this new form of interethnic reconciliation was the name change from Fiesta San Jacinto to Fiesta San Antonio. Fiesta organizers did not record any lengthy explanations for the new name, except that it was part of a desire to reach out to the city's Mexican American community. Apparently, the Municipal Advertising Commission recommended the name change in order to "promote friendship with Mexico."[69] As municipal government made attempts to include in a limited sense Mexican American representatives, Fiesta boosters made efforts to incorporate Mexican Americans into San Antonio's public culture. A rhetorical distancing from the Alamo battle was an important part of this process.

Several popular renditions of the Alamo story changed as well. In 1960, John Wayne's rendition of the Alamo battle merged with post–World War II patriotism and anticommunism to help make the Alamo a symbol of U.S. nationalism. San Antonians eagerly participated in the shooting of Wayne's film and attended its opening at San Antonio's Woodlawn Theatre.[70] Yet Wayne's film was not like previous Alamo movies; it demonstrated a refashioning of the Alamo story. Unlike the earliest Alamo films, including *Martyrs of the Alamo*, which depicted Mexicans as treacherous, lazy, and savage, Wayne's Alamo movie made great efforts to portray Mexicans in a more positive manner.[71] Wayne's Alamo story presented Santa Anna's Mexican army as loyal soldiers and also portrayed the Tejanos who fought alongside the Anglo forces within the Alamo's walls. While literature and films in the early twentieth century emphasized the Mexican other as a treacherous enemy, these new Alamo tales offered an inclusive lesson in Tejano loyalty. Discourses of racial unity began to intrude on the story of the Alamo.[72]

The annual Fiesta invitations demonstrated these changes. For several decades the FSJA issued annual invitational booklets to its members (and sold to the wider public) with descriptions of each festival event, schedules, and a story of the Alamo. In the 1948 invitation, the story of the Alamo is told as before but with an important revision. While earlier narratives emphasized the Anglo Texans' bravery against the Mexican soldiers, this description added a new clause.

> Outsiders, unacquainted with the real reasons for the Texas Revolution, who perhaps think that there was a racial cause for the strife, are astonished at the fact that it is a celebration shared by those of both Latin-American and Anglo-Saxon heritage.[73]

The reason for this shared celebration is a victory over a dictator, López de Santa Anna, not over a particular ethnic group. This revision offered an acknowledgement that the historiography of the Alamo battle had taken on racially based explanations. If these "outsiders" thought that the Texas Revolution had a "racial cause," the perception was the result of hundreds of previous narratives that emphasized revenge for the death of Anglo Texan defenders. The anonymous author of the 1948 story gave no explanation for the source of this misunderstanding, though. The "racial cause" is merely forgotten.

The story also seemed to imply that if visitors came to San Antonio and saw how Anglos and Mexicans related, they would see how well both groups got along together in the present. In such a revision, the moral lessons that the Alamo taught were reversed. What was once a story told to reinforce discriminatory practices against Mexican Americans now represented cooperation between these two groups. A symbol of war became a symbol of interethnic peace. Yet this new social arrangement between Anglos and Mexicans remained uneven, as a closer examination of these stories will reveal.

The theme of interethnic harmony continued through several years of Fiesta invitations. For many years, the Fiesta San Jacinto Association would invite a local historian or writer to contribute a biography of one of the Alamo defenders each year. The earliest biographies in the late 1930s included many of the most well known figures in the story, William Travis, Jim Bowie, and Davy Crockett. In 1951 the first Tejano's story appeared, Gregorio Esparza, who was a private in the company of Juan Seguín. Esparza's tale was written in the same romantic tone as that of many other heroic figures, yet it soon became clear that his story was not only an attempt at filling in the gaps in Alamo defender biographies, but also served as a symbol of interethnic cooperation. In the picture accompanying the story, Esparza and an anonymous Anglo Texan are readying themselves for battle. The writer asks:

> Who are these men beside the cannon? One is Anglo-American. The other's name is Esparza; he is of the same nationality as Santa Anna, but he doesn't think like Santa Anna. He, like many of his countrymen, prefers the dignity and equality that comes with freedom.[74]

Esparza is said to be the same nationality as Santa Anna, yet in terms of citizenship, all three men were probably Mexican. Though many Americans and Europeans fought with the Texans, the Anglo Texan settlers of the region were still considered Mexican citizens. Clearly, this description was marked by the modern social order, writing of the Alamo defenders as "Americans."

It was also important that the Anglo man in the picture was anonymous. The story continues:

> One [man in the picture] is a Mexican boy who grew up in San Antonio. The other? Who knows? Perhaps a lawyer from Philadelphia, a wheelwright from West Virginia, a counting clerk from New Orleans. But both understand the unspoken speech of free men, even though they can't converse in the same language.[75]

The ambiguity of the Anglo man's identity reaffirmed his larger, American identity. The "Mexican boy" of the picture, though, is specifically located by the term "boy" and by his hometown. Gregorio Esparza was embedded in the local landscape, a native. His function as boy is as a disempowered, yet loyal, symbol of San Antonio's Mexicano community. By contrast, the Anglo man's primary identity was his middle-class status. As a lawyer, wheelwright, or counting clerk, he could be an urban professional or a skilled artisan. While the official call was for cooperation, these men are not social equals. Esparza has had to separate himself from his "nationality" and take the side of the Anglo settler.[76] Although the Alamo story was retold to include a place for Gregorio Esparza as a patriotic hero, his new position was unequal and unstable. The contradictions in Esparza's story demonstrated that although this version of Alamo narrative rhetorically challenged previous racial hierarchies, it also encouraged them. While Anglo settlement was welcomed, Mexican immigration certainly was not, and even though Esparza "chose" American citizenship, he was still vulnerable to being treated as one of Santa Anna's soldiers.

In 1949 a local press published *City of Flaming Adventure: The Chronicle of San Antonio* by Boyce House. The book gave a general outline of San Antonio's history, written for a broad public audience. House's version of the Alamo story was very similar to Fiesta materials. After he described the battle and the coming of Texan independence, he included a long explanation of Mexicans' role in the conflict. He stated that "the winning of Texas is familiar to everyone—but there is one phase of that story which is not so widely known. And that is the aid which the patriots of Mexican blood rendered." House told the story of a company of Mexicans who fought on the side of Texas. He detailed their bravery and their loyalty to Texas. He also stated that they "had a more difficult choice to make than did the Anglo-Americans . . . they were siding against the government of their native land, whose language and traditions were theirs."[77] In a sense, House's comment was a clear recognition of the ways that the Texas Revolution divided the Tejano community. House also marked a clear boundary between Mexican and Texan identity, however. In order to be a loyal Texan, Esparza had to abandon his cultural heritage.

Fiesta boosters and Anglo historians were not the only people challenging the history of the Alamo. Spokesmen of Mexican American organizations, including the League of United Latin American Citizens, challenged the subservient space the city's Anglo leaders gave them in the Alamo story. During Davy Crockett Week, the San Antonio Chamber of Commerce sponsored a Gregorio Esparza Day on August 23, 1955. On this day, in a public address entitled "Our Place in Texas History," Jacob I. Rodríguez, manager of the Mexican Chamber of Commerce, spoke of the long-delayed recognition of this Texas patriot.[78] At the same time, he critiqued Texas historians for ignoring the much larger role Tejanos played in Texan independence. Quoting from *Viva Texas*, written by Rubén R. Lozano, a "large number" of Tejanos not only participated in the Texans' fight but also initiated the call for independence. Erasmo Seguín called the first Constitutional Convention in Texas, while Stephen F. Austin was still unwilling to fight for an independent state. Other Texas patriots like Juan Seguín, Lorenzo De Zavala, and José Antonio Navarro played a vital role in the new Texas Republic. Seguín led the charge that defeated Santa Anna at San Jacinto. De Zavala became vice president of the Texas Republic, and Navarro signed the Texas Declaration of Independence. These figures were "descended from the Spaniards who [arrived] more than three hundred years before Stephen F. Austin ever thought of coming to Texas."[79] Rodríguez challenged the prominence of the Anglo Texans in contemporary history books, as well as the notion that Anglos were the heirs to the Alamo's legacy. The problem of Anglo historians, he stated, is that they

> never realized that the Alamo (the Mission San Antonio de Valero) was over one hundred years old when their new friends, some no better than adventurers and soldiers of fortune, from the north, ever laid their eyes upon it. That it had served countless generations of Seguíns, Navarros, Arochas, Esparzas, and a host of others, as a school and sanctuary. That generations of Spanish people, high and low, had been born, lived and died within the pale of its ancient walls; that the Alamo meant more to them than it had ever meant or could ever mean to the newcomers and that the liberation and the future of Texas embodied to them their hopes, their aspirations; the very breath of life.[80]

For Rodríguez, and for many other Mexican Americans, the Alamo was a symbol of their legacy, a tie to San Antonio that preceded any Anglo's claim. In his address, Rodríguez used this slim opportunity for historical inclusion offered in Gregorio Esparza Day to reverse the claims of San Antonio's heritage elite.

In his most compelling challenge, Rodríguez also turned the idea of the Americanization of Alamo heroes on its head. The Alamo defenders, he asserted, were naturalized Mexican citizens, not Americans. "They died in the Alamo as 'Mexicans,'" fighting to restore "their own outraged and trampled rights as Mexican citizens, unwilling to submit to a dictator's whims." [81] Rodríguez had complex reasons for this particular challenge. As a prominent member of LULAC, Rodríguez fought for Mexican American civil rights for decades. He fought for their recognition as full American citizens. He struggled to separate ideas of citizenship from ethnic identity. His emphasis on the Alamo defenders' identity as Mexican citizens was part of this same logic. Ethnic Anglos could act as Mexican citizens at the Alamo, just as ethnically Spanish residents, as he identified them, could exercise their rights as American citizens.

Through many letters to local newspapers, self-published magazines, and pamphlets to history textbook committees, Rodríguez continued his struggle to revise Texas history, as did several other Mexican Americans. For the time, he was unsuccessful. Yet his challenge to prevailing Alamo narratives suggests that Alamo memory was a much more contested terrain. The DRT continued to define the battle as a racial conflict between heroic Anglos and tyrannical Mexicans. Rodríguez restored the Alamo as part of a Spanish heritage. He used the limited opportunities of the city's new politics of inclusion, but he had bigger revisions in mind.

Like Parakeets

Rodríguez welcomed Fiesta's new inclusiveness. He applauded the new Fiesta San Antonio Commission when the Mexican Chamber of Commerce could sponsor a Noche Mexicana during the festival. Some Mexican Americans embraced this celebration of San Antonio's Old World flavor as an acknowledgement of the positive aspects of Mexican culture. For the most part, though, San Antonio's Mexican American organizations and the Spanish-language paper *La Prensa* did not speak of Fiesta. While describing other fiestas patrias in Laredo, Corpus Christi, and other south Texas towns, the writers of *La Prensa* understood Fiesta as an Anglo celebration. A few, however, attempted to redefine Fiesta. Delís Negrón wrote one of the few *La Prensa* columns about Fiesta in 1955.[82] In this column, he defined Fiesta events as an extension of Mexican culture. He was proud of the many parades, a time when all leave their houses to come together. For him, Fiesta was a time for community gatherings, not an exclusionary set of events. Negrón accentuated the fact that much Fiesta imagery borrowed from Mexican culture and described this as natural because the city was part of Mexico before it was part of Texas. Fiesta, he wrote, was a celebration of San Antonio's history as a Mexican city. Like Jacob Rodriguez, Negrón attempted to rewrite Fiesta as the legacy of San Antonio's Mexicano residents.

Negrón's article was also a critique of an article a visitor named Ray Duncan wrote describing San Antonio for *Holiday* magazine. Duncan depicted San Antonio as one of the most depraved cities in the nation. He used the term Fiesta City as a derogatory comment on the city's high crime rate and poverty. Duncan associated the city's crime and underdevelopment with its high percentage of Mexicans. Rather than criticize the municipal government's poor service delivery for these problems, Duncan blamed Mexicans themselves. Negrón defended San Antonio on the basis that although the city had poor sanitation services, it remained "a paradise for us."

More important, he challenged Duncan's paternalism. Although Duncan may have had good intentions, he wrote, Duncan "praises the city as God paints a parakeet, not for its industry or intelligence, but for its innocence."[83] Negrón pointed out that Duncan's view of a young, naïve city had a great deal to do with his criticism of its Mexicano population, who Duncan claimed had a less industrious character. Negrón also implied that to designate San Antonio as the Fiesta City was not always complimentary. Often the celebration of the city's festiveness led to paternalistic depictions of its Mexicano residents. Negrón was well aware of the implications this festive language could have for Mexicanos. He also clearly articulated the growing distinction between a commodified multicultural festival and the implications this festival might have for the city's Mexicano residents.

Both Delís Negrón and Jacob Rodríguez fought to place Mexicanos at the center of San Antonio's public culture. It was clear to both, however, that this invention of the Fiesta City was a double-edged sword. While Anglos could enjoy the pleasures of playing Mexican, Mexicanos themselves would feel the continuing effects of such "festive" stereotypes of their culture. Fiesta's postwar organizers successfully challenged the prominence of San Antonio's heritage elite, but their limited rhetoric of inclusion would not fulfill the hopes of most Mexicano residents of San Antonio.

· 5 ·

Rey Feo and the Politics of Inclusion,
1970–2000

THE 2007 MISS FIESTA SCHOLARSHIP PAGEANT WAS HELD IN SAN Antonio's historic Empire Theater, which had once hosted vaudeville shows and the first motion pictures. A relatively small theater, it provided an intimate atmosphere for the annual pageant. Before the performance former Miss Fiestas mingled with family members of pageant contestants, along with members of the Fiesta Commission. The two reigning patriarchs of Fiesta, King Antonio and Rey Feo, took their separate entourages to the mezzanine box seats, while several other Fiesta queens made their way to the front rows of the orchestra. Military ambassadors from each of the city's air force and army bases were also in attendance. Behind the theater curtains, seventeen finalists waited to perform for the title of Miss Fiesta. The woman who would eventually be crowned would be the queen to reign over Fiesta "as a *whole*," the president of the Fiesta Commission emphasized. What he did not note was also significant: the woman who won would most likely be Mexican American.

Miss Fiesta has come a long way. From a pageant representing a group of Anglo coeds from the city's private colleges, the pageant has now become a scholarship fund that is open to any young woman who seeks a college education. For the past twenty-five years, most of the winners have been Mexican American. Miss Fiesta also brought a long line of new festival monarchs after her. Fiesta now includes five Fiesta queens and a new king to reign along-side King Antonio and the Queen of the Order of the Alamo. Miss Fiesta offered an opportunity not just for the Anglo middle class but for Mexican Americans to be part of the festival, but the focus was not just on this one role. After Miss Fiesta assumed her reign in the 1950s, many other organizations wanted to be part of the celebration as well. These organizations' queens, unlike Miss Fiesta, represented specific ethnic communities. One of the first organizations to join was LULAC, who integrated the *reina* of their own fundraiser, La Feria de las Flores. When LULAC became a participating organization in Fiesta in the 1970s, La Reina de la Feria de las Flores joined the festival's royal ranks. The San Antonio Charro Association, another Mexican American organization, also included the queen of their association in Fiesta in 1972, and in 1969 Gracie Poe Griffin created a position for the African American community, the Queen of Soul. Unlike Miss Fiesta, these new roles highlighted distinct cultural pride for San Antonio's Mexican and African American communities.

As described in the previous chapter, in the immediate decades after World War II, a new politics of inclusion signaled a dramatic shift in Fiesta. Like millions of Americans, San Antonians struggled with the contradictions between the fight for democracy abroad and racism at home. Mexican Americans in San Antonio had their own mixed feelings about the festival as well; Fiesta was largely seen as the "gringo's party." Andy Hernández, who was president of the Southwest Voter Registration Education Project and a columnist for the *San Antonio Light*, wrote that he personally "harbored a good amount of ambivalence about Fiesta." While he was attracted to the parades and the festivities, he felt like "an uninvited guest." He detailed his experience of being Mexican American in San Antonio, going to schools where he was spanked for speaking Spanish and reading Texas history books that celebrated the defeat of "bad Mexicans" at the Battle of San Jacinto.

To be Mexican was to be less than every one else. Except for one week of the year. During Fiesta week, San Antonio would embrace and celebrate all things Mexican. Our language would be spoken without apologies, our food elevated to gourmet status, Mexican American celebrations and decorations would liven up the entire city. For one week out of the year, San Antonio would put on its Mexican clothes. The irony in this was that the only week when it was not bad to be associated with Mexican culture and heritage, Mexican Americans were conspicuously absent. All that was us was present during Fiesta week, except us. I guess we were not even good enough to be ourselves when it was good to be who we were.[1]

Hernández expressed a common sentiment among many of the Alamo city's Mexican Americans, and San Antonio's growing Mexican American middle class initiated challenges to Fiesta's monarchy as a response. These challenges were similar to changes in other civic pageants nationwide. In St. Louis, Missouri, African Americans protested against the white business elite's Veiled Prophet parade and ball, eventually diminishing the power of this exclusive organization.[2] In New Orleans, the city council passed an ordinance that challenged the Carnival krewes by prohibiting parade permits for groups that discriminated on the basis of race, religion, or gender in 1992, thus pressuring a few of the krewes to change their membership policies.[3] From the mid-1960s through the 1990s, several municipalities were challenging the racial and ethnic exclusiveness of their city's heritage elite. San Antonio followed a similar pattern, issuing the first public challenges to the Anglo-dominated social clubs in the 1970s. San Antonians did not, however, launch large public protests or municipal ordinances. Compared to the controversies in St. Louis and New Orleans, San Antonio's royal integration was relatively quietly achieved. The reason for this difference has everything to do with the individuals who initiated the challenge and the distinct form of political negotiation that characterized the city.

Bringing Fiesta Home

After Reynolds Andrick's public efforts to introduce a new Fiesta queen, most subsequent royalty were introduced with very little fanfare. These new pageant queens were the first to bring the politics of cultural identity into Fiesta. They also indicated a shift from having a single figure represent the entire city to multiple figures representing several distinct communities within the city. In this era, Fiesta became de-centered. With a rather dizzying array of pageant queens, parades, band contests, and food festivals, Fiesta no longer seemed to revolve around a few central downtown events. Instead, Fiestagoers experienced a series of community parties. During this period, what characterized the festival the most was this effort to bring Fiesta to the neighborhood.

The most well known neighborhood party to begin at this time was the King William Fair, a festival located in an area just southeast of downtown. What began as a small community party in the early 1970s soon became a widely attended Fiesta event with almost one hundred thousand visitors.[4] Organizers for the fair emphasized its role in helping the neighborhood association raise funds for preservation of the area's homes and parks. For the most part, this has been the emphasis of most of these new participating organizations. Fiesta has become a valuable fund-raiser for the restoration of distinct communities. For the King William Association in particular, the fair has increased the association's ability to market the neighborhood for its distinct sense of place.[5] The organizers of the fair are reluctant to embrace the commercial aspects of the event, however. Rosemary Kozmetsky, the organizer of the King William Fair in 2005, emphasized that the fair continues to avoid advertising in local newspapers. According to her, what draws visitors to the fair is its distinctly "family atmosphere" and unique food and entertainment offerings. King William Fair makes an effort to preserve a distinct heritage by denying market forces, even though consumption is central to the fair's continuation. This downplaying of commercial culture is reminiscent of the heritage elite and is unsurprising, given that King William is a wealthy neighborhood with many continuing ties to San Antonio's upper class.

For communities who have long lived at the festival's margins, though, this was also a time to bring Fiesta closer to home. In 1982 Don Moyé, an African American businessman, petitioned the Fiesta Commission to include an event in an area where many members of his organization lived, near Lackland and Kelly air force bases. The event, held at Rosedale Park, would officially be called Fiesta West. Their organization, called the San Antonio Zulu Association, did not have direct connections to New Orleans but formed as a philanthropic organization and to host an annual Juneteenth celebration. The San Antonio Zulus wanted to create an event that would draw Fiestagoers to their neighborhood.[6] Unfortunately, the event failed miserably for the first two years until it was finally moved to the Sunken Gardens Theater in Brackenridge Park, just northeast of downtown, and renamed A Taste of New Orleans. The festival featured New Orleans–style food and music. In this instance, the attempt to extend Fiesta to the west side was unsuccessful. The event did, however, eventually prove to be a valuable fundraiser for the Zulus, and the Zulu Association itself also became an important member organization of the Fiesta San Antonio Commission. Eventually, Moyé himself became the commission's first African American president in 1996. These community parties, though, tell only part of the story of the political negotiations that diversified Fiesta during this time.

Another African American woman who felt marginalized during Fiesta was Gracie Poe Griffin. She remembered seeing many Fiesta parades as a

FIGURE 13. Queen of Soul contest, 1973, with the emblem
of a crown over an Afro hairstyle in the background.
UTSA's Institute of Texan Cultures at San Antonio.

young girl. Many of her most positive, and negative, memories were of watching the Fiesta queens and duchesses. As an African American who grew up on the west side in the 1950s, she knew she would never wear one of those gowns.[7] During that decade, most of the city's facilities were legally segregated, and the only Fiesta events she felt welcomed to were the Carnival and the parade sidelines.

As she watched Fiesta change, though, Griffin was encouraged by the greater openness of the festival, so much so that she saw the possibility of an African American Fiesta queen. In 1969, she helped found the Queen of Soul pageant. The first queen reigned in 1970–71 and rode in the Battle of Flowers Parade. In a city where the issues of African American representation are often upstaged by the conflicts between Anglos and Mexican Americans, Griffin's pageant offered a chance to demonstrate, in her words, the "intelligence and poise" of young black women. Because the Queen of Soul has the purpose of representing a specific community, the pageant can also be analyzed as a means to explore identity within San Antonio's African American community.[8] In these ethnic beauty pageants, idealized versions of femininity are combined with concerns about power and culture. In addition, the Queen of Soul contest incorporates similar concerns as the Miss Fiesta position, in that pageant organizers emphasize its accessibility to any member of San Antonio's black community. The Queen of Soul's purpose is to provide role models for the community itself, as well as display a cultural pride to a citywide audience.

The term "soul" connotes a wide array of distinctly African American cultural practices. Soul food often features African foods that were introduced to the Americas during the slave trade, and soul music includes many musical styles and rhythms derived from West Africa. The terms "soul brother" and "soul sister" also represent a strong sense of extended family within African American communities.[9] During the 1960s and 1970s, "soul" was a ubiquitous term that fused politics and cultural practices, including the civil rights and black power movements, and the renewed exploration of African influences in music, clothing, art, and other cultural forms.

The Queen of Soul was not created as a political entity but was certainly part of an era that emphasized a renewed pride in African heritage. The pageant was one of many efforts nationwide to create a distinct space of African American representation, coming shortly after the creation of the Miss Black America Pageant in August 1968. Within a few years, it also became part of the Miss Black America Pageant circuit.[10] In literature advertising the pageant, the contestants are part of a "sisterhood" and encouraged not to engage in rivalries but to look at the pageant as an opportunity to form friendships.[11]

This theme is prevalent in the rhetoric of many pageants, but the Queen of Soul places a particular emphasis upon reinforcing familial bonds among African American women. The rules for entry have changed very little in the years since the pageant was established. Young women who enter the contest are required to be between the ages of eighteen and twenty-five, at least be a high school senior, and be single and active in the black community. They should have no previous marriages or pregnancies. Like most pageants, the Queen of Soul emphasizes feminine purity and includes rules about maintaining dignity and composure at all official events. At the same time, part of the pageant has always emphasized the display of physical beauty. The pageant includes evening gown and swimsuit competitions, though now this has been modified to "fitness wear"—outfits to "enhance the physical beauty of the contestant, while maintaining modesty and integrity."[12] With these characteristics, the pageant portrays a form of "sanitized eroticism" for a public audience.[13] The pageant also emphasizes middle-class virtues of individual accomplishment and upward mobility. A third part of the competition is the business wear category, where contestants walk across the stage in business suits "for the fashion forward, career-minded young lady."[14] Clearly, the goal of such a contest is social uplift. The pageant approves all the contestants' outfits, and the pageant coordinators supervise the winners during their one-year reign. The Queen of Soul offers an opportunity to display both individual achievement and community pride.

The pageant has not been without critics, though. Because the pageant was founded in the years after feminist critiques of beauty pageants, including the protest of the Miss America Pageant in 1968, the Queen of Soul has had an ambivalent position within ethnic and feminist political movements since its inception. According to many beauty-pageant critics, the glorification of the individual, not to mention limited ideals of feminine beauty, debilitate any attempts at community empowerment. Griffin deliberately sought to mend these contradictions. She conceded that physical attributes were part of the contest, but she also emphasized the pageant winners' devotion to social concerns. For her, the most important qualification for participation was community involvement. Griffin also stressed the pride and confidence of each individual pageant participant. Such emphasis on public presentation pervaded Griffin's statements about the pageant. Her belief was similar to the shifts in other ethnic pageants in the United States, which stressed political activism alongside physical beauty.[15] Griffin's opening message in the 1974 pageant brochure expressed this compromise.

The Queen of Soul is not only selected for particular beauty, but whose charm, poise and intellectual ability is a credit to her community. We feel that our pageant provides the necessary experience of beauty pageant styled competition, and instills more self-confidence for our Queen and Court.[16]

Each queen wins a scholarship, and no outside organization sponsors her entry, providing a "fair chance for any young lady, from any economic or social background . . . to be a participant."[17] During the week preceding the pageant, all the contestants are given free lessons in makeup application, wardrobe advice, and formal dinner rituals, offering a sort of finishing school for the participants. These lessons in social graces are also methods of demonstrating fitness for middle-class status. The display of charm and poise is designed to encourage upward mobility.

When the pageant began, the outfits of the pageant contestants intertwined the ideals of Anglo beauty pageants with distinctly African physical attributes. In this pageant, the black body takes a classical form but with clear markers of a nonwhite cultural identity as well. The pageant's original emblem demonstrated such a hybrid construction. In the 1970s, pageant brochures featured the outline of a crowned young woman's face. The crown, as in other beauty pageants, distinguished her from the crowd. The most prominent feature of the emblem, however, was the Afro hairstyle. The disproportionately large hair dwarfed the image of the crown. This oversized feature is the one that most clearly connects the queen as a member of the African American community. Later designs altered the particular hairstyle but replaced this emblem with another, distinctly African American style. Certainly, the logo was influenced by the predominance of African characteristics and designs that were popular during a historic period of black pride and cultural empowerment.

The continuing criticism of beauty pageants took its toll on the Queen of Soul pageant, however. For many black women, these contests were not appropriate ways of expressing their aspirations. In the early 1980s, pageant participation was particularly low, and many feared the contest would not survive. Griffin attributed this decline to the increased openness of other beauty pageants, so that the Queen of Soul was not the only option for young black women. In the 1990s, Griffin saw a renewed interest in the pageant. She guessed that the growing popularity of multiculturalism had made these ethnically themed pageants more attractive. Another possibility is that within Fiesta representation, the almost exclusively Anglo coronation continues in its prominence. The Queen of Soul reserves the only specific space for African American representation in Fiesta royalty.

As the pageant has developed, though, it has become quite similar to other beauty pageants. There are fewer markers of a distinct African American cultural identity in terms of dress or performance. The same can be said of another Fiesta queen, La Reina de la Feria de las Flores. While la reina is required, at times, to wear folkloric costumes of different regions of Mexico, she usually appears in the semiformal dress and sash that is characteristic of most pageant queens. La reina is not selected in a pageant, though. She gains her position by raising the most scholarship money for the LULAC Rey Feo Scholarship Fund. The festival began in 1945, when a group of San Antonio businessmen organized by LULAC gathered to raise money for educational scholarships. The feria was modeled after the Mexican Feria de San Marcos, where people would pay a penny per vote to select a queen. At present, the committee funds more than one hundred scholarships of fifteen hundred dollars each. They also organize a Parent-Child Scholarship Fund that gives thousand-dollar scholarships to young children, to be awarded when the child begins college.[18]

The San Antonio Charro Association is closely associated with LULAC's feria. In the 1960s, several reinas were sponsored by this organization. The Charro Association also has its own queen, though, who is more closely identified with charro traditions. The Queen of the San Antonio Charro Association is another Fiesta queen who represents a particular community. She is usually the daughter of one of the men in the organization, and her main obligations are to perform a yearlong series of *charrerías*, displays of horsemanship and Mexicano ranching traditions. The requirements for her role are that she be between the ages of sixteen and twenty-one, unmarried, bilingual, and an accomplished sidesaddle rider and Mexican *folklórico* dancer. Unlike the other queens, the Charro queen wears a distinct *traje*, an elaborately stitched suit consisting of a white bolero jacket, skirt, and sombrero. She is the leader of the *escaramuzas*, a female precision team who ride side-saddle in elaborate full skirts.[19] Though their events require great skill, they may also reinforce the view of women as objects of display. She is supposed to refrain from drinking alcohol and agrees not to act in a way that discredits her role. The queen for 2002, Elysiana Judith Cantú, spoke of her role as part of the community of the Charro Association.[20] Fiesta was only one of many performances of her association. For the most part, her participation in Fiesta was just a small part of her experience as a queen. Instead, her role revolved around the activities of the Charro Association's ranch on the south side of town. Her family had longstanding ties to the association and was committed to continuing the distinct charro traditions. She described the San Antonio Charros as an extended family. Their ranch, whose stables and other facilities were maintained by volunteers, was the center of this community. Fiesta had become a part of the charro schedule, and this organization seemed to maintain a distinct identity within the festival.

Though each of these young queens represents distinct ethnic traditions, many of the requirements of their roles are very similar. They are all young, single women who are rewarded for their devotion to community service and individual achievement. They are often chaperoned to Fiesta events, and their activities are monitored by members of their respective organizations. While they certainly have diversified Fiesta royalty, they are also bodies on display. When interviewed by local media, they speak of their career plans, their tastes in music and clothes, and their favorite Fiesta events, but they do not often speak for Fiesta as an event. Perhaps this is why even after the inclusion of these multiple roles, many Mexican Americans continued to express frustration at Fiesta royalty's exclusiveness. When many Mexican American public leaders talk about Fiesta's new diversity, the main symbol for that change is the inclusion of a new king, the LULAC role of Rey Feo (the Ugly King) into Fiesta in 1980. For many, "El Rey Feo came to signify their own place and their own piece of Fiesta in San Antonio." Rey Feo's role was "a place where [Mexican Americans] existed not as someone else's costume but as their own affirmation."[21] Rey Feo was a symbol of successful integration because he defined a distinct role in the festival. All these queens were important precedents to Rey Feo's inclusion in Fiesta. Rey Feo's role stands out, however, because of the singular importance of the king in Fiesta. Only a socially prominent, middle-aged man, like King Antonio himself, could challenge the king's prominence in the festival. He was not merely included in the party; he redefined the party.

The first Fiesta kings in the early twentieth century were named Alegría and Selamat (tamales spelled backward). They were modeled after European carnivals with their emphasis on socially endorsed inversion. As the festival grew, the king's role became more formal, as if the city wanted to portray a more sober representative of the city to the public. In 1915, festival organizers decided on the name King Antonio. As previously described in chapter 2, this Fiesta king became more refined, wearing a military-style jacket and riding breeches instead of long robes and gaudy medallions. From this point onward, King Antonio's role changed very little. Like the Queen of the coronation, he maintained the boundaries of elite patronage of Fiesta, but King

Antonio became a more public figure than any of the queens.[22] As a middle-aged man, upper class and socially prominent, King Antonio was the host of the party. Only the king was said to preside over Fiesta events. He took over the symbolic space the women of the Battle of Flowers Association and then the San Antonio Conservation Society had once occupied. As these upper-class women lost some visibility in Fiesta, King Antonio's presence grew. The crowning of King Antonio began Fiesta week, when he declared the initiation of Fiesta merriment in front of the Alamo. He awarded honor students at elementary schools, gave hundreds of gifts and souvenir medals to local citizens, and visited hospitals, charity functions, and television and radio stations. He was the most conspicuous of these public representatives of Fiesta.

In 1947, LULAC created the figure who eventually rivaled King Antonio's prominence, El Rey Feo. Returning to a more carnivalesque tradition, LULAC claimed that the character of Rey Feo was taken from an ancient Roman tradition of crowning a commoner as king during carnival. In medieval Europe, this tradition took the form of a ceremony where people elected their own king, called the Ugly King (or People's King) because he was a representative of the "ugly common people."[23] LULAC's invented tradition had no official relationship to Fiesta royalty; he was merely the chief fund-raiser of their scholarship program. Then, in 1979, Logan Stewart, a local radio personality and the reigning Rey Feo, decided to campaign for Rey Feo's inclusion in Fiesta. He also proposed that Rey Feo be given his own parade during Fiesta week. His brief campaign was successful, and in 1980 Rey Feo was integrated into Fiesta activities.

By the time Logan Stewart's campaign began, Rey Feo's integration seemed easy to achieve, but this change was not simply a benevolent act of friendship. Rey Feo's inclusion came after a long struggle of a Mexican American middle class that had been growing in population and political power for the past forty years. Rey Feo represented a new interethnic negotiation and the last half century of Mexicanos' struggle for political inclusion in the city. If the first two decades after World War II brought about some limited integration of the Mexican American community, the next twenty years signaled deeper changes. Within this time, Mexicanos moved from "recognition" to an "institutionalized power."[24]

Community Development

This shift paralleled one in San Antonio's politics. Between 1973 and 1982, the city's municipal government transformed. These changes were initiated by neighborhood organizations rather than from machine or party politics. Local politics would be shaped by community concerns.[25] This was influenced by wider changes in regional and national politics as well. Lyndon B. Johnson's war on poverty and his administration's Community Action programs were an important precedent. These programs encouraged the direct involvement of community members in alleviating poverty in their own neighborhoods and often bypassed state and local government. The war on poverty did not achieve all its goals, but many who came of age during this era were influenced by these models of community empowerment. In the Southwest, though Sunbelt growth and expansion helped topple segregation, many were left behind in this process, and so civil rights and antipoverty activists turned to the local. To understand the national, regional, and local changes that led to Rey Feo's entry into Fiesta, one must look at the ways that community-centered politics developed in San Antonio.

As the city's population grew from just over 253,000 in 1940 to more than 654,000 in 1970, San Antonio rose from the thirty-sixth to the fifteenth largest city in the country. Like other cities in the South, the city had already benefited from the growing national defense industry, as seen in the creation of Lackland Air Force Base in 1942. The other existing military bases around the city, Kelly, Randolph, and Brooks, and the army base Fort Sam Houston, also served as important centers of training and research in the cold war era.

A rapidly growing Sunbelt city, San Antonio faced the challenges of urban sprawl. New residents came for jobs in the defense industry, and many new suburbs were built on the north side of town. As these populations pushed beyond the city limits, new debates stirred about the city's development. There were two struggles occurring within the city. The first was a conflict between the established economic elite, who had controlled city growth before World War II, and an emerging elite that developed after the war. These newcomers, sometimes called "auslanders," favored more aggressive strategies for the city's development. Because this new elite was centered in the north side of the city, much of its effort targeted developing its own neighborhoods. During the 1960s and 1970s, this new economic elite, with the help of a local political organization called the Good Government League, a group of predominantly north side Anglo businessmen who carefully selected new candidates for the city council, pushed for the north side development of a North Expressway, a new medical school, and a University of Texas campus. As these men channeled the city's resources to northern suburbs, they encountered increasing resistance from older neighborhoods in the city.

A second struggle emerged as this new economic elite clashed with working-class communities on the east and west sides of the city. These communities, predominantly African and Mexican American, had long struggled with substandard housing, poor street drainage, and a lack of public works projects. The northward movement of educational and health institutions and the growing prosperity of the suburbs were reminders of the city's continued neglect of the older communities on the east and west sides.

In the conflicts over north side development there was an interesting set of shared concerns among the city's older neighborhoods. The first debate came over the proposals for a new highway. Increasing numbers of suburban drivers traveled back and forth from downtown, causing severe traffic congestion. In 1956, Congress authorized the Interstate Highway Act, which created and funded a forty-one-thousand-mile highway system linking cities across the country. That same year, the city of San Antonio completed its first modern traffic study, which called for a new North Expressway to run northeast from downtown, close to Broadway, and to the airport northeast of town.[26] After 1960, as potential routes were made public, the San Antonio Conservation Society objected to the plans because the highway would cut through Brackenridge Park and part of the Olmos Basin floodplain.[27] They began a long battle with the city of San Antonio and its business community over the proper uses of public space. Following the philosophy of its founding members, the Conservation Society objected to the destruction of any parkland in order to preserve the city's heritage and protect its second largest source of income, tourism.[28]

At the same time, the Texas Highway Department concluded that existing streets simply could not handle the increasing volume of traffic. The department was also unable to obtain permission to go through the wealthy suburb of Olmos Park, so planning the highway on existing city lands cut the cost of building considerably. In the following years, San Antonians would be divided over this issue. The Conservation Society rallied enough support to defeat early bond issues, but Mayor Walter McAllister won the next bond election. The highway was finally completed in 1978 but only after ten years of the Conservation Society's struggle.

For several decades, the Conservation Society had claimed many of the city's public spaces as its own. The society owned part of the land of the Spanish missions, raised money to restore the historic homes of many prominent San Antonians, and helped restore the downtown river. Its members maintained a pastoral definition of the city's heritage and had fought for decades to keep San Antonio's downtown parks from the threats of parking garages and other development. In an era of rapid urban growth, however, they found that their claims were also temporary. Growth brought renewed competition over public goals and resources. The North Expressway was just one of several symbols of these changes.

The Conservation Society fought to preserve the natural and built environments of older elite neighborhoods. The members' concerns focused on the integrity of wealthy communities like Alamo Heights and Olmos Park, who represented the city's heritage elite. At the same time as they struggled to keep the highway out of these elite enclaves, a different struggle emerged from Mexican American neighborhoods of the city. In 1973, Ernie Cortés began an organization that would transform San Antonio politics and eventually gain national recognition, the Communities Organized for Public Service (COPS). Cortés was born and raised on San Antonio's west side, where he experienced the daily hardships of a neighborhood with poor drainage, unpaved streets, and high utility rates. Frustrated with existing channels for political change in the city, he went to Chicago for training as part of Saul Alinsky's Industrial Areas Foundation in Chicago.[29] He brought these lessons back to San Antonio and began talking to local Roman Catholic leaders about funding an organization that would address the pragmatic concerns of his community. With these funds from the church and the aid of parish networks, Cortés and others developed a powerful community-based organization that avoided abstract concerns like "civil rights" for more practical problems such as traffic, drainage, and public services. From its inception, neighborhood was a central institution, the center of family life and culture. In order to protect the resources of these older neighborhoods, COPS often opposed north side development. By 1980, COPS had become one of the most powerful political organizations in the city, working at the municipal level to redirect federal funds for inner-city neighborhood improvements. It obtained funds for improvements in sidewalks, streets, parks, and housing rehabilitation.[30]

Though COPS was a very different organization from the Conservation Society, its emphasis on restoring and reviving the city's older neighborhoods was similar. Like the Conservation Society, COPS claimed that the revitalization of their neighborhoods was central to the city's future. It was effective because of its dedication to local concerns and its use of a new confrontational style of politics. COPS's strategies differed from previous Mexican American organizations' efforts at community empowerment, but its goals were often related. Ernie Cortés, like other members of COPS, grew up during the civil rights movement, and he was influenced by an important generation of Mexican American leaders who fought for labor, education, and civic reform.

The Mexican American generation of activists in the 1950s and 1960s were predominantly native-born and educated in segregated American schools. Some had fought in World War I, and many others had participated in World War II. Returning from war, they were anxious to enjoy the benefits of full American citizenship, while they also aimed to protect the Mexican American community from discrimination. According to LULAC and other like organizations of the time, learning English and entering the American mainstream was the key to upward mobility.[31] They maintained pride in their Mexican heritage but advocated absolute loyalty to the United States and its political institutions. They were also economic conservatives who saw racial discrimination as the primary cause of Mexican American problems, not class domination.[32] Using the federal courts, they fought many legal battles to end segregation in schools and in other public facilities. In the late 1950s and 1960s, they had some success in electoral politics. They elected a mayor in El Paso, congressmen in California and Texas, and helped President Kennedy win a slim majority in Texas.

In the late 1960s and 1970s, however, a younger generation of activists began to challenge previous strategies for change. Cortés was part of this new generation, often called the Chicano Movimiento.[33] Though the Mexican American generation had much success in court battles against segregation and in electoral politics, most Mexican Americans still struggled with poverty, substandard housing, poor education, and police brutality. Some reformers felt that middle-class groups such as LULAC could not adequately respond to the needs of working-class Chicanos. Although Chicano activists continued the battles for civil rights and against institutional discrimination, the *movimiento* also changed the focus of reform. Rather than following the form of traditional civil rights activism, new Chicano activists spoke of cultural and racial conflict. In general, Chicanos sought cultural respect instead of integration.[34]

Many new organizations, like COPS, advocated a bottom-up principle of activism. Their supporters sought more direct participation from members of the community and called attention to the practical concerns of daily life. They also developed a more confrontational style of intervention, directly challenging local institutions like the city water board and city government. For example, they staged tie-up actions at local banks, lining up to exchange paper money for coins and vice versa. The intention was simply to use such incidents to attract more attention to their particular cause.[35]

In some ways, COPS differed from other organizations that played a larger role in the national Chicano movement. COPS kept its concerns with the local, while other student and farm worker organizations turned to more regional and national strategies. In addition, by the late 1970s the Chicano movimiento lost some of its fervency within the Mexicano community. Tensions between middle-class and working-class activists continued, and the philosophy of cultural nationalism failed to provide strategies for community empowerment within the American system.

COPS, however, continued to play a powerful role in San Antonio politics largely because of this continued focus on local concerns. Beginning in the late 1970s, but accelerating after 1980, a new generation of leaders established themselves within the Mexican American community. These leaders were part of what historian Ignacio M. García refers to as the Mexican American–Hispanic generation, and they represented a more widely distributed geographically and more politically and socially diverse Mexicano population. This generation had much to gain from participating in the mainstream, yet it was also "more anxious to flaunt its ethnicity" than the Mexican American generation.[36] Like the middle-class reformers of the Mexican American generation, Hispanic leaders sought inclusion, but like Chicano activists, they also promoted their distinct cultural identity and "reserve[d] the right to have a viewpoint buttressed by historical experience." Unlike some Chicano activists, however, they sought a more conservative agenda and tended to shy away from discussing conflicts that divide Mexican Americans from Anglo America.[37] This generation reflected a new social understanding between Mexican American organizations and Anglo urban business interests.

In San Antonio, this generation's main victory was in the area of municipal government. From 1951 to 1975, the Good Government League controlled the city council. The GGL maintained its power by at-large elections, in which all members of the city council were elected by the entire city and the council appointed the mayor. Mexican Americans in the city were strongly against the GGL and displayed this antipathy in their support of anti-GGL candidates and in low percentages of voter registration and turnout rates.[38]

In the late 1970s, the GGL disintegrated. When the Voting Rights Act was extended to Mexican Americans in the Southwest in 1975, the Texas state legislature enacted a number of reforms so that nearly any U.S. citizen eighteen years or older who resides in Texas can vote. These changes in federal and state law encouraged changes in the election of city council members in San Antonio. The following year, the Justice Department objected to San Antonio's earlier annexation of nine north side, predominantly Anglo, precincts into the city in 1972. With a majority of city council members already coming from the north side, COPS and other Chicano advocacy groups feared that the annexation of these communities would accelerate the neglect and isolation of Mexicanos in the west and south sides of the city. The Justice Department mandated that either the city de-annex these new precincts or alter its method of electing city council members. Rather than take the Justice Department to court, the city council proposed, and voters adopted, changes in the city charter that replaced at-large elections with a council of ten members elected from single-member districts and a mayor elected at large.[39] As a result, the 1977 elections produced a city council with one African American and five Mexican American members. These changes represented a fundamental shift in San Antonio politics.

The changes in city council elections, as well as the rising political and economic power of Mexican Americans in general, had a direct impact upon Fiesta. During this time, criticism of the GGL and its Anglo-dominated political machine merged directly with challenges to Fiesta. Although members of the Mexican American community had long resented Fiesta's celebration of Anglo hegemony, educational and political leaders within the community began to make their complaints more public and focused their critique on King Antonio and the Texas Cavaliers. In 1971, José Cárdenas, superintendent of the Edgewood School District, located on the city's west side, refused King Antonio's annual invitation to visit the schools. Cárdenas called King Antonio a "persona non grata." Joe Bernal, a former state senator, added, "King Antonio was telling Mexican American children they could be whoever they wanted to be, when they couldn't even be King Antonio. He was a farce."[40] Other Mexican American organizations also spoke out against the Texas Cavaliers. The Mexican American Legal Defense Fund (MALDEF) stated that because the cavaliers was a private organization that was selective in its membership, it should not be supported by public facilities.

Members of the newly diverse city council also criticized the cavaliers. As Henry Cisneros, from District One, was quoted in the *San Antonio Express News*, "I think the Cavaliers would be well-served if they would loosen up and widen access to the community to that particular event and honor." In the same article, Bernardo Eureste, a fellow council member from District Five, stated things more bluntly, calling King Antonio a "joke" and threatening that "the council committee will check out organizations that aren't really representative, such as the Cavaliers."[41] Although these criticisms did not change the structure of the cavaliers, the Fiesta San Antonio Commission did declare that neither King Antonio nor the Queen of the Order of the Alamo were the official royalty of Fiesta.[42]

Charros

During this period of marked Fiesta criticism, Socrates Ramírez, a long-standing member of the San Antonio Charro Association, invited King Antonio to his organization's ranch to ride in their annual *charreada*. He also suggested that their event become a part of Fiesta. Seeing the city council's challenges to the Texas Cavaliers, Ramírez envisioned another way to integrate Mexicanos into the city's public life.[43] He knew the executive director of the Fiesta Association, retired Col. Davis Burnett, and at a breakfast meeting at the downtown Menger Hotel, they negotiated the inclusion of this new event. King Antonio would ride at the head of the Charros, along with their queen, and would present them with a gift. The following year, King Antonio returned the favor, inviting the Charros' queen to ride in his River Parade.

Ramírez's gesture was an alternative strategy to the councilmens' criticisms of the Texas Cavaliers. While he agreed that Mexicanos deserved an equal place in Fiesta, he used the politics of negotiation, rather than confrontation, to bring the Charros into Fiesta. His efforts were also a prelude to Rey Feo's eventual inclusion, because the charro, unlike the multiple Fiesta queens, was a distinct symbol of Mexicano manhood. In the post–World War II era, when many Anglos were dressing as campesinos, the Mexican Chamber of Commerce and other Mexican American businessmen were dressing as the charro.[44] To counter the image of the campesino, who would present Mexicanos as rural peasants, the charro had become a figure of the Mexicano elite.

Olga Nájera-Ramírez describes the charro as "the master symbol of *lo mexicano* on both sides of the U.S.-Mexico border."[45] In the discourses of film, music, literature, and performance of greater Mexico, the charro represents both Mexicanness and manhood.[46] When the Spanish introduced the horse in the sixteenth century, horse riding represented elite privilege and power. Indians, mestizos, and blacks were prohibited from owning or riding horses.[47] By the late sixteenth century, however, the rise of cattle ranching and haciendas required skilled vaqueros, or cowboys, particularly in northern Mexico. Mestizos and Indians had opportunities to learn the skills of horsemanship. These riding and roping techniques were the foundational qualities of the charro, the Mexican horseman. Early charreadas were performances of these skills. For the wealthy, they were opportunities to display their ability to run the hacienda. For the common vaquero, the charreada offered a chance to show that they were as skilled as the elite. Nájera-Ramírez continues:

In all cases the point was to display their abilities of strength, independence, and bravery. Consequently, *charreadas* were a means by which men of any social class might prove themselves to be worthy *charros* and thus greatly enhance their status as real men.[48]

For men of lesser means, the charro was a symbol of the self-made man, an egalitarian ideal quite different from the socially stratified life at the hacienda. Thus, the charro acted as a symbol of unity and blurred the hierarchical structure of social life. By the nineteenth century, the charro had taken on a new significance. A newly independent Mexico was marked by civil strife, as armed bandits defied political leaders and sought social advancement. They forced wealthy landowners and politicians to meet their demands. The *plateados*, "silvered ones," were bandits well known for the silver that adorned their clothing. Dressed as silver-adorned charros, they were both feared and admired.[49] In the midcentury, Pres. Benito Juárez appropriated this charro outfit to establish order, creating a mounted police force to enforce national laws. The rurales created an image of tough, skilled horsemen who were also loyal to Mexican nationhood.[50] By the dictatorship of Porfirio Díaz at the end of the century, the charro had become a prominent symbol of manhood and nation.

After Mexico's Revolution of 1910, the charro image was transformed once again. The charreada became a way to promote and sell Mexican culture to tourists and natives alike.[51] In the 1920s, the charreada was becoming the first national Mexican sport. In 1921, the national charro association was formed, and in 1933 the Federación Nacional de Charros gave official status to the sport, standardized public performances, and specified charro ideals through a code of ethics intended to protect their image. This code included rules of behavior. Charros could not drink excessively or use foul language while in charro suits. Costumes could not be in bright colors, like royal blue, yellow, purple, or pink, which was considered "too *ranchero*" and "insufficiently masculine." Somber colors were considered more elegant and manly and followed upper-class aesthetics.[52] Although charro associations did not officially restrict membership, the time and money needed to purchase and train horses and riding gear effectively limited membership to wealthier individuals.

The San Antonio Charro Association was the first such group organized in the United States. Founded in 1947, the association followed the rules of the code of the *federación* and participated in many competitions with associations on both sides of the border. In the Charro Association's official history, former president Máximo Virgil offers a narrative of the Mexican charro that emphasizes the figure's elite origins. First he clarifies that the charro is not a vaquero or a cowboy. He is "a gentleman horseman" who might be equated with "a polo player, in expense and character of membership."[53] The association had about twenty active members at any one time, and membership included monthly dues, stable fees for the feeding and grooming of their horses, and several expensive trajes (suits) that run two or three hundred dollars each, all custom made in Mexico. The elaborate sombrero could cost more than five hundred dollars.[54]

For members of the San Antonio association, the charreada was the performance of a Mexicano upper class. These San Antonio charros embody a nostalgia very similar to that of the Texas Cavaliers. Anglo gentlemen of the New South demonstrated their superiority by invoking the English cavalier and summoning the social order of an antebellum planter society. The charros drew from the Spanish caballero, imagining a return to the hacienda society of Mexico. Yet the charro's nostalgia was more poignant than the cavalier's. While King Antonio invoked a southern chivalric code, he was also deeply invested in modernity. He did not usually ride a horse; he arrived in San Antonio on the train and later, in a car. The Kings Antonio were active agents in shaping the New South. The charros, by contrast, represented a cattle-ranching tradition that was violently replaced by this new social order by the end of the nineteenth century.

In the context of twentieth-century south Texas, these two figures were clearly not social equals. Though the members of the San Antonio Charros were frequently successful middle-class men, they were not part of the city's economic elite. In the beginning, the San Antonio Charro Association rented the land the members used to practice their skills. After years of saving, they bought ten acres of land next to Mission County Park, on the city's south side, in 1959. Ten years later they were able to put in new stands and clear most of the brush to create a parklike setting.[55] Members made a significant investment, yet they struggled for years to create and maintain both their organization and their ranch. In San Antonio they were not upper-class noblemen, yet their crafted image of the gentleman charro countered the derogatory stereotypes of the disorderly, indulgent Mexican. Like other charros in the federación, charro members were not allowed to drink at any time they were representing the organization. Their code emphasized discipline and skill, the antithesis of the degenerate Mexican. They performed a nostalgia of the social elite in order to counter the reality of their marginality.

Their history, though, omits the legacy of the charro as an egalitarian figure and ignores the common vaqueros who showed their skills in the charreadas over the centuries, even though this comparison is more fitting. In mid-twentieth-century Texas, the charros' position was much more like that of the vaqueros, and their gesture of reconciliation was also a challenge to King Antonio. The San Antonio Charros demonstrated that they were as skilled as their "superiors." In the context of other Mexican Americans' more vocal criticism of the Texas Cavaliers, these charros responded by positioning themselves as equals. Ramírez used social and physical space to make his point. The charros could bring King Antonio to their remote ranch on the south side, their imagined hacienda on the margins of the city. At the same time, they could also bring the charros into Fiesta, a downtown festival in the center of San Antonio's public culture. In this performance, the charro could be a symbol of both the nobleman and the vaquero. He could unify the parallel heritage of the cavalier and the caballero. Yet he could also demonstrate his equal skills and make a place for himself at the gringo's party. The San Antonio Charros were the first men to intrude on the cavaliers' masculine space in the 1970s, but they did not offer a parallel role within Fiesta. While King Antonio would come to the charreada, the charros played a much smaller role in the festival as a whole. The charro did not provide a role that could adequately respond to Mexicanos who wanted a figure that would assure an equal place on the Fiesta stage.

The Reign of the Ugly King

After a decade of public criticism of Fiesta, Rey Feo would become the symbol of Anglo-Mexicano reconciliation. Hernández and others looked to Rey Feo to assure that Mexicanos were more than "invited guests" to the city's party. Whether this was actually the case, this was how the event was promoted in the *San Antonio Light*. Radio talk show personality Logan Stewart became Rey Feo in 1979, and he immediately began his campaign for the role's inclusion in Fiesta. Stewart called his success "an historic occasion . . . It is the first time the Rey Feo has become a full Fiesta participant and the first time he's been accorded the king of the Hispanics."[56]

Obviously the event had one glaring contradiction. The man who claimed to bring a greater Hispanic presence in Fiesta, who named himself "king of the Hispanics" (LULAC itself did not make this claim) was Anglo. This irony was not entirely missed by the local newspapers or by Stewart, who admitted "while I may be an Anglo Rey Feo, I have purposely pioneered Rey Feo into Fiesta so it will evolve as a benefit for all succeeding Reyes Feo—whether they be Anglo, black or Hispanic."[57] Stewart's comment highlighted a key part of the Rey Feo role. Previous Reyes Feo were often Mexican American, but some Anglo businessmen who catered to the Mexican American community played the role as well. LULAC gave the title to any middle-class man who could fund their scholarships. According to Joe Bernal, the Ugly King was often "some friendly gringo who could raise a lot of money."[58] Rey Feo was not considered king of the Hispanics. Given the exclusively Anglo role of the Texas Cavaliers and Rey Feo's connection to LULAC, however, he symbolically became the Hispanic king when he joined Fiesta.

To the writers of the *Light*, the appointment of an Anglo Rey Feo was part of the "topsy-turviness" of Fiesta and San Antonio, where a Scottish Frenchman was "king of a Hispanic parade in an Anglo-dominated Fiesta in front of an old Spanish mission." This was explained away as simply the product of San Antonio's "special mix of people, cultures, and values."[59] For Fiesta organizers, the ethnic interchangeability of the Rey Feo role was part of its appeal. Following the rhetoric of middle-class inclusion, Everyman could become Rey Feo. As a figure who could be either Anglo or Mexican American, he truly represented the union of the Anglo and Mexican American urban business class. At the same time, he was marked with Mexicanness like Fiesta itself. Stewart, however, had broader ideas about Rey Feo's inclusion.

> New doors are being opened . . . We're not just talking about just having a party or a parade. The whole Hispanic issue addresses itself to the roots of an eco-cultural-socio-problem . . . Certainly the cause of equality and of equal opportunity requires more jobs and a higher pay scale. It requires progress. And you can't push San Antonio forward without taking the Mexican American with you.[60]

Stewart never got more specific about this "eco-cultural-socio-problem" or how Rey Feo's inclusion benefited the cause of equality, only affirming that the spirit of love that pervades Fiesta should be extended among all the city's ethnic communities throughout the year. For Stewart, and for many other cross-dressing gringos, Rey Feo was a figure of Anglo-Mexican reconciliation. For many Mexican Americans, Rey Feo was a symbol of both reconciliation and equal status in the city's public culture.

FIGURE 14. Rey Feo I, Logan Stewart, and King Antonio LIX, David Steves, 1981. San Antonio Light Collection, UTSA's Institute of Texan Cultures at San Antonio, Courtesy of the Hearst Corporation.

REY FEO AND THE POLITICS OF INCLUSION, 1970–2000

Stewart's dreams of enlightenment contained more than a dash of paternalism, however. In this statement about San Antonio's progress, the Mexican American was given a passive role. Stewart created an image of taking his Mexican American subjects by the hand, leading them through the stages of progress. Not much information about Logan Stewart's personal interests in diversifying Fiesta royalty is available, but printed sources indicate that he used his radio commentary as a pulpit for berating the Mexican American community's lack of Fiesta participation.[61] Interestingly, newspaper accounts implied that Stewart blamed the Mexican American community itself. Perhaps he was invoking a familiar paternalism, that Mexican Americans needed the skills and organization of an Anglo to get them involved in Fiesta events.

Yet Stewart was not the one to initiate Rey Feo's inclusion. In the early 1970s, Col. Davis Burnett, who was then executive vice president of the Fiesta Commission, was part of an effort to recruit royal roles from the Hispanic organizations already involved in Fiesta, including the Mexican Chamber of Commerce and the San Antonio Charros, but he was unsuccessful. When Stewart became Rey Feo in 1979, Burnett saw an opportunity. He invited Stewart, his longtime friend, and the LULAC president, Ray Doria, to lunch, where they started talking about a Rey Feo parade.[62] Later, they approached the cavaliers and the Battle of Flowers Association for approval. Although the cavaliers now deny any apprehension, Burnett claimed that they were initially wary of Rey Feo's role. After all, the Fiesta Commission had already declared that King Antonio was not the official king of Fiesta and their river parade had changed from King Antonio's River Parade to the more inclusive Fiesta River Parade.[63] The cavaliers were not eager to further diminish King Antonio's prominence in Fiesta. Many marathon meetings later, though, the relationship between the two kings was determined, with the agreement that Rey Feo would never upstage King Antonio. Because King Antonio was the senior king of Fiesta, Rey Feo would officially defer to him.

While the cavaliers may have been a bit apprehensive, they were not openly hostile to the creation of the Rey Feo parade. Fiesta had already grown to include more than one hundred events and several new queens, and the ceremonies of the Anglo elite were relatively undisturbed. As Michaele Haynes observed, Rey Feo allowed the Texas Cavaliers to continue their own organization and their Anglo kings with less criticism.[64] A photograph in the *Light* made this remarkably clear. The photo's caption read: "In a historic toast, King Antonio LVIII, Ricks Wilson, and Rey Feo XXXII, Logan Stewart, saluted their Fiesta city's cultural diversity Saturday night as 'a mosaic of hearts and colors.'"[65] Here we see two upper-middle-class Anglo men celebrating cultural diversity. The image also reflected a context of friendly compromise. Rey Feo's inclusion came through a process of lunch meetings between the city's Anglo and Mexican American upper class. Rey Feo powerfully expressed a new politics of negotiation, rather than confrontation.

The first year of Rey Feo's inclusion, the depiction of Anglo-Mexican unity was uniquely that of the *San Antonio Light* and was not advocated quite as wholeheartedly by San Antonio's more conservative other newspaper, the *San Antonio Express News*. In fact, the parade was only briefly mentioned in the paper's daily list of Fiesta events. While the *Express News* did tell of Stewart's campaign, it did not picture the "historic toast" or promote the new royal "diversity."[66] For the editors of the *Light*, who had criticized Fiesta elitism decades earlier, this was the culmination of a long public campaign to challenge Fiesta's upper-class organizers. The *Express News* took a less enthusiastic view. Yet following years demonstrated that Rey Feo represented a powerful sentiment among both Anglo and Mexican American middle-class residents. In following years, this middle-class Anglo-Mexican reconciliation became the dominant narrative of Rey Feo. Even the *Express News* was acknowledging Rey Feo's increasing prominence by 1981.

Henry I

A year after Rey Feo became a Fiesta king, Henry Cisneros became San Antonio's first Hispanic mayor since U.S. annexation in 1845 and the first Hispanic mayor of a major U.S. city. As Rey Feo represented a festive handshake between middle-class Anglos and Mexican Americans, Henry Cisneros's campaign unified voters from San Antonio's Mexicano west side with its Anglo north side. In the 1980 mayoral race Cisneros, a young Mexican American city council member with a moderate political agenda, was pitted against John Steen, who was "a card carrying member of San Antonio's upper class."[67] Steen was also a Texas Cavalier and had been crowned King Antonio in 1967. The local media portrayed their political race as a battle between the old guard and a new era of Mexican American political power in the city. By this time, San Antonio's Mexican American population was in the majority. Cisneros's landslide victory on April 4, 1981, was the product of an incredibly high rate of Mexican American voter turnout, the efforts of COPS, and the support of liberal and moderate Anglo voters. He won because he had almost the complete support of the Mexican American community (although this did not come without conflict) and enough of the Anglo community to secure 61.8 percent of the overall vote. If Logan Stewart claimed that Rey Feo formed a symbolic bridge between the Anglo and Mexican American communities, Cisneros formed a political bridge.

Steen was clearly surprised by the election results, as was the local press, which had been predicting a close race.[68] After the campaign, Steen only commented that "obviously, I didn't draw enough West Side votes," but Cisneros's victory had more to do with his ability to draw Anglo support.[69] Cisneros was more popular with the Anglo community because he represented more moderate viewpoints than did some of his Mexican American colleagues. Cisneros was initially elected to the city council as part of the GGL in 1975; he quickly became part of the successful campaign to create single-member districts, though, which led to the demise of the GGL. As a city councilman from 1975 to 1979, Cisneros continued to reach out to both the progrowth business interests and an underrepresented Mexican American community. He "enjoyed the resources and visibility of the GGL establishment without being confined to its agenda," and "built an image of an articulate, smooth, Harvard and MIT educated man." Cisneros also crafted a public persona who "cared about the problems of the common person."[70] In 1975 he emptied garbage cans to learn the problems of the sanitation department, walked a beat with a police officer, and administered first aid with ambulance attendants. He visited families in public housing units and promised that their problems would no longer be ignored. At the same time, he carefully distinguished his politics from any "radical tinge."[71] He placed a priority on economic growth, which gave him the support of prodevelopment groups. Cisneros made political compromises that cast him as a leader committed to both community and profit.

Cisneros's win represented a new alliance between Anglo and Mexican American middle-class leaders. When Cisneros became mayor, however, his supporters expected him to mediate between two different forces. Business leaders wanted Cisneros to control the more radical members of the city council. In an interview with the *Express News*, reporter Rick Casey asked Cisneros if he could "improve decorum" at city council meetings, specifically referring to the outspoken Bernardo Eureste.[72] For the next six years, city council politics revolved around the different styles of Eureste and Cisneros.[73]

Bernardo Eureste grew up in south side San Antonio. He completed his education at the University of Michigan and then returned to San Antonio as a professor at Our Lady of the Lake University. In 1977 he became one of the city councilmen in the city's new single-member districts. Eureste's District Five was the poorest district of San Antonio's south and west sides. Overwhelmingly Mexicano, District Five reflected the interests of those who were left out of this new politics of inclusion. Eureste brought a more confrontational political style to city council meetings and frequently challenged the growth policies of the business class. By 1978, Eureste became known as the "Champion of the Underdog."[74] He became a powerful political force, reelected by large majorities in his district. For some political observers, he represented a long-neglected community. His constituents, as well as many middle-class Mexican Americans and Anglo liberals, supported his efforts to call attention to urban barrios and inner-city development.[75]

After Cisneros became mayor, Eureste became his "alter ego."[76] Although the two leaders agreed on several issues, their contrasting political styles and differing goals concerning urban development led to frequent conflicts. Their split reflected not only a conflict between the suburb and the barrio but also a division within the Mexican American middle class. Some, like Cisneros, believed that an alliance with the Anglo upper and middle classes would benefit the city as a whole. Other activists, like Eureste, wanted to use their political position to advocate for the specific needs of inner-city neighborhoods.

Unfortunately, Eureste's efforts were short-lived. In 1983, personal scandal devastated Eureste's political career.[77] His behavior became more erratic, and his concern for personal control over his district led to conflicts with many former supporters.

In 1985, he came head to head with Cisneros again, this time over the issue of Sea World's plan to build a park in San Antonio. He embarrassed Cisneros, as local headlines published Eureste's charges. Sea World backed out of its initial plan, and Eureste was blamed for chasing away San Antonio's biggest investment opportunity in years.[78] This incident severed any alliance he had with Cisneros, who refused to endorse his bid for reelection. After Eureste's defeat, Cisneros no longer had any vocal opposition in the city council. He continued to attract new investments to the city, including plans for a biotechnology research park, a semiconductor plant, and a major golf tournament. Once again, "the business of the city council was about business."[79]

For many Anglo and Mexican American businessmen, Henry Cisneros was a symbol of interethnic reconciliation. In this new political context, a moderate, middle-class organization like LULAC, with the support of an Anglo Rey, could convince the Fiesta commission to include a new king. Like Cisneros, Rey Feo formed a political bridge. To some, he also challenged King Antonio's prominence in Fiesta.

The Grotesque King

Long before Rey Feo became part of Fiesta he was compared to King Antonio. LULAC strongly denies that the Rey Feo role ever had anything to do with King Antonio. Yet many continue to note the similarities between the roles. In 1983, *Texas Monthly* featured an article on Fiesta that claimed Rey Feo mocked King Antonio, despite statements to the contrary. "I told them again and again Rey Feo does not poke fun at King Antonio," said Stewart.[80] In order to continue their friendly relationship to the Texas Cavaliers, LULAC probably needed to make these refutations. Those who invented Rey Feo in 1947 claim he was based on a Roman carnival tradition of crowning a commoner king. As a symbolic inversion of the king, these crowned slaves could temporarily poke fun at royalty. Even as LULAC representatives explain the role's medieval origins, however, contemporary parallels are clear. A former LULAC president, Sam Doria, explained that "the legend is that the royalty became so segregated from the people that they were no longer representative. They were the wealthy, beautiful people. So the common people had a ceremony and selected their own king, the Ugly king of the Ugly people."[81] Doria's description was a thinly veiled description of Mexican American experiences in San Antonio. In the context of a segregated city, electing an Ugly King to represent one of the city's largest Mexican American civic organizations was clearly a comment on the social conditions of postwar interethnic relations.

Rey Feo, like the charro, was also a symbol of Mexican manhood. Reyes Feo can be found in the Carnival celebrations of many Mexican cities, where he serves a similar role as the people's king. In the United States, though, the role seems to be unique to San Antonio. During the late 1960s, LULAC produced a film to describe the purpose of their Feria de las Flores festival, where Rey Feo is crowned. In the film script, the narrator announced that at the end of the evening, the LULAC committee would present "the male 'divine' as he really is—the ugly brute—calling him the Ugly King, and his symbol of authority is a Baby Goat."[82] A common Mexican folk saying defines the ideal man as *fuerte, feo y formal* (strong, rugged, and upstanding). Although feo's literal translation is ugly, in this context, it had an additional connotation of ruggedness.[83] In the Feria script, the Ugly King was described as a "brute." He was an exaggerated image of unrestrained masculine power. Like the charro, Rey Feo was created to portray a common man's king who was not only an inversion of King Antonio but also a carnivalesque grotesque version of Mexican American manhood.

When Rey Feo became a part of Fiesta, comparisons to King Antonio only increased. Rey Feo's significance soon grew beyond Stewart's initial campaign. Through the 1980s, prominent Mexican Americans publicly embraced his inclusion. Father Virgil Elizondo, rector at San Antonio's San Fernando Cathedral, wrote this was "a festive breakthrough." Rey Feo "is beginning to outdo King Antonio" and has made Fiesta a celebration about "desegregating San Antonio."[84] While the original Rey Feo represented a segregated social order, these new Reyes Feo represented political and social inclusion.

He also indirectly challenged King Antonio's authority to represent the city. Although King Antonio had been dethroned from his official position as ruler of all Fiesta ceremonies in the early 1970s, he was still referred to as the King of Fiesta as late as 1979, simply because there were no other kings to challenge him.[85] The dual reign with Rey Feo, however, made this claim impossible. In the 1981 newspaper coverage of Fiesta royalty, the newly crowned King Antonio, David P. Steves, Jr., was quoted as saying that "it's really not important who the king is, but that we have one . . . There should be more kings." He also stated that he was grateful for the presence of Rey Feo: "There certainly is no rivalry. We could use more kings. I am king for 400 men [the Texas Cavaliers], that's all . . . any organization can elect a king."[86] His statements were decidedly humbler than 1979's King Antonio, Paul McSween, who frequently referred to the cavaliers' central role in Fiesta history and pointed admirably to the rows of medallions on his uniform.[87]

While these differences may have something to do with the differing personalities of the two kings, the 1981 account seemed to place great emphasis on this new king's lack of pompousness. The official inclusion of Rey Feo made any subsequent king's royal claims more tenuous. Rey Feo's mockery of King Antonio was a reminder of social division in the city, and royal titles were revealed as arbitrary designations of political and social organizations, not the divine right of the Texas Cavaliers.[88]

The People's Parade

Rey Feo's first parade further demonstrated his image as the common man's king. LULAC had difficulty finding applications for its parade, because so many organizations and schools were either already committed to the Battle of Flowers or could not afford the three thousand dollars for floats.[89] The 116 entries of the Rey Feo parade consisted mostly of pickup trucks hauling flatbed trailers and out of town high school bands. The crowd was also significantly smaller than the one at the Battle of Flowers Parade. The *Light* celebrated the smallness of the parade as a milestone in itself, however. The parade was said to be more personal. The paper quoted one viewer as noting that "the people in the parade talk to you and wave to you as an individual."[90] The parade itself was named the People's Parade, with the explicit goal of creating a spectacle that "people can actually take part in and be able to feel that they're participating in, not just watching." The *Light* published an interview with parade organizer Sam Doria, who helped define the parade on these terms. The article also implied that people was another name for the Mexican American community. Rey Feo's parade was the Hispanic parade. The *San Antonio Light* interviewer even asked whether "Anglos would feel comfortable" there. Much could be said about this question, but here it is sufficient to note that the *Light* hinted at a continuing anxiety within the Anglo community about any event Mexican Americans predominantly organized and attended. This question may also indicate that the actual relationship between the Anglo and Mexican American communities was not quite as unified as the Fiesta royalty wished to portray.

Logan Stewart was disappointed in his Paseo del Rey Feo parade. He wanted it to be an equal spectacle to the Battle of Flowers and the Fiesta Flambeau. Stewart wanted a position equal to King Antonio. Rey Feo and his new parade received ambivalent reactions from Anglos. This People's Parade, with its cheap decorations, expressed a desire among many San Antonians for a parade where the spectators could also be participants. Rey Feo could also represent some Anglos' continuing fears about Mexican American power and social proximity, but for Mexican Americans, he was the hope of an equal, integrated community.

After six years, though, Rey Feo lost his parade because of LULAC's internal disputes and continued lack of funding. As a result, the most popular element of Rey Feo's inclusion was discarded. At the same time, Rey Feo became a bigger part of Fiesta, and his role changed. He assumed the year-long duties of hospital and school visits and charity functions. One observer, Rubén Munguía, believed that something was lost when Rey Feo became a citywide figure. He was not seen as accessible to the people he had initially represented. Rey Feo "used to be something that was supposed to be fun. Now it's so dogmatic and ritualistic."[91]

When the Rey Feo role began, his royal clothing was an inexpensive faux velvet cloak and oversized medieval crown. His new uniform cost six hundred dollars, and he had to buy three of them. His new headdress, a metal crown with fake jewels, was ordered from London.[92] This new uniform was also more similar to King Antonio's. King Antonio wore a paramilitary uniform covered with medallions (civic service awards), a red plumed hat, and a ceremonial sword. Rey Feo's outfit was less military in style, a white suit and a broad, brightly colored sash. He also included an array of medals on his chest, though. Along with Rey Feo's traditional award of a cabrito (a baby goat for the royal feast, which he then pardons in very presidential fashion), he also invented the new Royal Order of the Cabrito, an honorary title given to his friends and associates, which was explicitly patterned after the cavaliers' Royal Order of the Red Plume. He also joined King Antonio in Fiesta's opening ceremonies.

Rey Feo did not become exactly like King Antonio, though. King Antonio maintains his connection to the heritage elite. His coronation is the only Fiesta ceremony to occur within the Alamo walls. After a solemn initiation within the Alamo chapel, King Antonio emerges before the larger public. Rey Feo continues to have his coronation during La Feria de Las Flores. His Order of the Cabrito includes a wider variety of Anglo, Mexican American, and African American businessmen, local TV newscasters, and other civic officials who do not find a place within the Texas Cavaliers.

One can also trace another shift in the public meanings attached to the two kings. In 1981, a minor, yet significant, change occurred in newspaper coverage of the Rey Feo parade. What had previously been referred to as the People's Parade became the "fun people's parade."[93] Additionally, while in earlier years King Antonio had occasionally been called the King of Merriment, this label seems to have been transferred to Rey Feo in 1981.[94] These contrasting roles also seem to be directly related to Rey Feo's proposed position as king of the Hispanics and King Antonio's role as king of the Anglos. Rey Feo was continually marked with Mexicanness. In this sense, Rey Feo did eclipse King Antonio as Fiesta king. Rey Feo represented Fiesta's new leadership, an interethnic business class committed to selling Mexicanness in the Fiesta city.

It is worthwhile here to draw a few larger comparisons to similar changes in the carnivals of other U.S. cities. As mentioned previously, both the St. Louis Veiled Prophet's ceremonies and New Orleans's Carnival had significant protests about the exclusion of those cities' African American communities. These protests also took the form of creating alternate traditions. In 1966, the St. Louis African American community began staging its own Black Veiled Prophet Ball, which was both a parody and a celebration of African American culture.[95] Civil rights advocates continued to protest the Veiled Prophet organization's use of public facilities, staging a dramatic disruption of the coronation in 1972 by landing on the stage and removing the crown and veil of the pageant's king. In New Orleans in 1992, the city council, with a majority black membership, passed an ordinance requiring Carnival krewes to desegregate their memberships if they wanted parade permits. A few of the most prominent krewes canceled their parades in protest that year, but the Rex krewe officially integrated their membership ranks by introducing three black members.[96] New Orleans also has a long history of struggle among social classes and racial and ethnic groups over representation in Carnival. The Krewe of Zulu was established in 1909 as a working-class African American organization that mocked white Carnival krewes, Jim Crow segregation, and stereotypes of African culture.[97] Painted in blackface, wearing a grass skirt, holding a ham bone as a scepter, and handing out coconuts, the Zulu king represented a burlesque parody of the white krewes.

Yet New Orleans's black middle class had a very ambivalent attitude toward the Zulu and explicitly protested their performances for reifying whites' attitudes about black culture, rather than offering a respectable alternative. The Zulu were never overtly political either, refusing, for instance, to join the black civil rights leaders in their Carnival boycotts in the 1960s. A heated debate emerged within the black community during this era, and the Zulu were pressured to reform their image beginning in 1965. By the 1980s, the Zulu had become a more moderate, racially integrated organization, though some of their blackface performances continued.[98]

Compared to the dramatic protests in St. Louis and the heated debates over African American representation in New Orleans, Rey Feo's introduction into Fiesta royalty seems rather tame. Though some city officials hinted at putting pressure on the Texas Cavaliers, no desegregation ordinance was passed. While Rey Feo may have lightly parodied King Antonio's court, he never performed stereotypes of Mexican culture. From the beginning, the LULAC role was a model of middle-class respectability. The integration of Rey Feo into Fiesta was achieved in a manner that made the heritage elite the most comfortable—through a series of quiet lunchtime meetings. It is difficult to know why in Fiesta the politics of negotiation were so much more successful than the politics of confrontation. Perhaps it had to do with the fact that by the time Rey Feo was introduced, many of the other political battles had already been won by other means. Henry Cisneros, like Rey Feo, was a dapper, moderate politician intent on building political bridges among San Antonio's communities. He was not interested in dramatically transforming the goals of city leadership; the business of the city was still business. Rey Feo, like Cisneros, was not interested in transforming Fiesta; he simply wanted to be included.

Returning to the moment of the 2007 Miss Fiesta Pageant, one can see that the politics of Fiesta have changed very little since the 1980s. In order to place greater emphasis on Miss Fiesta as a community representative, pageant contestants are now required to perform a short skit dressed as a famous woman in Texas history. Having seen a few of these historical pageants before, I was pleasantly surprised to note the diversity of Texas women these contestants chose. Rather than stick to the predictable, Alamo-era, Susanna Dickinson types, these young women chose figures as varied as Sandra Cisneros, Cindy Walker, Ann Richards, and Barbara Bush. The winning skit (from the contestant who ultimately won the pageant) was of Emma Tenayuca, a labor activist in Depression-era San Antonio. Tenayuca played a central role in the radical labor movement of the time; she organized a Ladies Garment Workers' Union at the age of sixteen, helped stage a strike at San Antonio's Finck cigar factory, and formed an organization for the unemployed called the Workers' Alliance.[99] In her historical skit, the Miss Fiesta contestant, Samantha García, portrayed Tenayuca in a jail cell, after her arrest for leading a pecan-shellers' strike in 1938. This strike helped transform the labor movement into a larger mass movement for civil rights and minimum wages. García gave a fairly accurate representation of the ideas of the outspoken Tenayuca, but there was something rather odd about this polished pageant queen's depiction of Tenayuca. García's studied monologue and her outstretched hand, already cupped into the familiar parade wave, seemed completely disconnected from the world of the Communist labor organizer she portrayed. Somehow, Tenayuca's concern for San Antonio's stigmatized Mexicano community had been transformed into a spectacle of middle-class, individualist achievement.

After the pageant, I briefly spoke to the new Fiesta Commission president, Jorge González, a Mexican American who grew up in Laredo and later moved to San Antonio. He spoke of always having a love for the city, remembering downtown visits to Joske's and the St. Anthony Hotel. He admitted to a feeling of exclusion because of his ethnicity from part of San Antonio's elite, as represented by organizations like the Order of the Alamo and the Texas Cavaliers. Here he was, however, president of Fiesta, and he was proving that he could put Fiesta together just as well as any one of them could—perhaps even better.[100] After researching the legacy of the exclusive practices of the city's heritage elite, it is easy for me to understand the context of his resentment. I kept wondering, though, how these contests between middle-class Anglos and Mexican Americans, between old and new money, were related to the rest of San Antonio.

Miss Fiesta's performance seems an appropriate image for this question. The political changes during the 1970s and the criticisms Mexican American leaders made of Fiesta traditions helped force open a space for the Mexican American representation into the largest event in San Antonio's public culture. Rey Feo was the culmination of decades of struggle for political inclusion, yet he also marks the boundaries of this alliance. For many Mexican American civic leaders, Rey Feo symbolized a victory against the heritage elite. Rey Feo also demonstrated, however, a widening gap between a Mexican American middle class that gained from these new political alliances and a larger population of poor and working-class Mexicanos who were excluded from these benefits. Rey Feo moved from the margins into the center of the city's public culture, but his success did not extend to all his subjects.

CHAPTER FIVE

. 6 .

Fiesta Rowdiness

La Semana de Carnaval

WEEKS BEFORE SAN ANTONIO'S ANNUAL BATTLE OF FLOWERS PARADE, the Salazars claim their space along the parade route.[1] The middle-aged couple picks up trash, mows the grass, and sprays ant killer on a small section of land at the Interstate 35 underpass at Broadway. They set up chairs and lights and bring food and drink to last them through the week. They are not alone. Hundreds of San Antonio families annually bring their lawn chairs and pickup trucks to park along the open sections of the parade route. The Salazars, like many families in the city, are domesticating the public grasses and sidewalks of Broadway. For a few weeks, they create a series of personal lawns and transform the city's downtown urban environment through these temporary, homelike dwellings.

The Salazars occupy a street that runs northeast from downtown San Antonio, past Brackenridge Park and Fort Sam Houston. Broadway is a major artery connecting downtown to the wealthy community of Alamo Heights. During and after World War II, the street became one of many centers for new business development, including new motels, fast food restaurants, and retail stores. When one drives up Broadway today, it is one of the most marked remnants of San Antonio's postwar boom. The street's landmarks recall the transformation that San Antonio experienced in these decades.

Broadway also serves as a reminder of the mobility of real estate, however. A street that was the center of the speculative boom in the 1950s and 1960s was beginning to decline by the 1970s. Now this section of Broadway has empty warehouses and bare, glass storefronts. Businesses left Broadway as quickly as they had come. This street is yet another example of capitalist development after 1970, with its frequent and intense periods of spatial reorganization.[2]

During Fiesta, however, this area experiences another type of spatial reorganization as part of the route of the biggest Fiesta parades. The empty lots provide free spaces for thousands of people to watch the parade. Both the Battle of Flowers Parade and the Fiesta Flambeau bring in more than three hundred thousand people each. As families gather to eat, drink, and party together, they transform a commercial space into a temporary residential neighborhood, merging the spaces of home and street.[3] Making an annual home on Broadway may be a way of creating a more intimate relationship to a space that seems devoid of cultural life and institutions.

The Salazars' story is just one of many examples of the ways space is reorganized during Fiesta. During the festival, San Antonio's downtown is transformed by the closing of streets, the construction of fences, and the pedestrian movements of the city's population. If one were to ride a helicopter over the city during Fiesta week, one could see that Fiesta happens in more than one hundred places. More than three million people come to various parades, fairs, and community performances. The biggest Fiesta events are still in the central city, though. The following chapter will depict and analyze the ways Fiestagoers challenge the daily ordering of public space.

In order to understand how the city changes, though, one must first understand how downtown culture is spatialized every other week of the year. Downtown San Antonio operates on two levels, street level and river level. This is one of the clearest ways that San Antonio's downtown demonstrates a division between those who can afford to participate as tourists and those who cannot. Tourists move at the level of the river, along a serene sunken garden of middle-class consumer culture.[4] Though some of San Antonio's downtown tourist centers are at street level, including the Alamo and El Mercado, most of the successful shops and restaurants are along the river. At the intersection of many downtown streets and bridges, visitors can take stairs down to this river level and remove themselves from the urban traffic above. Geographer Miguel De Oliver analyzes this Paseo del Río, also known as the Riverwalk, a long stretch of commercially developed riverbank running down both sides of the San Antonio River. This Riverwalk is a "deliberately created, romanticized, old Hispanic environment below street level" made up of outdoor restaurants with brightly colored tables, fountains, and a general Mediterranean ambience.[5] All the buildings facing the river have an Old World style, and the sides of the river are surrounded by lush tropical plants, giving the walk the appearance of a garden running through the city.[6]

By contrast, most of the San Antonians who live and work around San Antonio's downtown operate at street level. They ride the buses, walk through the urban parks, and shop at the few discount stores that face the streets. They live in the inner-city neighborhoods immediately surrounding downtown, separated only by crisscrossing highways. Unless they are serving tourists, these inner-city residents live apart from the city's tropical ambience. This distinction between street-level residents and river-level tourists is a shift from the downtown San Antonio of the turn of the twentieth century. Central to selling the city, as always, is the local Mexicano community, but tourists do not have the same experiences now that they had then. In those days Anglo tourists might sit in the plazas or venture to the houses in nearby neighborhoods of Laredito to consume chile con carne in makeshift booths. Postmodern, middle-class consumers of San Antonio get a different vision of Mexicanness in the commodified environment of the Paseo del Río, while many of the city's Mexicano residents are further removed from the tourist's experience.

De Oliver traces the ways that San Antonio's contemporary tourist industry simultaneously endorses multiculturalism and practices racial discrimination. Though this industry celebrates and sells Mexican culture, city planners have spatially and economically excluded Mexicano residents from the benefits of this industry. De Oliver details the ways San Antonio's downtown tourist spaces were built to isolate them from surrounding neighborhoods, which are predominantly poor and non-Anglo.[7] At the same time, business developers made tourist space more accessible to visitors, who seek an antidote to modern life in "therapeutic primitivism." This vision does not require, and in fact discourages, the physical presence of these nonwhite others; all that is needed are their symbols in the marketplace of representation. Mexicano culture is represented in the commodities of the tourist industry, but their bodies are marginalized by a network of highways that exclude them from the center of the city's commercial district.[8]

Beginning in the late 1950s, three freeways enclosed San Antonio's downtown core.[9] Over the next several decades, these widening highways insulated this downtown core from surrounding inner-city communities, creating a tourist-and-suburban-centered "intimate village blocked off from communities that are predominantly poor and non-white."[10] The process of separating downtown from the surrounding poor neighborhoods accelerated in the next two decades. By the end of the 1960s, tourism rivaled the military as the top industry in the city. In 1968 the city marked its 250th anniversary and tried to improve a sluggish tourist industry by bringing a world's fair to the city. U.S. congressman Henry B. González first took up the cause. As the first Mexican American from Texas elected to Congress, González wanted to use his new office to bring a Fair of the Americas to San Antonio. González imagined an event that would aid the city's growth by connecting it more closely to commerce with Latin America. As plans for the fair progressed, he was aided by the efforts of Gov. John Connally, Senator Ralph Yarborough, and, most important, Pres. Lyndon Johnson. Their collective political influence convinced business leaders such as Lee Iacocca to back the fair, so it came to fruition. The fair celebrated "the confluence of civilizations" of the Western Hemisphere and so was called Hemisfair, the first world's fair in the Southwest. The fair opened on April 6, attracting more than six million visitors and focusing international attention on San Antonio.

Hemisfair Plaza profoundly affected downtown development. After its five-month run, many of the buildings became central to the city's tourism industry. The Exhibit Hall became a convention center. The United States Pavilion became a federal courthouse complex, and the Texas Pavilion became the Institute of Texan Cultures, a museum honoring the various ethnic communities that shaped the state's history. A 750-foot Tower of the Americas was built, which was higher than both the Seattle Space Needle and the Washington Monument, and became a symbol of the modern city, and an ailing Riverwalk revived with new hotels, restaurants, and shops.[11] Hemisfair, more than any other event, transformed the city's tourism industry.

For the most part, the fair was a successful collaboration of a multicultural middle class. The liberal Henry B. González allied with the conservative Republican mayor, Walter McAllister, and conservative Democrat Governor Connally. Labor unions also supported the fair. Several organizers felt that more elements of the city's populace were represented in planning the fair than in municipal government itself.[12] Although there was great public support for the fair, the proposal had its controversies as well. In order to build the Hemisfair facilities, the city would have to clear an older neighborhood. Organizers wanted the fair to be downtown, so they located an area in the southeast corner of the central district that qualified for federal urban renewal funds. The San Antonio Conservation Society objected to the destruction of the historic buildings in the neighborhood and successfully lobbied to save thirty-five buildings, but otherwise Polish, German, Chinese, Mexican American, and African American neighborhoods were destroyed to create the ninety-two-acre park. More than 570 structures were razed, and 768 people were displaced.[13] Some families challenged their evictions but were unsuccessful. The fair illustrated an accelerating trend in downtown development: buildings would stay, but people would be pushed to the margins.

Hemisfair was not very good for Fiesta, either. Beginning just two weeks before the festival, Hemisfair crowds would cross with Fiesta Carnival crowds and create "a big mess," according to Mayor McAllister. In order to avoid the congestion, the mayor requested that the Fiesta Commission not hold its Carnival that year, which was the source of half its revenue. As a result, the commission began a frantic search for money and a public campaign to seek popular support for continuing Fiesta. What then-Fiesta Pres. Peter Hennessey found was that there was still much public support for Fiesta. On local radio call-in shows, nearly all San Antonians expressed the need for Fiesta. Eventually, the commission collected enough revenue to continue the parades and other events, but the next three years it struggled to raise the money to host Fiesta.[14]

The Hemisfair dilemma resulted from a power struggle between the city and the Fiesta Commission over control of the festival, a conflict that had its origins a decade earlier, but it also represented an important distinction between Hemisfair and Fiesta. Though Fiesta is partly designed as a tourist event, the festival is most important to residents of the city, and to this day seems to draw more locals than visitors.[15] While part of Fiesta happens on the river, most of Fiesta is street-level culture. The festival interrupts the practices of downtown daily life and the tourists' primitivist escape—repopulating quiet plazas and streets with residents from all sectors of the city. Nothing illustrates this more clearly than the Fiesta parades.

Both of Fiesta's big parades begin on the corner of Broadway and Grayson, just northeast of the downtown district. From here, the parade moves south along Broadway, crossing under the highway overpass and continuing until it curves around to pass Alamo Plaza. Here are the reviewing stands and the seats where most of the Fiesta officials sit to watch the parade. The parade then makes a right and goes through the center of town along Commerce Street until it reaches the western edge of downtown. The parade makes a final right turn and marches north on Santa Rosa Street up to West Martin. Essentially, the parade route makes a semicircle around the city's downtown, and the main streets it occupies were once the center of the city's business district, but are now relatively quiet.

For the Fiesta Flambeau Parade of 2002, I sat in one of the four-dollar seats on Broadway with one of my high school friends and her family. The "night parade," as it is more commonly known, had more than a hundred floats, bands, and decorated vehicles. The parade began with color guards and ROTC units from several local high schools, followed by the city police in a typical display of civic order. Parade officials followed, along with the University of Texas Longhorn Band, and Eva Longoria, who at that time was just a hometown girl who made it big on the *Young and the Restless*, as the grand marshal. The high school bands came, along with Miss Fiesta, Rey Feo, and most of the other festival monarchs.

As innumerable floats and bands continued to process down the street, however, parade spectators became increasingly more interested in each other. In the spaces between floats, our section of the audience started a cartwheel- ing contest between young girls on each side of the street, encouraged by the repetitive calls of, "We got spirit. Yes we do. We got spirit. How 'bout you?" Toward the end of the parade, the more intoxicated spectators turned this into a mooning contest, and soon after several police officers moved to our section to end the contest and control the crowd. One woman in front of me, who I knew only by her San Antonio Spurs Tim Duncan jersey, found this suppression particularly annoying. She wanted to continue the contests, and frequently challenged both the police officers and the opposing crowd. This tension between crowd rowdiness and civic order is similar to many urban parades, where spectators transform these highly structured spectacles into a more chaotic performance of multiple identities. Yet something else was going on here as well. People in the crowd were not only using the street as a space to temporarily display themselves; they also announced their allegiances to partic- ular neighborhoods as they cheered for their high school bands. I noticed that the inner-city and west side schools of Fox Tech, Lanier, and Memorial got the biggest cheers.[16] The same populations whose neighborhoods had been pushed to the margins by the city's tourist industry were now temporarily reclaiming and domesticating downtown, bringing together families and friends whose homes had been displaced by the city's commercial development.[17]

This seizure of public space is disruptive on two levels. The parade tem- porarily interrupts the traffic of daily automobiles and business by creating an alternative spatial and social order. Fiesta has become a social institution itself. The Fiesta Commission coordinates an extensive ten-day calendar of more than one hundred events, allocating funds, dates, and commercial spaces to make the festival run as smoothly as possible. The commission buys insurance for each event, negotiates contracts with the city for public permits, and seeks commercial sponsors for funding.[18] Like the officially sanctioned fiestas of other communities, Fiesta's "resistance" to the order of daily life is

FIGURE 15. Parade crowd at the
Fiesta Flambeau, 2002. Courtesy of the author.

very conservative, reaffirming the status quo even as it temporarily disrupts ordinary life.

At the same time, the mooning contest momentarily interferes with the order of the parade (and the festival) itself, coming between the flow of floats and marching bands that make up this modern civic spectacle. During every Fiesta parade, there are these momentary disruptions that are "out of place."[19] These transgressions, whether intentional or not, are acts that violate social norms. The mooning contest was a transgression of the Fiesta parade. As members of the crowd got up from their seats and moved to the center of the street, they literally stepped across the perceived boundary between spectator and parade participant. In addition, as they pulled down their pants they violated "respectable" forms of public behavior. To reestablish order, police officers told them both to pull up their pants and return to their seats, thus restoring both the spatial and social order of the parade.

Carnival Culture

Though every Fiesta event has its momentary disruptions, the one that draws the most controversy is the Carnival. For the past several years, the Fiesta Carnival has been on Dolorosa Street, between Flores and Santa Rosa. The location is west of the river, inside the downtown core. It is just a few blocks from El Mercado, the historic farmer's market that now houses dozens of Mexican folk art shops and restaurants. For most of the year, El Mercado is a tourist mecca, but during Fiesta, San Antonians take over, as Carnival and El Mercado merge. Fiesta Carnival is street-level San Antonio, a time and place where residents outnumber tourists.[20] The crowds move past gordita booths, Tejano bands, the Tilt-o-whirl, and the Ferris wheel. Police officers barricade streets, divert cars, direct pedestrian traffic, and generally reorganize public activity within this crowded space throughout the week. Throughout its history, the Carnival has occupied a central space in San Antonio's downtown streets. At times, its relationship with civic authorities has been troubled, but it has continued because it is the financial backbone of Fiesta. Without Carnival revenue, Fiesta could not survive. It is also the most highly attended Fiesta event, outside of the parades.[21]

Last year I went to Fiesta's Carnival. My husband and I drove into a crowded parking lot, our sedan pulling tightly between two extended-cab trucks. We entered a long alley of booths that makes up the entrance to Carnival. We passed the usual vendors, selling cotton candy, soda, hot dogs, and beer. It was the middle of the afternoon, and there was still plenty of room to walk around. Most of the crowd was working-class Mexicano teenagers and young families. We stopped at one of the booths and decided to play a typical game of chance. The man running the game demonstrated first: he rode a bike through a defined path—the goal was not to touch any of the orange cones on the boundaries. It sounded simple enough, except that the handlebars were designed to turn in the opposite direction as the bike's wheels. In order to get through, you had to fight all of your bike-riding instincts. The operator made it look easy, of course, but my husband failed as did several other young men who tried.

Like so many other carnival games, winning was more difficult than it appeared. Most patrons were wise enough to know this but were willing to waste a few dollars on the possibility that their luck might be different. Carnival games are often a reminder of the cruelty of a rigged system. Yet the Carnival is a place where so many San Antonians come—despite these minor disappointments. It offers free entry, popcorn, candy and beer, dizzying rides, and the occasional stuffed animal prize. At the same time, Fiesta's Carnival has been a place that has made some San Antonians feel uncomfortable. As a teenager, I was told that the Carnival was a place to watch out for the violence of young Mexicano gangs—the Carnival was described to me as a space of juvenile deviance. There was some reality behind this rhetoric. During the late 1980s and through the 1990s, San Antonio's youth violence escalated to an alarming degree. In the worst years, San Antonio became known as the drive-by shooting capital of Texas, averaging 3.5 drive-bys per day in 1993. The Fiesta Carnival became a space notorious for continuing gang wars, and daily fights and stabbings at the carnival stands would find their way into local newspapers. Judging by the police presence during my visit, local authorities still consider the Carnival a place to be cautious. Every five minutes, we passed a pair of uniformed officers (I counted about ten in our alley area). Writers in the local press sometimes reify this perception, and much of the media coverage of the Carnival has been negative.

The Carnival has a much more complicated history than this would suggest, however. Although some have described Carnival in negative terms, it is also the second oldest Fiesta event. Within the first few years of the Battle of Flowers Parade, individual vendors were setting up booths of carnival attractions in San Antonio's downtown plazas. By the turn of the twentieth century, the Carnival became the main Fiesta event for most San Antonians, who often could not afford to attend the private balls and dances that, at the time, were the only other Fiesta attractions.

When Fiesta expanded after World War II and many new middle-class events were included, the Carnival was one of the first events some businessmen tried to eliminate. In August 1959, the same year that the Fiesta San Antonio Commission formed, a group of about ninety merchants, the Downtowners, threatened to file suit against the city if street permits were issued for the Fiesta Carnival. Herbert Schenker, an attorney for the group, claimed that the Carnival was "degenerate," a haven for illegal gambling and pornography.[22] Although the Downtowners' primary concern was the amount of revenue they lost during the Carnival, carnie corruption was used as a way to seek popular support for the suit. Local newspapers were quite responsive to the call, but the Carnival would not be easy to remove. The event, run by private contractors, was outside the Fiesta organization's direct control. Most important, Carnival revenue funded every other event in the festival. Fiesta organizers depended upon the Carnival contractors' advance payments to run all three parades and allocate monies to each participating organization. The Downtowners discovered that the Carnival, though often ignored in festival promotions, was actually the financial center of Fiesta.

Ever since then, the story of Carnival in the narrative of Fiesta has been primarily disruptive, out of place—a space of games of chance, juvenile delinquency, and corruption. Yet this necessary evil also continues to attract more visitors than any other event, to be the popular center of Fiesta, so maybe it is time to invite this Cinderella to the ball.

Most of the information about Fiesta's Carnival is in the summaries from the local press. At the turn of the twentieth century, the *San Antonio Daily Express* marveled at the display of electric lights arching over Commerce street.[23] Alamo Plaza was filled with traveling midway shows featuring an electric fountain, baby incubators, snake eaters, and cinematograph shows.[24] Like carnival shows throughout the country, San Antonio crowds marveled at displays of exoticism and new technologies. They packed the central commercial district every night of the festival. In fact, the distinction of the Carnival within the larger Fiesta only emerged later. Until 1913, the entire festival was called the Spring Carnival, and even after the name was changed to the Fiesta de San Jacinto, it was frequently referred to as the city's annual carnival.

The carnival shows were broad and interspersed throughout the festival week. They were made up of various booths, street vendors, and amusements. One 1920 program describes it as "shows on the plazas, army features, band concerts, revelry in the streets, dancing at hotels, [and a] Mexican village."[25] Though much of Fiesta de San Jacinto consisted of private balls and parties, and the society pages were filled with Kings Antonio and Queens of the Order of the Alamo, the rest of San Antonio filled downtown streets each night at the Carnival.

Occasionally, a story of a corrupt Carnival vendor or a public Fiesta incident would make its way into the newspaper headlines, but for the most part, the Carnival was described as other Fiesta parades and events. The popular crowd was depicted as a harmonious, fun-loving throng. Of course, the press romanticized these early twentieth-century crowds. Yet I note this trend because it changes significantly in the late 1950s. In the year the Downtowners filed their lawsuit against the city, the local press's attitude toward Fiesta's Carnival was sharply divided. What was once the heart of popular Fiesta was now the center of Fiesta controversy. In the process, the Carnival became a more distinct event. In the years after 1959, Fiesta's carnival culture changed, and the heart of this discussion was the growing concern over juvenile delinquency.

By the time the Downtowners filed their lawsuit, Fiesta's carnival had become more formalized within Fiesta. The booths were leased to private contractors in a more organized system than the haphazard setup of previous decades. This was also the year that the Fiesta San Antonio Commission was created, and so the new commission created a system to better ensure that the private contractors' monies went back to fund the other Fiesta events. The Downtowners' official reasons for filing a suit were that the city did not have the right to lease public streets to private contractors and that such practices were unfair to downtown merchants.[26] Actually, San Antonio's Mayor Kuykendall readily acknowledged that these leasings were "not exactly legal." In terms of the lawsuit itself, the Downtowners seemed to have a good case.

This reason alone did not seem to generate much public support or interest, though. Although the Downtowners initiated the debate, local journalists focused instead on the Carnival as the site of illegal activity. Games of chance were targeted as the source of Carnival corruption. The district attorney quickly joined in the campaign, threatening to crack down on gambling during the following Fiesta week. The FSJA sought a compromise by promising to create a clean carnival. Yet this did not satisfy the Downtowners, who claimed that the Carnival operators would not make a profit unless gambling were permitted. Schenker stated that

> the carnival operators will not put up a red dime unless the city guarantees they can operate their bingo and skin games. The only way they can make money is by taking the pennies, nickels, and dimes from poor kids and they know it.[27]

Schenker also noted the numerous knife injuries suffered in the past year and the added cost in police protection to the area. Carnival critiques offer an interesting combination of moral concerns. On the one hand, Schenker portrayed Carnival operators as manipulators, taking advantage of the young and the poor. On the other, some residents characterized this crowd itself as inherently violent. One citizen claimed that the Carnival should be removed because "too many juvenile delinquents are loose in there. It's getting so you can't walk in without running into trouble."[28]

Public opinion about the Carnival was not always consistent with such accounts, however. The controversy often seemed to split along class and ethnic lines. In a poll the *San Antonio Express News* took in 1959, the respondents who supported the Carnival were predominantly from working-class neighborhoods on the east and west sides of the city, while most of those who opposed the Carnival were from the newer middle-class suburbs north of town.[29] The two main organizations that came to back the Carnival were Mexican American—LULAC and the Mexican Chamber of Commerce. At this time, when both legal and de facto racial segregation were a continuing fact of social life, people of color were more unified in their support of the Carnival.

In this fight, the two city papers also took opposing sides. For the most part, the more conservative *San Antonio Express News* sided with the Carnival critics. The *San Antonio Light* seemed to offer a different point of view. As the *Light* had defended Reynolds Andricks's attempts to open up Fiesta, the paper also supported the Carnival as the event most accessible to a diverse public. One columnist identified the critique of the Carnival as a north side attempt to "do away with a social irritant."[30] The *Light* was more concerned with the Carnival as an Everyman's Fiesta. At the time, the Carnival was one of the only free events in the festival.

A few of these divergent opinions filtered into the *Express News* as well. One merchant claimed that "opponents of a downtown carnival are possibly in a financial condition where they can stage their own celebrations in one of the local country clubs . . . But to the average wage-earner Carnival is his fiesta."[31] For people of color, this alternative conception of Carnival was particularly important. For Gracie Poe Griffin, an African American woman who grew up on the city's west side during the 1950s, the Carnival was where she felt safe. The Carnival was one of the only Fiesta events that had a long history of welcoming people of color.[32] What critics defined as a dangerous space, she redefined as the only safe space for working-class African Americans and Mexican Americans.

This controversy over cleaning up the Carnival that erupted in the paper was part of a larger set of social anxieties of the time. Juvenile delinquency was a subject of great concern for many adults during the 1950s, as a more autonomous youth culture emerged with the rise of comic books, rock 'n' roll music, and the youth market. The teenager was the focus of both social fascination and concern. In 1954–55, the United States Senate held a series of hearings to investigate the effects of new forms of mass culture on youth. A Judiciary Subcommittee to Investigate Juvenile Delinquency examined the impact of television programs and the comic book industry (often referred to as the Kefauver committee for its leading advocate, Tennessee Senator Estes Kefauver). During that same year, a child psychiatrist named Fredric Wertham published his influential book, *The Seduction of the Innocent*, where he linked violent comic books to juvenile delinquency. His study, though more complex than many popular discussions suggested, contributed to a moral panic over the rise of juvenile crime. Other media, such as the film *Rebel without a Cause*, gave more sympathetic depictions of the struggles of rebellious teenagers. All these representations were part of a new national discussion of youth and the effects of mass culture. For those teenagers who participated in Fiesta's Carnival amusements, their activities in mass culture were the subject of intense public debate as well.

In the 1950s, as youth came to represent social change, they became convenient scapegoats for social anxiety and moral panics. At the same time, though, many local readers noted that Carnival criticism was also a reflection of a city divided by ethnicity and social class. Those who petitioned to support the Carnival were those who were excluded from other Fiesta spaces. They also noted, at a local level, what had also been common to many of these moral panics—they primarily focused on working-class youth and also on race.[33] For the moment, however, the Downtowners' lawsuit was unsuccessful for one central reason: the public controversy quickly revealed what Fiesta organizers knew all along—Carnival funded every other Fiesta event. Without Carnival, there would be no Fiesta. Once this was known, the remaining public support for the lawsuit diminished.

This would not be the last time that groups tried to eliminate the Carnival. The next significant threat, though, came from the city itself. In 1968, the mayor, Walter McAllister, asked the president of the Fiesta Commission to do away with the Carnival so that it would not compete with attendance at Hemisfair. The president reluctantly agreed, not really having much choice in the matter, and the following year the city council again asked for it to be canceled for unknown reasons, since Hemisfair was over.[34] The Fiesta Commission, however, was already in a fiscal crisis, and so the Carnival was reinstated. The causes of this rift between the city council and the Fiesta Commission are not entirely clear, but seem to trace back to continuing competition for city permits between Reynolds Andricks and the Fiesta Commission itself.[35] By 1968, the city also did not have as great an interest in protecting the Carnival. At the time, the Carnival was held around city hall, so members of the council may not have appreciated a carnival "in their backyard." The burlesque shows and other forms of risqué entertainment were deemed inappropriate so close to municipal headquarters.[36] The newspapers did not have the same interest either. Carnival was no longer advertised as Everyman's Fiesta. To understand some of these changing attitudes toward the Carnival, I suggest that, once again, changing attitudes toward youth and youth rebellion are the key.

Rampage in the Streets

After the Fiesta River Parade in 1969, between four hundred and one thousand "youths" marched through downtown. The march was organized by the local chapter of the Student Nonviolent Coordinating Committee (SNCC), a predominantly African American organization committed to fighting segregation and racism throughout the South. None of the newspaper accounts made the marchers' motivation clear. Instead, both newspapers described the event solely as a Fiesta disruption. The march actually had nothing to do with Fiesta but was a protest against the death of Bobbie Joe Philips, an unemployed construction worker police had beaten to death.[37] The large crowd who came to see the parade offered a unique opportunity for SNCC to communicate to a citywide audience. The press responded to the march as it had to the Carnival controversy a decade earlier. One consistent theme is that of mob disorderliness. In the process of reporting the march, other dissimilar disturbances were indiscriminately merged with these accounts.[38] The march lost its distinctive cause and became yet another example of "juvenile delinquency."

Once again, the city's newspapers described the controversy rather differently. The *Express News* did not make much of the event, noting that the "disturbance" failed to disrupt the parade. In this account, the "mostly Negro youths" "milled around" and looted downtown businesses for two hours until police came and "brought things under control."[39] Little else was said about the march. In these accounts the assembled crowd appeared the most disorderly. SNCC was not even mentioned as an organization. Instead, the march became one of many failed attempts to disrupt the week's festivities.

Rather than diminish the event, the *San Antonio Light* took the opposite approach. The front-page article "Rampage in Downtown S.A." sensationalized the march as a threatening "organized disturbance."[40] In this depiction, the protesting crowd became a mob of African Americans and "several white hippies" who broke windows and looted buildings. In contrast to this unruly group, the police were depicted as agents of civic order. "Despite the organized nature of the disturbance, police acted with restraint throughout the two hours." What is interesting is that while the article referred to the planned nature of the protest, it never referred to any particular motive. Instead, the irrationality of the incident was highlighted by this absence of a cause. SNCC was criticized for not controlling the crowd, as it reported frantic student leaders using police megaphones saying, "We've made our point," and encouraging the crowd to disperse.[41] Unfortunately, it seems that the point was not well communicated to the press. Instead, "black militants" were ultimately characterized as being disruptive for the sake of stealing guns and breaking windows, and the police were lauded. For the marchers, however, the protest was a powerful example of spontaneous protest against a corrupt police force and the dominant social order. As soon as SNCC initiated the march in Victoria Courts, a housing project right next to Hemisfair Plaza, thousands joined, "singing freedom songs."[42] This was also a street-level interruption of river-level culture, as they literally marched on the streets above the river.

CHAPTER SIX

The sensational tone of the *Light*'s reporting was consistent with the style used to describe other minor Fiesta incidents that year as well. A front-page headline four days later declared that "violence mars Fiesta parade."[43] The actual incident, however, failed to live up to the promise of the headline. Exploding firecrackers were mistaken for gunfire, and in the confusion the Fiesta queen was taken off her float halfway through the parade. After describing the incident, the article followed with a list of other disturbances during the parade, including one man who was "taunted into fighting with four men who ridiculed his western attire." Although numerous fights were cited, none seemed to amount to a great disturbance, yet the list emphasized these events. "Isolated incidents involving police and unidentified tormentors seemed to be the order of the day." Also, although many of the "tormentors" were left unidentified in the article, a few names and descriptions were prevalent. Most important, while the names of the pranksters responsible for the firecracker incident were not disclosed, a "Negro youth" who somehow "attempted to interfere" with the queen's evacuation was given a name and address.[44] The few descriptions of the parade disrupters usually identified them as "militant black youths." Thus, while the long list of fights among the crowd indicates that the disturbances were spread throughout the parade route, African Americans were targeted as the chief source of trouble.

While the *San Antonio Light* gave more coverage to the SNCC march, the rhetoric of this coverage did more to delegitimize the protest than did that of other city papers. The reports of property damage showed that this was a rather mild rampage. Overall, nine arrests were made, five pistols were stolen from one downtown store, some costume jewelry taken from another, and a few windows were broken. It was also never clear that the marching crowd were the persons responsible for the looting. Because the protest occurred after the River Parade, thousands of other people were "milling around" the area at the same time. In these newspaper stories, however, the protestors were defined as a "roving crowd" that was not only unresponsive to calls for order but also distinctly separate from parade spectators, although it is difficult to know how these distinctions could be made in the aftermath of a downtown crowd after the parade.

Because the police found that the "black militants" could not control their ranks, the cops were to "drop the soft approach" for later demonstrations.[45] In another article paralleling the rampage, Police Chief Bichsel reported that although police had previously honored requests to use restraint in restoring order after demonstrations, this disturbance showed that these tactics did not work. In the future, the police should "respond more swiftly and more positively."[46] In the previous article Bichsel had acknowledged that damage was minimal and that a greater disturbance had occurred the previous year, but he simultaneously defined the disturbance as out of control. He used this definition to further justify the change in police tactics, even though this protest was actually less violent and more organized.

The most disturbing aspect of this shift in police tactics, though, was in a story reported the next day. Apparently, the night after the parade disturbance police came to the Langston Hughes Center, the SNCC headquarters, based on reports of "a rifle being displayed" outside the building.[47] A spokesman for SNCC charged that the police "brutally beat" organization members and arrested five of them afterward.[48] While it is uncertain whether this was retaliation for the previous demonstration, it seems likely that this was the product of Bichsel's new tactics.

The structure of the *Light*'s narrative also discredited the SNCC march by placing it in the context of other Fiesta disturbances. By equating this event with firecracker explosions and crowd fights, the *Light*, like the *Express News*, did not distinguish social protest from social disorder. Because the *Light* did give so much coverage to the events, however, these accounts also furnished a counternarrative. One of the primary sources for this narrative was in the photographs accompanying the week's articles. While the reports claimed that the rampage was the work of black militants, the photos were of police using force. On the front page, a police officer grabbed one of the protestors. On the next page of the article, the police were shown in riot formation, giving "a protestor's eye view of the police line."[49] Three days later, when firecrackers caused crowd panic, the photos again showed police officers drawing their guns and wielding riot sticks.[50] Although the articles highlighted police restraint, the photos emphasized their aggression, particularly against African American youths. In one picture, the seventeen-year-old African American who was taken into custody for "interfering" was shown with a bloodied face; the accompanying article did claim that the officer had to use force to restrain him during his arrest. Thus, although SNCC's message was never voiced in the city's papers, the photographs of police force question the accounts of their restraint. In the photograph of "a protestor's eye view" of the police in riot formation, the newspaper also offered an interesting opportunity to identify with these youths. Although the photo's purpose may have been to offer an intimidating show of force, the picture also paradoxically invited the reader to identify with the demonstrators. Ultimately, the accumulation of images seemed to argue the possibility that in their attempts to restore order, the cops may have been more disruptive, and done more damage, than the militant protestors.

In many ways these events differed from the 1959 Carnival controversy. By 1969, a more organized, politicized counterculture had developed among both working-class and middle-class youth across the country and throughout much of the rest of the world as well. The *San Antonio Light*, once interested in defending those spaces of Everyman's Fiesta, would now sensationalize the youth disturbances it had once ignored. The attacks on SNCC and other such organizations were part of a larger sense of a crisis of authority. Even though civil rights struggles had been part of southern history for many years, organizations like SNCC had by this time developed more radical aims than some other more moderate civil rights organizations. Led at this point by Stokely Carmichael, SNCC was more interested in black empowerment, self-reliance, encompassed in the term "black power." He did not necessarily follow the tenets of Martin Luther King, Jr.'s, principles of nonviolence, which were also the original principles of SNCC. As SNCC had changed, so had many political groups who encountered white resistance to desegregation and continuing white violence.

In south Texas, the late 1960s were a time of both great optimism and frustration. Much of the political work of the civil rights movement was successful, particularly in urban areas like San Antonio. World War II, industrialization, and social protest from all segments of the Mexican American and African American communities accelerated the decline of race restrictions. Within the Texas state legislature, a coalition of African Americans, Mexican Americans, and white liberal Democrats managed to gain greater power and defeat segregationist measures in education pushing for enforcement of *Brown v. Board of Education*. The growth of a Mexican American business class also contributed to weakening local segregationist practices in the cities. Veterans' organizations were crucial in mobilizing voting registration drives as well.[51] Jim Crow segregation continued throughout the 1950s and 1960s in many places, however, and middle-class organizations often had condescending attitudes toward working-class Mexicanos.[52] This split widened by the late 1960s, and the working-class movement's organization of farm workers sparked youth into a larger Chicano civil rights movement, which emphasized Chicano identity, as well as more direct protest and action. For a time, even middle-class groups became more activist, participating in many consumer boycotts; high schools throughout south Texas had their own boycotts, calling for more Mexican American teachers and courses in their history. At times, though, the tactics and the ideologies of these groups came into conflict. These conflicts were based on both class and, at times, generation. The militancy of the Chicano movement also spurred the demise of

Jim Crow throughout the Southwest, though. The SNCC protest came at a time of much frustration but also a time of incredible social change and transformation of a segregated social order.

In the decades after the 1960s, when the most defined boundaries of this politicized counterculture dissolved and faded from newspaper headlines, the youth who had been so marginalized in these Fiesta disruptions returned, once again, to the Carnival. For the moment of 1969, some of them became politically active, and, needless to say, many of them became politically active afterward as well, but they would not garner the same kind of press attention as they had at this particular historical moment. No, the young militants who had been defined as out of place after the Fiesta River Parade of 1969 once again reappeared, I suggest, many times in the local press, but not in quite the same form. For years, some in society had made the juvenile delinquent or the militant into "folk-devils," symbols of a society that had lost its way.[53] The faces of those folk-devils, the ones beaten and harassed in sweeping law-and-order campaigns, would be black, brown, and poor. In 1969, these youths found a space to collectively protest after a River Parade. For the most part, though, they have been most in place at the Carnival, weaving uncomfortable paths in games of chance, finding their balance in dizzying rides, making do.

La Semana Alegre

Rules is rules, do's and don't's and won't's
Got picked up for checking some dude's oil
At La Semana Alegre.
There I was having beers and beers
Checking out chicks in tops like tubes . . .
Then some dude steps on my fuckin' shoe.[54]

In this poem about one of Fiesta's most notorious events, La Semana Alegre (the Festive Week), Santiago García takes the voice of a young Mexicano gang member who was placed in jail for stabbing another person ("checking some dude's oil"). García's poem was inspired by a night when he walked out of La Semana Alegre and saw a row of young guys lying on the sidewalk calmly waiting for an EMT to clean the stab wounds on their stomachs. He wanted to write about how all of their emotions—excitement, joy, anger—get focused on La Semana.[55]

By the 1980s, La Semana Alegre became synonymous with depictions of San Antonio's gang culture. The violence that characterized these young men's daily lives was often tragically reflected in newspaper stories about La Semana. The festival revealed a social reality that many Fiesta revelers ignored.

After World War II Fiesta was promoted as a space of middle-class civic unity and interethnic friendship, represented by the positive images of Mexicano masculinity in the charro and Rey Feo. At the same time, young working-class African and Mexicano men were increasingly portrayed as the most dangerous representatives of machismo and male violence, and the Carnival was the space for this "immoral geography," marking the boundaries of this evolving middle-class alliance.[56] Even as late as 1991, *Express News* columnist David Richelieu described the Carnival as "a squalid hotbed of knifings, shootings, assaults, and even live daytime sex." (Apparently, two carnival workers were discovered having intercourse on the grounds that year.[57]) Like his predecessors, Richelieu described corruption and debauchery as endemic to the Carnival. One can look at the last three decades of Fiesta's Carnival as a way to discover the more troubling edges of an economy that has not worked for many of its residents. Furthermore, as in many previous moral panics, the city's nonwhite youth become the symptom and the scapegoat for these social problems.

Although the struggles for civic inclusion have produced many positive results, much of the working-class Mexicano population is largely overlooked in this new Anglo–Mexican American alliance, yet this population "constitutes a massive pervasive social reality" in this region.[58] David Montejano notes that this new political inclusion has not solved the social and economic problems of most Mexicanos. In 1990, 25 percent of Mexicanos lived in poverty, and high school dropout rates have actually increased to 56.4 percent. Such evidence suggests that "the Mexican American community has been split into a socially incorporated middle class and a socially segregated lower class."[59] José Limón refers to the emergence of a new political-economic condition by the 1970s that David Harvey calls "flexible accumulation," which includes, among other things, the surge in "service sector" employment.[60] Limón illustrates these economic shifts in terms of their particularly devastating effects on San Antonio's Mexicano poor and lower class. As part of flexible accumulation, employers can exert greater control over the workforce, undercutting organized labor and increasing unemployment and unskilled labor as well. This form of late capitalism, Limón claims (restating Harvey), "wages war on lower-class Mexican-Americans" and may also threaten the politics of moderation, compromise, and negotiation.[61] By the 1970s, these trends were already central to the experiences of nearly all lower-class Mexicanos in San Antonio.

As so many other Fiesta events expressed San Antonio's middle-class politics, its lower-class events, mainly the Carnival, but a few others as well, came to represent this other social reality. One event that represented great social anxiety was La Semana. The accounts of the irate crowd that gave Fiesta's La Semana a bad reputation during this time are very similar to descriptions of the Carnival and of the SNCC protest. The greater violence of the city's youth, in terms of increasing numbers of gangs and homicides, resembles Limón's description of the "post modern working class *mexicano*," who often turns to socially unacceptable forms of expression such as gang culture.[62] These expressions are the language of today's "juvenile delinquents," and Fiesta's La Semana Alegre was their social space.

La Semana Alegre was not so different from other Fiesta events, featuring lots of food, beer, and entertainment. Its distinguishing feature, though, was heavy metal music. Understandably, this event attracted a younger audience. Many inner-city kids looked to La Semana as their "adolescent playground," a place to drink, party, and celebrate the temporary emancipation from parental rule.[63] As it grew, La Semana attracted bad press. In the minds of many a newspaper columnist, La Semana had actually replaced the Carnival as "the ugly stepchild" of Fiesta.[64] The event became particularly controversial after a 1990 concert. One evening, Faster Pussycat, a local metal band, and its audience began chanting obscenities at the security guards. After several unsuccessful calls to stop the chants, the police turned off the power. Afterward, the crowd rushed the stage, and the band began destroying equipment.[65]

This incident was the beginning of the end of La Semana. Although reports indicate that this was an unusual event, and place most of the blame on the band, the stage rushing was soon combined with other incidents. On April 24, 1990, one day after, an article about several fights was placed underneath the coverage of the concert, entitled "Fistfights Mar Fiesta Celebration."[66] Although police officers interviewed at the event claimed that these occurrences were normal and not more numerous than in previous years, the press began to write about them in more detail. The following day the *San Antonio Light* ran an article about increased security at Fiesta events, because of a pro basketball playoff game occurring that same evening. Although the article made clear that the extra security was because of the game, the narrative soon shifted to La Semana violence. The remainder of the text displayed an interesting phenomenon: as the police officers repeated admissions that La Semana had not become more dangerous in relation to other events or to previous years, citing statistics of fights and arrests, the article's attention to these events made them seem new or unusual. The *Light* seemed to create its own controversy. By April 26, the stage-rushing incident had become a criticism of heavy alcohol consumption and youth gangs.[67]

While excessive alcohol consumption probably did have something to do with Fiesta fights and the concert incident, the target of criticism soon shifted to a more specific source, La Semana. By the next year, the local media began to focus on La Semana as the main source of Fiesta violence. Rollette Schreckenghost, the head of the San Antonio Conservation Society and NIOSA director, claimed that the event had "gotten out of control." She stated that "La Semana is giving Fiesta a bad name. They're just different from other Fiesta events . . . I'm afraid to go over there."[68] Schreckenghost admitted that she had never attended La Semana, but this did not seem to affect her claims. NIOSA also most directly competed with La Semana for nighttime crowds, as it occurred during the same time and was directly across the street. The city manager, Alex Briseño, supported La Semana and suspected that "either the media or this NIOSA official is creating an issue." He also stated that this was a campaign to do away with the event itself: "I think this issue is not about moving La Semana, but killing it."[69] Briseño's comment was prophetic. In 1993, La Semana was moved to an area south of downtown, where it never did attract the crowds it had in previous years. By 1995, La Semana was discontinued.

Although many people I have spoken with believe that La Semana's demise was the result of its excessive violence, it was never clear that La Semana was any rowdier than other Fiesta events. The police took an average of twenty people per night off the premises, which seems minor compared to the crowd of one hundred thousand.[70] This number is about the same as at other Fiesta events such as NIOSA itself. The only type of disruption that seemed to mark La Semana as the target of criticism was the Faster Pussycat concert incident. While NIOSA organizers and others may have wanted to do away with the event for a number of years, this stage rushing provided the necessary catalyst. While some San Antonians spoke of La Semana as out of control, for others the event offered an opportunity for a level of freedom that was unavailable in other spaces. NIOSA officials wanted to define La Semana as out of place during Fiesta, but for thousands of young Mexicano and African American men, La Semana was *their* space.

After the demise of La Semana, San Antonio's lower-class youth returned to their other Fiesta spaces—El Mercado, the Oyster Bake, and most often, the Carnival. Occasionally, news of a fistfight or a stabbing would make the newspaper. In 1999, an argument at the Carnival ended in a shooting outside the grounds.[71] The most chilling Carnival incident was when a nine-year-old girl was abducted and killed by a Carnival worker in 1999.[72] For the most part, though, the stories of youth violence at Carnival are word-of-mouth. They are hinted at in the heavy police presence at all the Carnival booths, and they seem to have a reality because of the larger reality of violence that has become a rising part of the lives of San Antonio's lower-class youth since the late 1980s.

In 1988, the *San Antonio Express News* ran a cover story with the headline "S.A. Gangs: A Problem Waiting to Explode." The article described several downtown gangs, paint sniffers, and street punks who sold drugs, had murdered two homeless people, and beaten a newspaper employee to death.[73] Such youth violence was part of a city and region in economic crisis. Texas was in the middle of an oil crisis, a recession that affected banking institutions, real estate, and development. As in other places throughout the country, local and federal governments slashed social services as well. Many of the kids most vulnerable to gang activity were pushed out of the after school programs designed to help them.[74] As in most urban gangs, kids grouped together by neighborhood, following the cultural and socioeconomic boundaries that have shaped San Antonio for most of the twentieth century. Poor African American kids gathered on the east side, poor Mexicanos on the west side, and within these broad territories they used the concrete walls of markets and government housing to spray-paint even more specific boundaries. They identified with images from mass media—the movie *Colors* and the battles between L.A.'s Crips and Bloods—but their wars were also local, fighting for every square of sidewalk and street corner. They got the most attention from the larger public, though, when they moved out of their neighborhoods and into other public spaces. The high schools became some of the first battlegrounds; a lunchtime shoot-out at Sam Houston High gunned down three students in 1989. As a result, the police launched its first gang unit. Two years later, two armed officers were stationed at each high school in the San Antonio school district and one at each middle school.[75]

Then they hit the malls. Rachel Grant, a sixty-four-year-old African American grandmother, was caught in the crossfire while waiting for the bus outside a Toys "R" Us at a north side mall. She was killed instantly, and the *Express News* photo of January 5, 1992, showed the police standing over her body, the popcorn she was holding strewn on the ground. Days later, the *Express News* published a map of thirty-five gangs by name, clothing, and ethnicity, along with a warning list for tourists, businesses, and parents on how to escape gang violence. The paper received eleven thousand requests for copies.[76] As fear escalated among San Antonians, and juvenile violence spread across the city, police and the paper developed and promoted a negative map of the city, an immoral geography of juvenile criminality. While San Antonians had legitimate fears about the rapid rise of youth crime, such anxieties also marginalized the bodies of young, poor Mexicanos and African Americans as never before. The public space where most of these young men have felt the greatest effects of public anger has been in the justice system. In 1995, massive changes to Texas criminal law for juvenile offenders transformed the punishments for youth crimes. Maximum sentences were increased, parole standards tightened, and, most specifically, fourteen-year-old offenders could be certified for trial as adults.[77]

The gang map revealed how the city marked and divided its residents. It also offered an interesting countermap to the many tourist maps circulating through downtown San Antonio, particularly during Fiesta. Clearly the map was intended for tourists, businesses, parents, and perhaps most important, those who lived on the north side; they were now all given an immoral geography of the more troubled sections of the city. These maps also served the purpose of exoticizing and isolating those who had already been caught in the crossfire in most of these gang wars. Even though a shootout at a mall parking lot occasionally shocked the city, the most frequent victims of gang violence were in these communities themselves. At the height of the violence, 1,262 drive-by shootings were recorded in 1993.[78]

The debates over Carnival continue. Most recently, new carnival contractors have created a "clean carnival," including a new fenced-off children's section.[79] This most recent controversy was encouraged by the practices of former Carnival operator Philip Sheridan. In 1996 businessman Sheridan won approval to continue a contract to run children's rides at Brackenridge Park, even though he was accused of sexually assaulting one of his fourteen-year-old female employees. The scandal became a huge political embarrassment to the city of San Antonio, which for years had given him this lucrative contract as well as the contract to run the Fiesta Carnival. Later, it was also revealed that the city council knew Sheridan had been convicted of tax evasion when they voted to continue the contract.[80] The council members claimed they were unaware of the assault charges when they approved the new contract, but the scandal quickly grew. By the following year, the *Express News* was publishing stories of Fiesta's long connection to the Sheridan family. Phil Sheridan himself, acquitted of the sexual assault charges, was still on parole the tax fraud conviction and was in much other legal trouble.[81] He had handed the family business, Alamo Concessions Supply Inc., down to his son Patrick, but this did little to ease the public controversy. As the local press detailed the long history of Sheridan's legal troubles, it also demonstrated a no-bid contract system that had existed between the Sheridan family and the Fiesta Commission since 1973. For years, Alamo Concessions paid a flat fee of $350,000 for the right to operate the Carnival and another $50,000 for exclusive rights to operate concessions in the downtown area during the three major Fiesta parades. With such an arrangement, the Fiesta Commission was guaranteed enough money to run the parades. As Edward Steves, head of the commission's 1997 carnival committee, stated, "Without the money [from the carnival and concessions], the [Fiesta] parades wouldn't exist."[82] The argument had quite a familiar ring. Without Carnival there would be no Fiesta. In addition, Sheridan gained more goodwill with the commission by donating an extra $100,000 in 1992 for extra Fiesta Centennial expenses.[83]

These arguments could not protect the Sheridans' sweetheart deal with the Fiesta Commission for long, however. As the controversy continued, several city council members questioned the nature of this arrangement. Although the council did have final say in rejecting any particular contract proposal from the Fiesta Commission, its role in selecting concessionaires was otherwise severely limited. In addition, many thought that the city should get a share in the revenues generated from the Carnival and downtown concessions. San Antonio never received any money to offset the annual $1 million it spent on police and traffic control. Many Mexican American leaders also argued that the Fiesta Commission's leadership was not reflective of the city's population and thus should not exclusively decide on such contract issues.[84] The protests forced a delay in the vote, and in August 1998, the city council unanimously voted to oversee the Fiesta Commissions selection process for awarding Carnival contracts and concessions rights. A councilman, Roger Flores, along with LULAC officials, also pressured the Fiesta Commission to broaden the ethnic makeup of the contract committee. With the previous arrangement, Alamo Concessions was allowed to carry off all the profits, after paying the initial flat fee of $350,000. With the new deal, the city would get 25 percent of the profits anytime the Fiesta Commission netted more than $500,000. If the Commission made more than $700,000, the profits would be split 50–50 with the city.[85]

The new deal certainly generated more money for both the Fiesta Commission and the city. The controversy also put a spotlight on the nature of Fiesta and negotiations of public space. As city council members repeatedly pointed out, Carnival and parades used public resources, and the city was now demanding a share in these profits. The Sheridan scandal uncovered long-standing resentments over the relationship between the Fiesta

Commission and the city. Some in the local press continued to argue that the Fiesta Commission, for all of its rhetoric of inclusion, had not opened itself up to San Antonio's diverse public. Carlos Guerra, a *San Antonio Express News* columnist and one of the commission's most frequent critics, stated the concessions controversy most succinctly. Recommending that the city council, and not the Fiesta Commission, evaluate Carnival contracts, he wrote: "This isn't about choosing the caterer for a party. It's about city business."[86]

Meanwhile, it is difficult to know how the paths have changed for the youths who wander through the booths at today's Carnival. After the violence of the early 1990s, city officials poured more resources into both prevention and anticrime programs, enforcing curfews, funding after school programs and other initiatives, and significantly reducing the numbers of drive-by shootings. On the city's west side one of the most successful gang truces was organized by social workers from the Good Samaritan Center, where five of the area's largest gangs gathered for weekly meetings, job training, drug counseling, and education. One of their first small victories was a Fiesta week truce.[87]

Conclusion

Fiesta is the psalm of San Antonio—a hymn sung for a century now by the citizenry to glorify the conviction that theirs is a place of halcyonic sophistication on the one hand and an impregnable refuge against the soul-wearying onslaught of day-to-day living on the other.

—Jack Maguire[1]

Remember the Alamo? I can't even remember my name."

—T-shirt sold on the San Antonio Riverwalk

DURING THE FIESTA CELEBRATION OF 1998, I VIEWED THE ANNUAL pilgrimage to the Alamo. The late afternoon ceremony was sparsely attended, with about two hundred visitors sitting on outside bleachers facing the Alamo. On the grounds directly in front of the chapel's entrance, empty chairs waited for the members of the Daughters of the Republic of Texas. Without much warning, a deep voice addressed the crowd, calling for a reverent silence as the Texans who died at the Alamo battle were named. Looking around, I could not see who was speaking. The speakers were placed around the building, but there was no visible microphone, as if the walls themselves were addressing the audience. As the steady baritone proceeded with the list of more than two hundred Alamo defenders, the crowd lost interest and began to talk, so that at times the names were difficult to hear. I walked around the food booths and past the bleachers, listening to the various conversations. A few people had come to the pilgrimage with the expectation of a battle reenactment. Others, who knew more about the ceremony, explained the fragments of Texas history they could remember. Yet most of the conversations had nothing to do with the events at all, just the random accounts of daily life. When the procession began, the crowd quieted a little. The representatives of America's revolutions and foreign wars stepped forward as they paid homage to the "shrine of Texas liberty." We recited the pledge of allegiance and listened to a short sermon about heroes and courage, but by this time, most of the crowd was gone.

The one silent pause that Fiesta had set aside for respectful commemoration was not reverential and not very quiet. I kept waiting for something to write down, a key phrase that would pull together the threads of conversation. I have investigated the controversies and debates that continually redefine the *corazón* of this city's public culture. I have found stories that challenge any attempts to define Fiesta under one unifying narrative. Yet I also look for those quiet moments of resolution, for temporary coherence within the chaos, but the Alamo is not the space for these moments. Situated on a literal and metaphorical battlefield, the tiny fortress has not silenced its conflicted past.

The Fiesta crowd has moved away from the Alamo, but it has not separated itself from its tangled history. Perhaps a complete forgetting is not possible, especially in the context of a tourist industry that continues to promote San Antonio as the Alamo city and a social order that is still influenced by the Texas Modern. As Fiesta participants articulate their relationships to Texas Modernity, two dominant views emerge. One, which the heritage elite endorses, describes the festival as a realm of halcyonic sophistication. Jack Maguire, a Texas writer touted by Fiesta organizers, wrote his Fiesta history following this view. His work is a hymn of praise, both of Fiesta and San Antonio as a whole. For Maguire, Fiesta's history is one of consensus. Unlike the chaotic series of public displays that make up Fiesta, Maguire presents a rather orderly procession of events. As parade officials seek to control these disruptions, so Maguire has attempted to appropriate the many public controversies into a respectable story.

For another group, Fiesta sounds more like a bawdy bar tune than a hymn, a cacophony of voices with no particular message. Although Fiesta has faithfully occurred around the week of April 21, the anniversary of Texan independence, most contemporary events have very little to do with remembering the Alamo's heroes or remembering anything at all. Fiesta has transformed into a carnivalesque forgetfulness, ten days of *puro* party. Such a public display of forgetfulness has affected private memories as well. Like the Fourth of July and other national commemorations, the patriotic purposes of the event are often the taken-for-granted setting for modern leisure.

La Voz de Esperanza, a small newspaper the Esperanza Peace and Justice Center publishes, has voiced this point of view. In 1993, it published an issue devoted to Fiesta critiques. Esperanza is a San Antonio community organization advocating a number of social justice and environmental issues, particularly within the Chicano/a and lesbian/gay communities. Laura Codina, in her article "The What, How y Qué Más of Fiesta," writes:

> There has been an ongoing struggle to incorporate [Chicana/os] representation, our continued presence in this event and in this land. It is a drive to regain lost ground, sabotaging the original intention of Fiesta. But it has become an end in itself, "puro party," dulling the repressed masses, blocking revolution and evolution.[2]

A recent documentary emphasizes this aspect of Fiesta as well. Produced by three San Antonio filmmakers for Deep Dish Television, *Puro Party: Celebrating a Genocide* attacks Fiesta as a racist celebration. The theme of the thirty-minute piece, as it documents several parades and street fairs, is that while most working-class Mexicanos in San Antonio like to party and forget about the history of racial and class discrimination in San Antonio, the Anglo Fiesta organizers are playing a joke on them, presenting distorted parodies of Mexican American culture for their naïve consumption. Graciela Sánchez, head of the Esperanza Center, in the film defines Fiesta as "white businessmen making money off of poor Chicanos." Her statement simplifies the event, yet it is certainly fair to say that Fiesta makes much of its money off the poor, as the history of the Carnival demonstrates.

Yet there are also problems with the themes of *Puro Party*. The most frequently repeated image in the film is of the white queen sitting on her float and "waving to the brown people" along the parade route. In the film, the queen is supposed to represent the hegemony of Anglo, wealthy Fiesta organizers, though Fiesta organizers and volunteers are no longer just this group of Anglo elites. The documentary argues that the Fiesta power structure has not changed, when it has actually changed quite significantly, as has the city's. While the kings and queens of the Order of the Alamo are still from the same families who controlled the city one hundred years ago, these families now have to share their power with many middle-class organizations that contribute most of the work of Fiesta.

The city's changes are illustrated in the film itself. One of the producers, Lizzie Martínez, went to the same high school as that year's queen. As she is filming the queen's float, she calls to Katie. The queen, Katie, sees her, and they have a brief conversation as the float rides down the parade route. Lizzie then talks in the film about her memories of their shared car pool rides as kids. The incident reflects the contradictory position of San Antonio's Mexican American upper middle class. They share rides to school and go to each other's parties, but there are moments, especially during Fiesta, when they also become a white queen waving to a brown person in the crowd. Much of the Mexican American middle-class activity in Fiesta has worked to resolve this contradiction, to finally enter the private circle of the heritage elite. What these critics have ignored is that middle-class Mexican Americans have taken over the rest of Fiesta as well.

Ethnic binaries do not adequately express the Fiestas in the later part of the twentieth century and the early part of the twenty-first. The end of Jim Crow segregation in San Antonio and south Texas has contributed to the growth of the city's Mexican American middle class, and some of its members have made an alliance with an Anglo business elite. Today, while a group of Anglo elites continue to dominate in terms of political and economic power in the city, they do so along with an upper-middle-class Mexican American population who also benefits.[3] Looking at the members of the board of the Fiesta San Antonio Commission in 1990, which had a Mexican American president, Roger Flores, and several other Mexican American members, one can see evidence of the politics of inclusion. As I have demonstrated, contemporary Fiestas are part of the story of this limited political inclusion. Yet many Fiesta participants are from these other sectors of the Mexicano community—poor, working-class, and first-generation immigrants who enjoy the food, music, and merriment of Fiesta. For the most part, they cannot afford to pay the admission cost to NIOSA or attend the many other private fundraisers that week. Instead, they go to the Carnival or El Mercado and attend the parades. They are not just watching the royal court. Their children are in the marching bands or on the floats of the hundreds of local businesses that participate. They often make parade visits a family tradition. Their stories, for the most part, were not included in the archives, and Fiesta critics have simplified their experiences, but they keep attending.

While Fiesta critics voice many important concerns, at times they have ignored the pathways that San Antonians have made for themselves in Fiesta.

CONCLUSION

They struggled to legitimize their positions in the social structure, become individual actors in the city's public life, and write their own histories. My analysis could not hope to capture all of Fiesta's dizzying multivocality, but I have brought out the key events and participants who shaped Fiesta's place in this modern city. To use a familiar Tex-Mex food analogy, I have found that Fiesta is like an elaborately layered dip. Each of Fiesta's distinct events—the Battle of Flowers Parade, the coronation, NIOSA, the Fiesta Flambeau, Rey Feo, and Carnival—emerged and responded to distinct historic moments, but very few disappeared from the festival, so Fiesta continues with the vestiges of each of these eras. Like any well-consumed dip, these various performances blend into one another, yet maintain some of their distinct tastes as well. Although I only focus on the emergence of these central Fiesta events and themes, it is important to note that each of these different performances continues into contemporary Fiestas. High school kids still march in the Battle of Flowers Parade, and the Fiesta queens ride above their heads. The street fairs like the Night in Old San Antonio monopolize San Antonio's tourist pedestrian spaces, and the Carnival continues at downtown's margins. Each of these events has its own cultural domain within Fiesta. Each adds another layer to understanding this central spectacle of San Antonio's civic identity.

NOTES

Notes to Introduction

1. Michel de Certeau, *The Practices of Everyday Life* (Berkeley: University of California Press, 1984), 101. This phrase, like this beginning example, is modeled after Michel de Certeau's idea of "walking rhetoric."
2. De Certeau, *The Practices of Everyday Life*, 99.
3. De Certeau, *The Practices of Everyday Life*, 97.
4. Susan Davis, *Parades and Power* (Philadelphia: Temple University Press, 1986), 5–6. Davis writes that parades are stages for the social forces of the city; they are tools for "building, maintaining, and confronting power relations."
5. David Glassberg, *Sense of History: The Place of the Past in American Life* (Amherst: University of Massachusetts Press, 2001). Glassberg first used this idea of civic parades as "celebrating the city," 59–86.
6. Here I am borrowing from de Certeau's critique of Michel Foucault's approach to power and social space. Foucault emphasizes the disciplining of society and the many methods and technical procedures of structures of power. Through this metaphor of walking the city, de Certeau argues that social spaces are more open to human agency and creativity than Foucault allows.
7. David M. Guss, *The Festive State: Race, Ethnicity and Nationalism as Cultural Performance* (Berkeley: University of California Press, 2000), 8–12; Richard Bauman, "Performance and Honor in 13th Century Iceland," *Journal of American Folklore* 99, no. 392 (1986): 131–50. Guss identifies four key elements of cultural performance. The first is that it is framed, set apart from daily life. Cultural performances are separated spaces, dramatizations that allow participants to understand and sometimes change their worlds. They are set apart from normative reality, but are not sealed off from this larger social sphere. The second element of performance is that it is reflexive. As Bauman writes, performances are "cultural forms about culture, social forms about society, in which the central meanings and values of a group are embodied, acted out, and laid open to examination and interpretation in symbolic form, both by members of that group and by the ethnographer" (133). The third element of performance is that it is "profoundly discursive." Participants use performance to "argue and debate, to challenge and negotiate." Guss emphasizes that performances are not texts to be read, but "fields of action"

where multiple groups can dramatize competing ideas (10). Finally, cultural performances have "the ability to produce new meanings and relations" (11).

8. Charles Ramsdell, *San Antonio: A Historical and Pictorial Guide* (Austin: University of Texas Press, 1959), 9.

9. Lewis Fisher, *San Antonio: Outpost of Empires* (San Antonio: Maverick Publishing Company, 1997), 1.

10. Timothy M. Matovina, *Tejano Religion and Ethnicity: San Antonio, 1821–1860* (Austin: University of Texas Press, 1995), 7.

11. Matovina, *Tejano Religion and Ethnicity*, 10.

12. Matovina, *Tejano Religion and Ethnicity*, 11.

13. David Montejano, *Anglos and Mexicans in the Making of Texas, 1836–1986* (Austin: University of Texas Press, 1987), 35.

14. Montejano, *Anglos and Mexicans in the Making of Texas*, 22.

15. Montejano, *Anglos and Mexicans in the Making of Texas*, 27.

16. William A. McClintock, "Journal of a Trip through Texas and Northern Mexico in 1846–7," *Southwestern Historical Quarterly* 34 (October 1930): 146–47.

17. Montejano, *Anglos and Mexicans in the Making of Texas*, 27.

18. Montejano, *Anglos and Mexicans in the Making of Texas*, 25.

19. Montejano, *Anglos and Mexicans in the Making of Texas*, 26.

20. Montejano, *Anglos and Mexicans in the Making of Texas*, 34.

21. Montejano, *Anglos and Mexicans in the Making of Texas*, 38.

22. Montejano, *Anglos and Mexicans in the Making of Texas*, 45.

23. Matovina, *Tejano Religion and Ethnicity*, 70.

24. Montejano, *Anglos and Mexicans in the Making of Texas*, 28.

25. Montejano, *Anglos and Mexicans in the Making of Texas*, 51–52.

26. Matovina, *Tejano Religion and Ethnicity*, 50.

27. Fisher, *San Antonio: Outpost of Empires*, 23.

28. Matovina, *Tejano Religion and Ethnicity*, 51.

29. Matovina, *Tejano Religion and Ethnicity*, 25.

30. Montejano, *Anglos and Mexicans in the Making of Texas*, 29.

31. Montejano, *Anglos and Mexicans in the Making of Texas*, 27.

32. Matovina, *Tejano Religion and Ethnicity*, 53.

33. *San Antonio Ledger*, September 1, 1853.

34. Matovina, *Tejano Religion and Ethnicity*, 55–56.

35. Matovina, *Tejano Religion and Ethnicity*, 79–80.

36. Matovina, *Tejano Religion and Ethnicity*, 74–75. Though it is difficult to know the substance of these accusations, they were frequent enough to suggest that Tejanos' attitudes were not consistent with local Anglos' attitudes toward slavery.

37. Matovina, *Tejano Religion and Ethnicity*, 35–37.

38. Eric Hobsbawm and Terence Ranger, eds., *The Invention of Tradition* (Cambridge: Cambridge University Press, 1983), 1–8. Hobsbawm first defined this idea of "invented tradition" as the "set of practices, normally governed by overtly or tacitly accepted rules and of a ritual or symbolic nature, which seek to inculcate certain values and norms of behavior by repetition, which automatically implies continuity with the past. . . . [invented traditions] are responses to novel situations which take the form of reference to old situations, or which establish their own past by quasi-obligatory repetition" (1).

39. Steven Hoelscher, *Heritage on Stage: The Invention of Ethnic Place in America's Little Switzerland* (Madison: University of Wisconsin Press, 1998), 22. Hoelscher synthesizes much of the recent work about the consumption of place. He writes: "Commodification—the process by which objects and activities come to be valued primarily in terms of their value in the marketplace and for their ability to signify an image—can take place as its starting point. Distinct places and the qualities they imbue . . . can be turned into commodities in their own right" (22).

40. Hoelscher, *Heritage on Stage*, 12.

41. Reid Mitchell, *All on a Mardi Gras Day: Episodes in the History of New Orleans Carnival* (Cambridge, MA: Harvard University Press, 1995), 10–12.

42. Mitchell, *All on a Mardi Gras Day*, 88–90.

43. Samuel Kinser, *Carnival, American Style: Mardi Gras at New Orleans and Mobile* (Chicago: University of Chicago Press, 1990), 102.

44. Munro Edmundson, "Carnival in New Orleans," *Caribbean Quarterly* 4, nos. 3, 4 (1956): 240.

45. Neil Foley, *The White Scourge: Mexicans, Blacks and Poor Whites in Texas Cotton Culture* (Berkeley: University of California Press, 1997), 2. Most Anglo Texans were transplanted southerners who also sought to maintain the color line and extend its barriers to Mexicans. José Limón recently investigated many of the historic and symbolic connections between greater Mexico and the U.S. South. José Limón, *American Encounters: Greater Mexico, The United States and the Erotics of Culture* (Boston: Beacon Press, 1998). As Limón demonstrates, though, greater Mexico also influenced the modern South. Throughout his work, he charts a "comparable set of responses to the expanding hegemony of a 'Northern' and capitalist modernity," and makes these connections in the domains of political economy, labor, the arts, and folkloric culture (32).

46. In this introduction I focus on the Los Angeles festival, but in later chapters I will have a more detailed comparison of other similar fiestas, most notably the Santa Fe Fiesta. For a thorough analysis of this festival, see Charles Montgomery, *The Spanish Redemption: Heritage, Power and Loss on New Mexico's Upper Rio Grande* (Berkeley: University of California Press, 2002), 9–11; and Chris Wilson, *The Myth of Santa Fe: Creating a Modern Regional Tradition* (Albuquerque: University of New Mexico Press, 1997).

47. Carey McWilliams, *North from Mexico: The Spanish-Speaking People of the United States*, rev. ed. (1949; repr., New York: Greenwood Press, 1968), 35–47.

48. William Deverell, *Whitewashed Adobe: The Rise of Los Angeles and the Remaking of Its Mexican Past* (Berkeley: University of California Press, 2004), 50–51. I will go into a more detailed comparison of the Los Angeles and San Antonio fiestas in chapter 1.

49. Deverell, *Whitewashed Adobe*, 62.

50. Deverell, *Whitewashed Adobe*, 74.

51. Deverell, *Whitewashed Adobe*, 7–8.

52. C. Vann Woodward, *Burden of Southern History* (Baton Rouge: Louisiana State University Press, 1960), 19.

53. Louis Rubin, "Changing, Enduring, Forever Still the South," in *The Prevailing South: Life and Politics in a Changing Culture*, ed. Dudley Clendinen (Atlanta: Longstreet Press, 1988), 226.

54. Edward Said, *Orientalism* (New York: Random House, 1979), 7.

55. Said, *Orientalism*, 7.

56. Larry J. Griffin, "The American South and the Self," *Southern Cultures* 12, no. 3 (2006): 6–28. Griffin was one scholar to identify the depiction of the South as America's negative self-image and, drawing from Said, to articulate the idea of "internal orientalism" in reference to the South. I added this formulation to the American West.

57. Peter Stallybrass and Allon White, *The Politics and Poetics of Transgression* (New York: Routledge, 1986), 5.

58. There is an exhaustive bibliography of studies of this formation. The most influential for my work are Ruth Frankenberg's *White Women/Race Matters: The Social Construction of Whiteness* (Minneapolis: University of Minnesota Press, 1993); Grace Elizabeth Hale, *Making Whiteness: The Culture of Segregation in the South, 1890–1940* (New York: Vintage, 1999); Eric Lott, *Love and Theft: Blackface Minstrelsy and the American Working Class* (New York: Oxford University Press, 1995); Michael Omi and Howard Winant, *Racial Formation in the United States from the 1960s to the 1980s* (New York: Routledge, 1986); David Roediger, *The Wages of Whiteness: Race and the Making of the American Working Class* (New York: Verso, 1999); and Alexander Saxton, *The Indispensable Enemy: Labor and the Anti-Chinese Movement in California* (Berkeley: University of California Press, 1975).

59. Holly Beachley Brear, *Inherit the Alamo: Myth and Ritual at an American Shrine* (Austin: University of Texas Press, 1995), 22.

60. Richard Flores, *Remembering the Alamo: Memory, Modernity and the Master Symbol* (Austin: University of Texas Press, 2002), xvii.

61. Robert Young, *Colonial Desire: Hybridity in Theory, Culture and Race* (New York: Routledge, 1995), 2–4. In his analysis of such contradictions within English theory and literature, Young writes that "Englishness" is divided within itself, continually "sick with desire for the other." He attributes this to the transformation into modernity. During the nineteenth century, the cultural movement capitalist development produced was one of processes of both unification and differentiation. "The globalization of . . . a single integrated economic and colonial system . . . was achieved at the price of the dislocation of its peoples and cultures" (3). Stallybrass and White also focus on bourgeois representations of the low and find a great deal of contradiction, discourses that both revile and desire the lower strata. They delineate the binaries of high and low; they also explore the ambivalence of these discourses. While not every aspect of this colonial model can be applied to the Texas modern, the impact of the dramatic transformation to an industrialized and racially stratified society is both creative and destructive, a "unity of disunity" (3–5). Also see Marshall Berman's *All That Is Solid Melts Into Air: The Experience of Modernity* (New York: Simon and Schuster, 1982).

62. Stallybrass and White, *The Politics and Poetics of Transgression*, 44.

63. Michel-Rolph Trouillot, *Silencing the Past: Power and the Production of History* (Boston: Beacon Press, 1995), 116. Trouillot writes that commemorations "contribute to the continuous myth-making process that gives history its more definite shapes: they help create, modify, or sanction the public meanings attached to historical events deemed worthy of mass celebration." Commemorations "adorn the past with certainty: the proof of the happening is in the cyclical inevitability of its celebration" (116).

64. Alessandra Lorini, "Public Rituals and the Cultural Making of the New York African-American Community," in *Feasts and Celebrations in North American Communities*, ed. Ramón A. Gutiérrez and Geneviève Fabre (Albuquerque: University of New Mexico Press, 1995), 29. Lorini examines the community life of blacks in nineteenth-century New York and argues that "acts of invention and reinvention of selected traditions, far from being the exclusive products of hegemonic groups, are part of the broader process of cultural circularity between 'high' and 'low' cultures" (29).

65. Mary P. Ryan, *Women in Public: Between Banners and Ballots* (Baltimore: Johns Hopkins University Press, 1990). My analysis is greatly influenced by Ryan's discussion of the ways that the public/private distinction continues to be relevant for feminist scholars. I am also influenced by Michele Zimbalist Rosaldo's essay "Woman, Culture and Society: A Theoretical Overview" in *Woman, Culture and Society*, ed. M. Z. Rosaldo and Louise Lamphere (Stanford: Stanford University Press, 1974), 17–42. Here she argues that the basis of sexual inequality is the association of women with private/domestic spaces and their underrepresentation in the public realms.

66. Tim Cresswell, *In Place, Out of Place: Geography, Ideology and Transgression* (Minneapolis: University of Minnesota Press, 1996), 11–28. I use Tim Cresswell's terms "in" and "out" of place to refer to these boundary transgressions.

67. I use the term "white" here to refer to an Anglo and German elite.

68. The San Antonio Conservation Society continues to the present day, though I focus on this particular historical period.

69. Helen Delpar, *The Enormous Vogue of Things Mexican: Cultural Relations between the United States and Mexico, 1920–1935* (Tuscaloosa: University of Alabama Press, 1992), 15–54. She details the broader interest in Mexico in the fields of politics and the arts.

70. For more details about the ideology of this generation, see Mario T. García, *Mexican Americans: Leadership, Ideology, and Identity, 1930–1960* (New Haven: Yale University Press, 1989); and Juan Gómez-Quiñones, *Chicano Politics: Reality and Promise, 1940–1990* (Albuquerque: University of New Mexico Press, 1990).

Notes to Chapter One

1. Helene Von Phul, "The Battle of Flowers Association," 1931, Battle of Flowers Association Collection, Daughters of the Republic of Texas Library, San Antonio.

2. Battle of Flowers Parade program, 1899, Battle of Flowers Association Collection, Daughters of the Republic of Texas Library, San Antonio.

3. Jack Maguire, *A Century of Fiesta in San Antonio* (Austin: Eakin Press, 1990), 1. Holly Beachley Brear also credits Ballard in *Inherit the Alamo*, though she makes it clear that Ellen Maury Slayden organized the parade.

4. *San Antonio Daily Express*, April 17, 1891.

5. *San Antonio Daily Express*, April 19, 1891.

6. "Battle of Flowers," *San Antonio Daily Express*, April 25, 1891.

7. William Beezley, *Judas at the Jockey Club* (Lincoln: University of Nebraska Press, 1987), 41.

8. Mary Etta McGimsey, "History of the Battle of Flowers Association," 1966, Battle of Flowers Association Collection, Daughters of the Republic of Texas Library, San Antonio, 1.

9. "Battle of Flowers," *San Antonio Daily Express*, April 25, 1891.

10. "Battle of Flowers," *San Antonio Daily Express*, April 25, 1891.

11. Mikhail Bakhtin, *Rabelais and His World* (Bloomington: Indiana University Press, 1968), 12.

12. Richard Harding Davis quoted in Fisher, *San Antonio: Outpost of Empires*, 49.

13. Steven Gould, *The Alamo city guide, San Antonio, Texas. Being a historical sketch of the ancient city of the Alamo, and business review; with notes of present advantages, together with a complete guide to all the prominent points of interest about the city, and a compilation of facts of value to visitors and residents* (New York: Macgowan & Slipper Printers, ca. 1882), 31.

14. Gould, *The Alamo city guide*, 32.

15. Gould, *The Alamo city guide*, 37.

16. Flores, *Remembering the Alamo*, 38.

17. Flores, *Remembering the Alamo*, 52. Flores gives a thorough account of the new businesses opening on Alamo Plaza, as well as the transformation of Military and Main plazas.

18. "Battle of Flowers," *San Antonio Daily Express*, April 25, 1891.

19. Glassberg, *Sense of History*, 68.

20. Flores, *Remembering the Alamo*, xvii.

21. David R. Johnson, John A. Booth, and Richard Harris, eds., *The Politics of San Antonio: Community, Progress and Power* (Lincoln: University of Nebraska Press, 1983), 4–15.

22. Foley, *The White Scourge*, 19. Note that in this chapter I begin to use the term Mexicano to describe the entire community of persons of Mexican ethnic descent. After the Civil War, the term Tejano, referring to an indigenous community of persons of Mexican heritage living in Texas before annexation, lost much of its significance, as they merged with more recent immigrants from Mexico.

23. Montejano, *Anglos and Mexicans in the Making of Texas*, 8.

24. Flores, *Remembering the Alamo*, 47.

25. Arnoldo De León, *The Tejano Community, 1836–1900* (Albuquerque: University of New Mexico Press, 1982), 90.

26. Richard A. García, *The Rise of a Mexican American Middle Class: San Antonio 1929–1941* (College Station: Texas A&M Press, 1991), 22.

27. Arnoldo De León, *Mexican Americans in Texas: A Brief History* (Arlington Heights, TX: Harlan Davidson, 1993), 63.

28. Kenneth Mason, *African Americans and Race Relations in San Antonio, Texas, 1867–1937* (New York: Garland Publishing, 1998), 23.

29. Mason, *African Americans and Race Relations in San Antonio, Texas*, 27.

30. Mason, *African Americans and Race Relations in San Antonio, Texas*, 49.

31. Mason, *African Americans and Race Relations in San Antonio, Texas*, 51.

32. Donald Everett, "San Antonio Welcomes the 'Sunset'-1877," *Southwestern Historical Quarterly* 65, no. 1 (1961): 46–60.

33. It is important to note that the participants in the Texas Revolution were not all Anglo, yet subsequent histories diminished the role of Tejano revolutionaries in the battles.

34. Brear gives a more thorough account of the commemoration of the Alamo battle as Good Friday, the Battle of Flowers Parade (and later Fiesta) as the "secular Easter," and the rebirth of Anglo social prominence in *Inherit the Alamo*, 18–22.

35. Judith Berg Sobré, *San Antonio on Parade: Six Historic Festivals* (College Station: Texas A&M University Press, 2003), 30.

36. Renato Rosaldo, *Culture and Truth: The Remaking of Social Analysis* (Boston: Beacon Press, 1993), 68–69.

37. Gail Bederman, *Manliness and Civilization: A Cultural History of Gender and Race in the United States, 1880–1917* (Chicago: University of Chicago Press, 1995), 25.

38. De León, *The Tejano Community*, 95.

39. David Glassberg, *American Historical Pageantry: The Uses of Tradition in the Early Twentieth Century* (Chapel Hill: University of North Carolina Press, 1990), 1.

40. McGimsey, "History of the Battle of Flowers Association," 4.

41. Battle of Flowers Parade program, 1896, Battle of Flowers Association Collection, Daughters of the Republic of Texas Library, San Antonio.

42. "With Flowers as Weapons," *San Antonio Daily Express*, April 22, 1896.

43. "Grand Patriotic Fete and Battle of Flowers," *San Antonio Daily Express*, April 22, 1897.

44. Lott, *Love and Theft*, 15–37.

45. Deverell, *Whitewashed Adobe*, 70.

46. Deverell, *Whitewashed Adobe*, 88.

47. Deverell, *Whitewashed Adobe*, 2.

48. Notes from the Battle of Flowers Association are very ambiguous about the possible inspirations for the processions and flower battles. There were similar processions in both Mexico City and Nice, France. Given the Slaydens' personal friendship with the Díaz family, including Ellen Maury Slayden's accounts of her frequent visits, I have deduced this as a likely source for the idea.

49. Beezley, *Judas at the Jockey Club*, 128–29.

50. Limón, *American Encounters*, 30–33. As Limón demonstrates, though, greater Mexico also influenced the modern South. Throughout his work, he charts a "comparable set of responses to the expanding hegemony of a 'Northern' and capitalist modernity" and makes these connections in the domains of political economy, labor, the arts and folkloric culture (32).

51. Delpar, *The Enormous Vogue of Things Mexican*, 1.

52. George Grayson, *The United States and Mexico: Patterns of Influence* (New York: Praeger, 1984), 18.

53. Beezley, *Judas at the Jockey Club*, 128.

54. Beezley, *Judas at the Jockey Club*, 128.

55. Alfred Oscar Coffin, "Land without Chimneys; or The byways of Mexico" (Cincinnati, OH: The Editor Publishing Co, 1898), 18.

56. Coffin, "Land without Chimneys," 18.

57. Michael Johns, *The City of Mexico in the Age of Diaz* (Austin: University of Texas Press, 1997), 17.

58. De León, *The Tejano Community*, 178.

59. De León, *The Tejano Community*, 178.
60. The notion of "public culture" most closely defines this "zone of cultural debate." I am using Arjun Appadurai and Carol A. Breckenridge's definition of public culture in "Why Public Culture?" *Public Culture Bulletin* 1, no. 1 (Fall 1988): 6. Within this arena, mass culture, vernacular traditions, elite institutions, and national culture "are encountering, interrogating and contesting each other in new and unexpected ways."
61. Sobré makes this suggestion in her analysis of the first Battle of Flowers Parade. I credit her with the observation that newspaper reports limited their carriage descriptions to a dozen elite displays, while offering only indirect references to the many other carriages in the procession. *San Antonio on Parade*, 164.
62. Glassberg, *Sense of History*, 67.
63. Glassberg, *Sense of History*, 35–37. Stallybrass and White point out that large city fairs frequently combine work and play, commerce and leisure, and scholars have often unwittingly reproduced a separation of these spheres in their work on festival. They argue that large city fairs are highly adaptable to industrialization, and in fact aid these processes by their intersection of populations, discourses, and products. Stallybrass and White reconceptualize the fair as an integral part of modernization.
64. Glassberg, *Sense of History*, 35–37.
65. Sara Evans, *Born for Liberty* (New York: Free Press, 1989), 67. She does not apply this analysis to the Battle of Flowers directly. Michaele Haynes was the first to apply Evans's work to Fiesta. Michaele Haynes, *Dressing Up Debutantes: Glamor and Glitz in South Texas*, (Oxford: Berg, 1998).
66. "With Flowers as Weapons," *San Antonio Daily Express*, April 22, 1896.
67. Von Phul, "The Battle of Flowers Association," 3.
68. *San Antonio Daily Express*, April 12, 1891.
69. *San Antonio Daily Express*, April 22, 1892.
70. W. Fitzhugh Brundage, "White Women and the Politics of Historical Memory in the New South 1880–1920," in *Jumpin' Jim Crow: Southern Politics from Civil War to Civil Rights*, ed. Jane Dailey, Glenda Elizabeth Gilmore, and Bryant Simon (Princeton: Princeton University Press, 2000), 115.
71. Brundage, "White Women and the Politics of Historical Memory," 116.
72. Flores, *Remembering the Alamo*, 53.
73. Horace R. Smith, "History of Alamo Plaza from Its Beginning to the Present" (master's thesis, Trinity University, 1966), 40.
74. Ann Douglas, *The Feminization of American Culture* (New York: Knopf Publishing, 1977), 210.
75. Douglas, *The Feminization of American Culture*, 210.
76. Von Phul, "The Battle of Flowers Association," 3.
77. Douglas, *The Feminization of American Culture*, 10.
78. This friction is not directly expressed in any Battle of Flowers Association materials.
79. Von Phul, "The Battle of Flowers Association," 2.
80. McGimsey, "History of the Battle of Flowers Association," 6.
81. "It Was a Dream of Beauty," *San Antonio Daily Express*, April 22, 1899.
82. "Flower Battle," *San Antonio Light*, April 22, 1898.
83. "Flower Battle," *San Antonio Light*, April 22, 1898.

Notes to Chapter Two

1. Haynes, *Dressing Up Debutantes*, 7.
2. *San Antonio Daily Express*, January 8, 1895; January 14, 1895; January 15, 1895.
3. Sobré, *San Antonio on Parade*, 187.
4. Haynes, *Dressing Up Debutantes*, 31.
5. Sobré, *San Antonio on Parade*, 177.
6. Frederick C. Chabot, *With the Makers of San Antonio: Genealogies of Early Latin, Anglo-American, and German Families with Occasional Biographies; Each Group Being Prefaced with a Brief Historical Sketch and Illustrations* (San Antonio: Artes Gráficas, 1937), 339–43.
7. *San Antonio Daily Express*, February 11, 1898.
8. *San Antonio Daily Express*, March 3, 1899; March 17, 1899; March 24, 1899; March 31, 1899; April 7, 1899; *San Antonio Light*, March 3, 1899, 4; March 17, 1899; March 24, 1899; April 7, 1899.
9. *San Antonio Daily Express*, March 4, 1900.
10. The BFA's charter was not approved until 1914, however.
11. Sobré, *San Antonio on Parade*, 195.
12. Haynes, *Dressing Up Debutantes*, 38.
13. Order of the Alamo, *Courts of the Order of the Alamo 1909–1925* (San Antonio: Order of the Alamo, 1925).
14. Beverly Stoeltje, "The Snake Charmer Queen: Ritual, Competition, and Signification in American Festival," in *Beauty Queens on the Global Stage: Gender, Contests and Power*, ed. Colleen Ballerino Cohen, Richard Wilk, and Beverly Stoeltje (New York: Routledge, 1996), 15.
15. *San Antonio Daily Express*, April 21, 1909. Each year, the queen would promise to bring to San Antonio's public "mirth, melody and sweet song" and "banish sorrow."
16. Karal Ann Marling, *Debutante: Rites and Regalia of American Debdom* (Lawrence: University Press of Kansas, 2004), 128.
17. Marling, *Debutante*, 130–31.
18. Kinser, *Carnival, American Style*, 137.
19. Marling, *Debutante*, 130.
20. Glassberg, *American Historical Pageantry*, 2.
21. Abner Cohen, *The Politics of Elite Culture: Explorations in the Dramaturgy of Power in a Modern African Society* (Berkeley: University of California Press, 1981), 1–2. Cohen defines this as the need to reconcile the tension between universalism and particularism, between serving the larger needs of the public and serving the elite's particular needs and interests.
22. Glassberg, *American Historical Pageantry*, 282.
23. Glassberg, *American Historical Pageantry*, 283.
24. Glassberg, *American Historical Pageantry*, 64. Not all pageant organizers had these goals. Glassberg distinguishes the patriotic and hereditary societies' interests from progressive educators and playground organizers, who used pageants not only to educate the public, but also to encourage their direct participation as a democratic exercise in civic unity.

25. Pierre Bourdieu, *Distinction* (Cambridge, MA: Harvard University Press, 1984), 7. Michaele Haynes also connects Bourdieu's concepts specifically to the Order of the Alamo's Coronation, *Dressing Up Debutantes*, 7.

26. Holly Beachley Brear, *Inherit the Alamo*, 77–80.

27. Haynes, *Dressing Up Debutantes*, 77.

28. Carrington seems to offer a selective version of his own history. While he was born in Virginia, he spent much of his childhood in Kentucky. He frequently identifies himself as a Virginian, however.

29. Glassberg, *American Historical Pageantry*, 43.

30. Glassberg, *American Historical Pageantry*, 35.

31. Haynes, *Dressing Up Debutantes*, 40.

32. Glassberg, *American Historical Pageantry*, 252.

33. Anne F. Scott, *The Southern Lady: From Pedestal to Politics, 1830–1930* (Chicago: University of Chicago Press, 1970), 17.

34. Hale, *Making Whiteness*, 134.

35. Order of the Alamo, *History of the Order of the Alamo, Volume Two, 1926–1939* (San Antonio: Order of the Alamo, 1939).

36. Haynes, *Dressing Up Debutantes*, 107.

37. Stoeltje, "The Snake Charmer Queen," 15.

38. Haynes, *Dressing Up Debutantes*, 23.

39. Susan Bordo, *Unbearable Weight: Feminism, Western Culture and the Body* (Berkeley: University of California Press, 1993), 166.

40. Caroll Smith-Rosenberg, ed., *Disorderly Conduct: Visions of Gender in Victorian America* (New York: Alfred Knopf, 1985), 245; Janet M. Davis, *The Circus Age: Culture and Society under the American Big Top* (Chapel Hill: University of North Carolina Press, 2002), 262. I am using Smith-Rosenberg's definition of the "New Woman" as an upper- or middle-class woman who chose to challenge the bonds of domesticity. I am also following Janet M. Davis's enlargement of this term to include all women in the public sphere at the turn of the century. Many of the women of the Battle of Flowers Association were married and had children, but also tried to increase their public role through their pageantry.

41. *San Antonio Daily Express*, February 23, 1913.

42. Elizabeth Bronwyn Boyd, "Southern Beauty: Performing Femininity in an American Region" (PhD diss., University of Texas at Austin, 2000), 4. Anne Goodwyn Jones also makes this argument in *Tomorrow is Another Day: The Woman Writer in the South 1859–1936* (Baton Rouge: Louisiana State University Press, 1981), 10.

43. Boyd, "Southern Beauty," 2–3. The first historian to define this myth of southern womanhood was Scott in *The Southern Lady*.

44. Maria B. Fenwick, ed., *Who's Who among the women of San Antonio and Southwest Texas: a blue book and directory and yearbook of women's organizations* (San Antonio: Maria B. Fenwick, 1917), 21.

45. Marling, *Debutante*, 148–49.

46. William R. Taylor, *Cavalier and Yankee: The Old South and American National Character* (Cambridge, MA: Harvard University Press, 1979), 203–25.

47. Taylor, *Cavalier and Yankee*, 336.

48. Taylor, *Cavalier and Yankee*, 336.

49. Henry Graham, "History of the Texas Cavaliers," 1976, 51, Texana Collection, San Antonio Main Library, San Antonio.

50. Haynes, *Dressing Up Debutantes*, 41.

51. Graham, "History of the Texas Cavaliers," 12.

52. García, *Mexican Americans*, 26.

53. García, *Mexican Americans*, 16, 23.

54. García, *Mexican Americans*, 27.

55. García, *Mexican Americans*, 24.

56. García, *Mexican Americans*, 25.

57. Hale, *Making Whiteness*, 125.

58. Suellen Hoy, *Chasing Dirt: The American Pursuit of Cleanliness* (New York: Oxford University Press, 1995), 86.

59. Hoy, *Chasing Dirt*, 88.

60. Katherine Ott, *Fevered Lives: Tuberculosis in American Culture since 1870* (Cambridge, MA: Harvard University Press, 1996), 124.

61. Haynes, *Dressing Up Debutantes*, 36.

62. Haynes, *Dressing Up Debutantes*, 101.

63. Ott, *Fevered Lives*, 121.

64. *International Encyclopedia of the Social Sciences*, 1968 ed., s.v. "Pollution."

65. Hoy, *Chasing Dirt*, 88.

66. Ott, *Fevered Lives*, 54. Katherine Ott nicely summarizes the broad definition of germ theory here: "Germ theory posited that microscopic organisms exist (a fact generally accepted), that these organisms are the primary cause of certain and specific diseases, and that these organisms can be transmitted from animal to animal in some way, with pathogenic results."

67. Ott, *Fevered Lives*, 67, 101.

68. García, *Mexican Americans*, 29.

69. Montejano, *Anglos and Mexicans in the Making of Texas*, 229.

70. *San Antonio Daily Express*, January 11, 1914.

71. Montejano, *Anglos and Mexicans in the Making of Texas*, 228.

72. Hale, *Making Whiteness*, 8.

73. Mason, *African Americans and Race Relations in San Antonio, Texas*, 32–33.

74. García, *Mexican Americans*, 38.

75. García, *Mexican Americans*, 39.

76. Montejano, *Anglos and Mexicans in the Making of Texas*, 160.

77. Montejano, *Anglos and Mexicans in the Making of Texas*, 180–90.

78. Montejano, *Anglos and Mexicans in the Making of Texas*, 89.

79. Benjamin Johnson, *Revolution in Texas: How a Forgotten Rebellion and Its Bloody Suppression Turned Mexicans into Americans* (New Haven: Yale University Press, 2003), 25–26.

80. Johnson, *Revolution in Texas*, 21.

81. Johnson, *Revolution in Texas*, 60.

82. Johnson, *Revolution in Texas*, 61.

83. Johnson, *Revolution in Texas*, 58.

84. Johnson, *Revolution in Texas*, 20.

85. Montejano, *Anglos and Mexicans in the Making of Texas*, 122.

86. Johnson, *Revolution in Texas*, 72.

87. Johnson, *Revolution in Texas*, 72.

88. Johnson, *Revolution in Texas*, 73.

89. Johnson, *Revolution in Texas*, 75–79.

90. Johnson, *Revolution in Texas*, 78–80.

91. Mason, *African Americans and Race Relations in San Antonio, Texas*, 181–83.

92. García, *Mexican Americans*, 25.

93. De León, *Mexican Americans in Texas*, 76.

94. De León, *Mexican Americans in Texas*, 93.

95. Davis, *The Circus Age*, 10.

96. *San Antonio Light*, February 24, 1900.

97. *San Antonio Daily Express*, April 18, 1900.

98. Hale, *Making Whiteness*, 8.

99. *San Antonio Daily Express*, April 17, 1900.

100. *San Antonio Daily Express*, April 25, 1905.

101. Stallybrass and White, *The Politics and Poetics of Transgression*, 5.

102. Mitchell, *All on a Mardi Gras Day*, 22.

103. Mitchell, *All on a Mardi Gras Day*, 25.

104. *San Antonio Daily Express*, April 25, 1905.

105. *San Antonio Daily Express*, April 23, 1909.

106. *San Antonio Daily Express*, April 23, 1915.

107. *San Antonio Daily Express*, April 22, 1917.

108. *San Antonio Daily Express*, April 15, 1906.

109. *San Antonio Daily Express*, February 10, 1909.

110. *San Antonio Daily Express*, April 15, 1906.

111. Baudelaire, "The Painter of Modern Life" (1863) in *The Painter of Modern Life and Other Essays* (New York: Da Capo Press, 1986), 130. I am borrowing from David Harvey's extended analysis of this statement in *The Condition of Postmodernity* (Cambridge: Blackwell, 1990), 10.

112. Berman, *All That Is Solid Melts Into Air*, 15.

Notes to Chapter Three

1. International Festivals and Events Association and Birchhill Enterprises, "Section One-Executive Summary: Fiesta San Antonio—Night in Old San Antonio," 2002, Fiesta San Antonio Commission Records, University of Texas at San Antonio.

2. Ramsdell, *San Antonio: A Historical and Pictorial Guide*, 281.

3. Ramsdell, *San Antonio: A Historical and Pictorial Guide*, 282.

4. *San Antonio Express*, March 5, 1936.

5. Frank Bushick, *Glamorous Days* (San Antonio: Naylor Publishing, 1934), 96–100.

6. Bushick, *Glamorous Days*, 98.

7. Limón, *American Encounters*, 113. As Limón suggests, such a longing "brings into question . . . the full psychic and cultural legitimacy of Anglo-American domination in the Southwest." Limón also contends that folk ballads about Anglo

cowboys' brief romantic relationships to Mexicanas represent an ambivalence, a "partial and unconscious challenge to the ruling cultural order" (111). The cowboy, occupying a low position in American capitalism, is the central ambivalent figure. His desire for Mexican women also represents "a fissure in the colonial enterprise" (111).

8. Barbara Babcock, "A New Mexican 'Rebecca': Imaging Pueblo Women," *Journal of the Southwest* 32, no. 4 (1990): 406. Babcock was the first to name the Southwest as "America's Orient."

9. *San Antonio Express*, March 5, 1936.

10. *San Antonio Express*, March 5, 1936.

11. Sarah Deutsch, *No Separate Refuge: Culture, Class and Gender on an Anglo-Hispanic Frontier in the American Southwest, 1880–1940* (Oxford: Oxford University Press, 1987), 188.

12. Molly Mullin, *Culture in the Marketplace: Gender, Art, and Value in the American Southwest* (Durham, NC: Duke University Press, 2001), 13.

13. Mullin, *Culture in the Marketplace*, 13.

14. Philip Deloria, *Playing Indian* (New Haven: Yale University Press, 1998), 101. As Deloria writes, "American identity was increasingly tied to a search for an authentic social identity, one that had real meaning in the face of the anxious displacements of modernity."

15. Mullin, *Culture in the Marketplace*, 28. Mullin writes that "[they] felt that by affirming the value of people and things that had long been undervalued they would find an authentic identity."

16. Leah Dilworth, *Imagining Indians in the Southwest: Persistent Visions of a Primitive Past* (Washington, D.C.: Smithsonian Institution Press, 1996), 182–91.

17. Deutsch, *No Separate Refuge*, 190.

18. Delpar, *The Enormous Vogue of Things Mexican*, 5. Delpar writes that American perceptions were "colored by racism, ethnocentrism, and antipathy toward Catholicism."

19. Delpar, *The Enormous Vogue of Things Mexican*, 5.

20. Delpar, *The Enormous Vogue of Things Mexican*, 9.

21. Delpar, *The Enormous Vogue of Things Mexican*, 9.

22. Delpar, *The Enormous Vogue of Things Mexican*, 10–12.

23. Delpar, *The Enormous Vogue of Things Mexican*, 56.

24. Delpar, *The Enormous Vogue of Things Mexican*, 205.

25. García, *The Rise of a Mexican American Middle Class*, 40.

26. García, *The Rise of a Mexican American Middle Class*, 33.

27. García, *The Rise of a Mexican American Middle Class*, 216.

28. Benjamin Marquez, *LULAC: The Evolution of a Mexican American Political Organization* (Austin: University of Texas Press, 1993), 17.

29. García, *The Rise of a Mexican American Middle Class*, 255.

30. García, *The Rise of a Mexican American Middle Class*, 4–5.

31. García, *The Rise of a Mexican American Middle Class*, 258.

32. García, *The Rise of a Mexican American Middle Class*, 32.

33. García, *The Rise of a Mexican American Middle Class*, 34.

34. Montejano, *Anglos and Mexicans in the Making of Texas*, 315.

35. García, *The Rise of a Mexican American Middle Class*, 43.

36. Montgomery, *The Spanish Redemption*, 86–87.

37. Montgomery, *The Spanish Redemption*, 204.

38. Montgomery, *The Spanish Redemption*, 37.

39. Montgomery, *The Spanish Redemption*, 38.

40. Montgomery, *The Spanish Redemption*, 210.

41. "Emma Tenayuca: La Pasionaria de Tejas," *La Voz de Aztlán*, March 13, 2000.

42. García, *The Rise of a Mexican American Middle Class*, 214.

43. García, *The Rise of a Mexican American Middle Class*, 212–14.

44. García, *The Rise of a Mexican American Middle Class*, 211.

45. García, *The Rise of a Mexican American Middle Class*, 214.

46. García, *The Rise of a Mexican American Middle Class*, 216–17.

47. Dean MacCannell, *The Tourist: A New Theory of the Leisure Class*, 2nd ed. (New York: Schocken Books, 1989), 13. MacCannell links preservation movements to the development of tourism and modernity, arguing that this preservation of history is not only an act of recovery but of construction. He describes the tourism industry as a "catalogue of displaced forms," where the structures and practices of an earlier historical period are taken out of their previous context and rearticulated into the logic of modernity. MacCannell also observes that the tourist searches for authenticity to counter a modern sense of rootlessness. While he oversimplifies tourists' multiple motivations for travel, he does describe a key aspect of San Antonio's tourist industry.

48. Lewis F. Fisher, *Saving San Antonio: The Precarious Preservation of a Heritage* (Lubbock: Texas Tech University Press, 1996).

49. Charles J. Hosmer, *The Presence of the Past* (New York: G. P. Putnam's Sons, 1965), 288–90.

50. Wilson, *The Myth of Santa Fe*, 181–231. SACS's activities during this period bear remarkable resemblance to activities in Santa Fe, New Mexico, also. At the same time as SACS was hosting Mexican dinners and selling crafts, white Santa Fe residents created a fiesta that first revolved around a historical pageant of the Spanish conquest of New Mexico and then involved a large Spanish market, where local Hispano villagers sold enchiladas, performed dances, and exhibited their weaving and woodcarving. For the Fiesta council that created the festival, it was a return to a more authentic, traditional event and a rejection of previous fiestas that had become too Anglicized and commercial.

51. Wilson, *The Myth of Santa Fe*, 88–89.

52. Montgomery, *The Spanish Redemption*, 101–2.

53. SACS meeting minutes, October 4, 1924, San Antonio Conservation Society Library, San Antonio.

54. "How Santa Barbara Utilizes Spanish Atmosphere For Profit Told to Conservation Society," *San Antonio Express*, September 14, 1924.

55. "Architect Who Restored Palace Appeals to San Antonio to Keep Individuality All Its Own," *San Antonio Express*, March 1, 1931.

56. "San Antonio Offers to Tourists Many Attractions of Old World, Says Prize-Winning Essay," *San Antonio Express*, February 2, 1920.

57. "Historical Society to Conduct Tour," *San Antonio Express*, March 17, 1929.

58. Montgomery, *The Spanish Redemption*, 66–70. The use of the term "Spanish American" was also an important part of the effort to gain New Mexico's statehood.

59. Hoelscher, *Heritage on Stage*, 23. Hoelscher points out that "the 'native' or 'ethnic' is an integral component of the tourist spectacle. The ethnic becomes an object of the tourist gaze, an actor whose 'quaint' and 'different' behavior, dress and artifacts are themselves significant attractions."

60. García, *The Rise of a Mexican American Middle Class*, 16.

61. Montejano, *Anglos and Mexicans in the Making of Texas*, 180.

62. Robert M. Mclean, *That Mexican As He Really Is, North and South of the Rio Grande* (New York: Fleming H. Revell, 1928), 163.

63. SACS meeting minutes, March 22, 1924, San Antonio Conservation Society Library, San Antonio.

64. This appears on the society's earliest letterhead.

65. "A Message from Emily Edwards," undated typescript, San Antonio Conservation Society Library, San Antonio.

66. Fisher, *Saving San Antonio*, 519–21. This is a very abbreviated chronology of SACS projects. It continues to fund restoration projects to this day, but that work is beyond the scope of my analysis.

67. Fisher, *Saving San Antonio*, 94.

68. Fisher, *Saving San Antonio*, 96. As reported from Rena Maverick Green's daughter, Mary Vance Green.

69. Emily Edwards, Oral history transcript, April 27, 1967, San Antonio Conservation Society Library, San Antonio. She made this remark during a tour of the Ursuline Convent.

70. Emily Edwards, Oral history transcript, July 24, 1971, San Antonio Conservation Society Library, San Antonio. She was interviewed by Charles J. Hosmer for his work *Preservation Comes of Age, From Williamsburg to the National Trust, 1926–1949* (Charlottesville: University of Virginia Press for the Preservation Press, 1981).

71. Rowena Green Fenstermaker, Oral history transcript, February 2, 1984, 28–29, San Antonio Conservation Society Library, San Antonio.

72. Excerpts from Fisher, *Saving San Antonio*, 3–7.

73. Yet this also hints that these roles are changing. The recent election of Ma Ferguson points to the changing roles of women in political offices in the state and the nation.

74. Emily Edwards, oral history transcript, "A Message from Emily Edwards," undated typescript, 2–3, San Antonio Conservation Society Library, San Antonio.

75. Fisher, *Saving San Antonio*, 97.

76. Flores, *Remembering the Alamo*, 64.

77. Flores, *Remembering the Alamo*, 66.

78. Flores, *Remembering the Alamo*, 74–77, 82.

79. Flores, *Remembering the Alamo*, 82.

80. *San Antonio Express*, April 23, 1929.

81. *San Antonio Express*, October 11, 1936.

82. Flores, *Remembering the Alamo*, 91.

83. *San Antonio Express*, December 25, 1929.

84. *San Antonio Express*, January 25, 1930.

85. Fisher, *Saving San Antonio*, 198.

86. SACS meeting minutes, January 27, 1938, San Antonio Conservation Society Library, San Antonio.

87. Monica Michelle Penick, "A preservationist's dissonance: Maury Maverick and the restoration of La Villita, 1939–1941" (master's thesis, University of Texas at Austin, 2001), 15.
88. O'Neill Ford to J. C. Kellam, August 30, 1939, San Antonio Conservation Society Library, San Antonio.
89. Fisher, *Saving San Antonio*, 204.
90. Fisher, *Saving San Antonio*, 204.
91. Penick, "A preservationist's dissonance," 24.
92. Penick, "A preservationist's dissonance," 36–37.
93. Rena Maverick Green to Lola Maverick Lloyd, September 24, 1931, Schwimmer-Lloyd Collection, New York Public Library.
94. Deloria, *Playing Indian*, 120.
95. Richard Flores, *Los Pastores: History and Performance in the Mexican Shepherd's Play of South Texas* (Washington, D.C.: Smithsonian Institution Press, 1995), 172–77. Here I borrow from Flores's contemporary analysis of SACS's performance, because this analysis applies to early versions of the play as well. Though some elements of *Los Pastores* have changed over the years, the differences that Flores describes between the performances at the Mission San José and at the Guadalupe Church are relatively unchanged.
96. Flores, *Los Pastores*, 33–35.
97. Fisher, *Saving San Antonio*, 132.
98. *San Antonio Express*, December 29, 1928.
99. García, *The Rise of a Mexican American Middle Class*, 27.
100. Fisher, *Saving San Antonio*, 223.
101. Fisher, *Saving San Antonio*, 352–54.
102. Esther MacMillan, Oral history transcript, October 8, 1992, 12–13, San Antonio Conservation Society Library, San Antonio.
103. Hale, *Making Whiteness*, 107.
104. Hale, *Making Whiteness*, 111.
105. Hale, *Making Whiteness*, 113.
106. Mary M. Fisher, "NIOSA *Anticuchos* Her Claim to Fame," *North San Antonio Times*, April 14, 1988.

Notes to Chapter Four

1. *San Antonio Express News*, April 18, 1956.
2. Haynes, *Dressing Up Debutantes*, 47.
3. FSJA charter, June 10, 1955, Fiesta San Antonio Commission Records, University of Texas at San Antonio.
4. Most of these organizations, though, did not exist at the time of the 1905 charter. As elite organizations expanded, these organizations were added in amendments.
5. The other participating organizations, though not heritage based, had similar family ties to Fiesta's early years. The exception was the Junior Chamber of Commerce.
6. Johnson, Booth, and Harris, *The Politics of San Antonio*, 19.
7. Johnson, Booth, and Harris, *The Politics of San Antonio*, 20.

8. Johnson, Booth, and Harris, *The Politics of San Antonio*, 21.

9. Rodolfo Rosales, *The Illusion of Inclusion: The Untold Political Story of San Antonio* (Austin: University of Texas Press, 2000), 47.

10. Rosales, *The Illusion of Inclusion*, 47.

11. Rosales, *The Illusion of Inclusion*, 20–23.

12. Heywood Sanders, "Building a New Urban Infrastructure: The Creation of Postwar San Antonio," in *Urban Texas*, ed. Char Miller and Heywood Sanders (College Station: Texas A&M Press, 1990), 167.

13. Sanders, "Building a New Urban Infrastructure," 172.

14. Sanders, "Building a New Urban Infrastructure," 156, 83.

15. Sanders, "Building a New Urban Infrastructure," 280–81.

16. Sanders, "Building a New Urban Infrastructure," 78.

17. Montejano, *Anglos and Mexicans in the Making of Texas*, 279.

18. Rosales, *The Illusion of Inclusion*, 51.

19. It is important to note, as Rosales does, that not all the Mexican American middle class followed this conservative philosophy. Political inclusion was a field of much debate during this period.

20. In the mid-1950s, the U.S. Border Patrol initiated a program of mass deportation of Mexican nationals, which they called Operation Wetback.

21. *San Antonio Express News*, March 14, 1959.

22. Haynes, *Dressing Up Debutantes*, 61.

23. Reynolds Andricks to Fiesta San Jacinto Association, March 27, 1959, Fiesta San Antonio Commission Records, University of Texas at San Antonio.

24. *San Antonio Express News*, March 14, 1959.

25. Kinser, *Carnival, American Style*, 357. In New Orleans, these torches were and are usually for the parades of the city's oldest krewes—Comus, Proteus, and Momus—and are invariably carried by black men, as Kinser notes here. This symbol of a Jim Crow racial order does not seem to be part of Fiesta's Flambeau parade, however.

26. "History," Fiesta Flambeau Parade Association, Inc., www.fiestaflambeau.org/history.htm (accessed January 5, 2007).

27. "History," Fiesta Flambeau Parade Association, Inc., www.fiestaflambeau.org/history.htm (accessed January 5, 2007).

28. "History," Fiesta Flambeau Parade Association, Inc., www.fiestaflambeau.org/history.htm (accessed January 5, 2007).

29. Reynolds Andricks to Fiesta San Jacinto Association, March 27, 1959, Fiesta San Antonio Commission Records, University of Texas at San Antonio.

30. Reynolds Andricks to Fiesta San Jacinto Association, March 27, 1959, Fiesta San Antonio Commission Records, University of Texas at San Antonio.

31. *San Antonio Express News*, March 27, 1959.

32. Haynes, *Dressing Up Debutantes*, 12.

33. Haynes, *Dressing Up Debutantes*, 145.

34. Haynes, *Dressing Up Debutantes*, 145. In 1982 the Cornyation was revived and continues to the present day.

35. Stallybrass and White, *The Politics and Poetics of Transgression*, 9. As Stallybrass and White explain, "grotesque realism images the human body as multiple, bulging, over or undersized, protuberant and incomplete. The openings and orifices

of this carnival body are emphasized, not its closure and finish. They use Bakhtin's distinctions between the classical and the grotesque body to demonstrate a dialogic relationship between the 'high culture' of the completed, individuated body and the mobile, disproportionate body of the 'low culture' of the carnival."

36. Description of Miss Fiesta compiled by Mr. John Thiel for the *Galveston Daily News*, Spring 1965, from Diane Thiel's scrapbook in the author's personal collection.

37. Robert Lavenda, "'It's Not a Beauty Pageant!' Hybrid Ideology in Minnesota Community Queen Pageants," in *Beauty Queens on the Global Stage: Gender, Contests and Power*, ed. Colleen Ballerino Cohen, Richard Wilk, and Beverly Stoeltje, 31–46 (New York: Routledge, 1996). While the practice of inversion reverses hierarchical relationships among different categories, it does not change the categories themselves—the coronation and Cornyation queens portray opposing qualities of high and low culture. Hybridization is a more complex critique of high culture, because it offers "new combinations and strange instabilities" of these roles.

38. Lavenda, "'It's Not a Beauty Pageant!'," 41.

39. Lavenda, "'It's Not a Beauty Pageant!'," 42. As Lavenda writes: "[The pageant] must reward what have become appropriate 'democratic' achievements as it celebrates upwardly-mobile young women, offering to teach them fully in the life of the class fragment they seek to join."

40. Stallybrass and White, *The Politics and Poetics of Transgression*, 58. Miss Fiesta expressed another form of Bakhtinian parody, hybridization. By intermingling high and low culture, hybridity offers the possibility of shifting the terms themselves.

41. Diane Thiel Bozorgi, Miss Fiesta 1965, in discussion with the author, February 2007. Pageant dresses had to be approved by the FSJA, however. Diane Thiel, Miss Fiesta of 1965, remembers that the association rejected the first dress she chose, a black dress reminiscent of Audrey Hepburn in *Breakfast at Tiffany's*. The association made it clear to her that no Miss Fiesta contestant would wear a *black* dress, regardless of contemporary fashion.

42. *San Antonio Light*, April 14, 1991.

43. Diane Thiel Bozorgi, in discussion with the author, December 2006.

44. "Festival San Jacinto Association—1965: Code of Behavior Pertaining to Activities of Miss Fiesta and Miss Fiesta Maids of Honor," from Diane Thiel's scrapbook in the author's personal collection.

45. Diane Thiel Bozorgi, interview with the author, December 2006.

46. Diane Thiel Bozorgi, interview with the author, December 2006.

47. Draft of FSAC letter to the press, Fiesta San Antonio Commission Records, University of Texas at San Antonio.

48. Maguire, *A Century of Fiesta in San Antonio*, 44.

49. *San Antonio Light*, May 3, 1959.

50. Mrs. William H. Spice, Jr., to Col. Dwight Allison, May 4, 1959, Fiesta San Antonio Commission Records, University of Texas at San Antonio.

51. Robert Lavenda, "Festivals and the Creation of Public Culture: Whose Voice(s)?" in *Museums and Communities: The Politics of Public Culture*, ed. Ivan Karp, Christine Mullen Kreamer, and Steven D. Levine, 76–104 (Washington, D.C.:

Smithsonian Institution Press, 1992). I am borrowing from Lavendas's analysis of the role of the Jaycees in organizing small-town Minnesota festivals.

52. "Official Souvenir Program" of Fiesta San Antonio Commission, 1960, Fiesta San Antonio Commission Records, University of Texas at San Antonio.

53. Miguel de Oliver, "Historical Preservation and Identity: The Alamo and the Production of a Consumer Landscape" *Antipode* 28, no. 1 (1996): 9.

54. De Oliver, "Historical Preservation and Identity," 9.

55. FSJA Invitation, 1949, Fiesta San Antonio Commission Records, University of Texas at San Antonio.

56. FSJA Fiesta Invitation, 1953, Fiesta San Antonio Commission Records, University of Texas at San Antonio.

57. Miguel de Oliver, "Democratizing Consumerism: coalescing constructions of subjugation in the consumer landscape." *Gender, Place and Culture* 4, no. 2 (1997): 211–33.

58. *San Antonio Express News*, April 22, 1958.

59. De Oliver "Democratizing Consumerism," 227.

60. *San Antonio Express*, March 17, 1946.

61. Ellis Shapiro to Harry Jersig, March 25, 1946, Fiesta San Antonio Commission Records, University of Texas at San Antonio.

62. *San Antonio Express*, April 7, 1946.

63. *San Antonio Light*, March 21, 1946.

64. Sylvia Rodríguez, "Tourism, Whiteness, and the Vanishing Anglo," in *Seeing and Being Seen: Tourism in the American West*, ed. David M. Wrobel and Patrick T. Long, 194–222 (Lawrence: University Press of Kansas, 2001). Rodríguez makes this observation of the gringo cowboys depicted in New Mexico's Enchantment tourist industry.

65. The lonely crowd refers to sociologist David Riesman's bestseller of the same name. Riesman suggested that the United States was becoming a nation of conformity, of "other-directed" people, as opposed to "inner-directed" individuals with their own ethics. Deloria connects this study to the practice of playing Indian in the postwar years; *Playing Indian*, 128–53.

66. Deloria, *Playing Indian*, 132. As he writes: "Triggered in part by a war in which people of color had caught a glimpse of freedom and opportunity, Americans of all classes and colors struggled to address the contradictions between the nation's rhetoric of social equality and its history of race-based oppression."

67. Deloria, *Playing Indian*, 153. He applies this idea to playing Indian. I argue that in the Southwest, a very similar process happened with Mexican Americans.

68. Trouillot, *Silencing the Past*, 118.

69. Researchers from the Institute of Texan Cultures revealed this in an exhibit for the 1991 Fiesta San Antonio.

70. Flores, *Remembering the Alamo*, 115.

71. *Martyrs of the Alamo, or the Birth of Texas*, directed by William Christy Cabanne, 1915. Cabanne was an assistant to D. W. Griffith, who directed *The Birth of a Nation* only a few months earlier.

72. An important note is that this change is not true of all Alamo narratives, especially not the versions the DRT endorsed.

73. FSJA Invitation, 1948, Fiesta San Antonio Commission Records, University of Texas at San Antonio.

74. FSJA Invitation, 1951, Fiesta San Antonio Commission Records, University of Texas at San Antonio.
75. FSJA Invitation, 1951, Fiesta San Antonio Commission Records, University of Texas at San Antonio.
76. Matovina, *Tejano Religion and Ethnicity*, 27–28. Interestingly enough, it seems that Gregorio Esparza did have a difficult decision to make in fighting for Texan independence. The war divided his own family, and his brother Francisco served in the Mexican army. After the Alamo battle, Francisco asked for permission to bury his brother. His request was granted, and he and other members of his family went within the Alamo's walls to search for his remains.
77. Boyce House, *City of Flaming Adventure: The Chronicle of San Antonio* (San Antonio: Naylor publishing, 1949), 72–74.
78. Jacob I. Rodríguez, "Our Place in Texas History" (speech, San Antonio, TX, August 23, 1955), Jacob I. Rodríguez papers, LULAC Archives, Nettie Lee Benson Latin American Collection, University of Texas at Austin.
79. Rodríguez, "Our Place in Texas History."
80. Rodríguez, "Our Place in Texas History."
81. Jacob I. Rodríguez, letter to the editor, *San Antonio Light*, February 11, 1965, Jacob I. Rodríguez Papers, LULAC Archives, Nettie Lee Benson Latin American Collection, University of Texas at Austin.
82. Delís Negrón, editorial in *La Prensa*, April 21, 1955.
83. My translation. The original reads: "Nos pone como Dios pintó al perico, no por su ingenio, sino por su ambrosa inocencia."

Notes to Chapter Five

1. Andy Hernandez, "Mexican Americans are Becoming Part of Fiesta," *San Antonio Light*, April 26, 1990.
2. Clarence Lang, "Between Civil Rights and Black Power in the Gateway City: The Action Committee to Improve Opportunities for Negroes, 1964–1975." *Journal of Social History* 37, no. 3 (Spring 2004): 725–54. There was a previous challenge to the Protestant membership of the Veiled Prophet Ball. Elite Roman Catholics started their own tradition, the Fleur-de-Lis Ball.
3. Calvin Trillin, "New Orleans Unmasked," *The New Yorker*, February 2, 1998.
4. Rosemary Kozmetsky, director, King William Association Fair, in discussion with the author, July 2006.
5. Here I am using David Harvey's analysis of the "selling of place," which includes "attracting consumers through the creation of a cultural center"; "From Space to Place and Back Again," in *Mapping the Futures*, ed. Jon Bird, Barry Curtis, Tim Putnam, George Robertson, and Lisa Tickner (London: Routledge, 1993), 3–29.
6. Don Moyé, in discussion with the author, July 2006.
7. Gracie Poe Griffin, interview with the author, November 6, 1998.
8. Judy Tzu-Chuu Wu, "'Loveliest Daughter of Our Ancient Cathay': Representations of Ethnic and Gendered Identity in the Miss China Town U.S.A. Beauty Pageant," *Journal of Social History* 31, no. 1 (Fall 1997): 5–32. I am using Wu's approach to the ethnic beauty pageant as a means to examine how these versions of womanhood also reflect broad concerns about power and culture.

9. Phillip Mason, "Soul in the Culture of African Americans," *Music Educators Journal* 79, no. 3 (November 1992): 49–52.

10. The introduction in the 1974 pageant program states that the new title will be Miss Black San Antonio The Queen of Soul. The connection to the Miss Black America Pageant was later dropped.

11. Queen of Soul Web site, "Creating a Sisterhood," www.saqos.org (accessed December 12, 2006).

12. From the description of the competition categories, www.saqos.org (accessed December 12, 2006).

13. Belinda Edmondson, "Public Spectacles: Caribbean Women and the Politics of Public Performance," *Small Axe* 13 (March 2003): 1–16. I owe this term to Edmondson, who uses it in her analysis of Caribbean beauty pageants.

14. www.saqos.org (accessed December 12, 2006).

15. Edmondson, "Public Spectacles," 16.

16. Queen of Soul Pageant invitation, April 9, 1974, in the author's personal collection.

17. Queen of Soul Pageant invitation, April 9, 1974, in the author's personal collection.

18. Information from www.reyfeoscholarship.org.

19. Olga Nájera-Ramírez, "Engendering Nationalism: Identity, Discourse, and the Mexican Charro," *Anthropological Quarterly* 67, no. 1 (January 1994): 10.

20. Elysiana Judith Cantú, interview with the author, March 2003.

21. Elysiana Judith Cantú, interview with the author, March 2003.

22. Haynes, *Dressing Up Debutantes*, 59.

23. Christi Phelps, "A Tale of Two Kings," *San Antonio Monthly*, April 1986, 61.

24. Christine Marie Sierra, "In Search of National Power: Chicanos Working the System on Immigration Reform, 1976–1986," in *Chicano Politics and Society In the Late Twentieth Century*, ed. David Montejano (Austin: University of Texas Press, 1999), 131–53.

25. Rosales, *The Illusion of Inclusion*, 80.

26. Fisher, *Saving San Antonio*, 285.

27. Fisher, *Saving San Antonio*, 287–89.

28. Fisher, *Saving San Antonio*, 290.

29. Joseph D. Sekul, "Communities Organized for Public Service: Citizen Power and Public Policy in San Antonio," in *The Politics of San Antonio: Community, Progress and Power*, ed. David R. Johnson, John A. Booth, and Richard Harris (Lincoln: University of Nebraska Press, 1983), 175–90.

30. Sekul, "Communities Organized for Public Service," 181.

31. García, *Mexican Americans*, 1–24. For a summary of the Mexican American generation's ideology, see also Ignacio M. García, "Backwards from Aztlan: Politics in the Age of Hispanics," in *Chicanas and Chicanos in Contemporary Society*, ed. Roberto M. De Anda (Boston: Allyn and Bacon, 1996), 191–204.

32. Márquez, *LULAC*, 2.

33. Although each generation—Mexican American, Chicano, and Hispanic— represents a particular historical and cultural movement, these terms do not describe the goals and values of all Mexicanos during each period. These terms cannot adequately account for the complexity and range of ideas and opinions of

the Mexicano population. They do, however, represent shifts in the guiding ideologies of significant numbers of political and social leaders and organizations.

34. García, "Backwards from Aztlan," 196.

35. Ernest Cortés, quoted in Sterlin Homesley, *Hemisfair '68 and the Transformation of San Antonio* (San Antonio: Maverick Publishing Company, 2003), 117–23.

36. García, "Backwards from Aztlan," 199.

37. García, "Backwards from Aztlan," 199. Again, I would add that the Hispanic generation does not refer to the attitudes of all Mexicanos of this generation.

38. Johnson, Booth, and Harris, *The Politics of San Antonio*, 78–87.

39. Rosales, *The Illusion of Inclusion*, 143–44.

40. Joe Bernal, as quoted in Phelps, "A Tale of Two Kings," 60.

41. *San Antonio Express News*, September 15, 1977.

42. Phelps, "A Tale of Two Kings," 61.

43. Socrates Ramírez, in discussion with the author, August 2003.

44. In several of the post–World War II Fiesta articles in the local press, prominent city representatives described their Fiesta costumes (as I detailed in chapter 5). The members of such organizations as the Mexican Chamber of Commerce often wore the charro outfit. *San Antonio Light*, April 20, 1953.

45. Nájera-Ramírez, "Engendering Nationalism," 1.

46. I am using the term "greater Mexico" as José Limón uses it, to describe both the present-day country of Mexico and the U.S. Southwest that was once part of Mexico.

47. Nájera-Ramírez, "Engendering Nationalism," 2.

48. Nájera-Ramírez, "Engendering Nationalism," 3.

49. Nájera-Ramírez, "Engendering Nationalism," 4.

50. Nájera-Ramírez, "Engendering Nationalism," 4.

51. Nájera-Ramírez, "Engendering Nationalism," 6.

52. Nájera-Ramírez, "Engendering Nationalism," 6.

53. Máximo Virgil, "Viva El Charro!" Fiesta San Antonio Commission Records, University of Texas at San Antonio.

54. Delores Carson, "Daring Charreada Riders Carry Old Traditions," *San Antonio Light*, April 24, 1988.

55. Socrates Ramírez, in discussion with the author, August 2003.

56. *San Antonio Light*, April 19, 1980.

57. *San Antonio Express News*, April 20, 1980.

58. Phelps, "A Tale of Two Kings," 61.

59. *San Antonio Light*, April 19, 1980.

60. *San Antonio Light*, April 19, 1980.

61. Phelps, "A Tale of Two Kings," 113.

62. Phelps, "A Tale of Two Kings," 113.

63. Phelps, "A Tale of Two Kings," 113.

64. Haynes, *Dressing Up Debutantes*, 65.

65. *San Antonio Light*, April 20, 1980.

66. *San Antonio Express News*, April 20, 1980.

67. Kemper Diehl and Jan Jarboe, *Cisneros: Portrait of a New American* (San Antonio: Corona Publishing Co., 1985), 71.

68. *San Antonio Express News*, April 4, 1981.
69. *San Antonio Express News*, April 5, 1981.
70. Rosales, *The Illusion of Inclusion*, 144, 146.
71. Rosales, *The Illusion of Inclusion*, 144, 146.
72. *San Antonio Express News*, April 19, 1981.
73. Rosales, *The Illusion of Inclusion*, 149.
74. This term is taken from an article in the *San Antonio Light*, "Bernardo Eureste: He's a Champion of the Underdog," November 5, 1978.
75. Rosales, *The Illusion of Inclusion*, 151–52.
76. Rosales, *The Illusion of Inclusion*, 152.
77. In a city park, Eureste, a married man, was attacked by muggers while in a sexually compromising situation with one of his female aides. Eureste left the young woman to seek help from the police. He was thus accused not only of adultery, but also of abandoning a young woman in danger. He later apologized to his constituents and successfully won a runoff election to keep his seat, but his political career never recovered.
78. Sea World later renegotiated a deal, and the water park was built.
79. Rosales, *The Illusion of Inclusion*, 157.
80. Phelps, "A Tale of Two Kings," 113.
81. Phelps, "A Tale of Two Kings," 113.
82. From "La Feria de las Flores: A Festival with a Purpose," for Tony Benavides productions, Jacob I. Rodríguez Papers, LULAC Archives, Nettie Lee Benson Latin American Collection, University of Texas at Austin.
83. Nájera-Ramírez, "Engendering Nationalism," 9, 13.
84. Virgil Elizondo, *The Future is Mestizo: Life Where Cultures Meet*, rev. ed. (Boulder: University Press of Colorado, 2000), 48, 50.
85. *San Antonio Light*, April 22, 1979.
86. *San Antonio Express News*, April 19, 1981.
87. *San Antonio Light*, April 22, 1979.
88. Babcock, "A New Mexican 'Rebecca,'" 29.
89. Phelps, "A Tale of Two Kings," 56.
90. *San Antonio Light*, April 19, 1980.
91. Rubén Munguía, as quoted in Phelps, "A Tale of Two Kings," 114.
92. Phelps, "A Tale of Two Kings," 114.
93. *San Antonio Light*, April 17, 1981.
94. *San Antonio Light*, April 19, 1981.
95. Lang, "Between Civil Rights and Black Power in the Gateway City," 739. For a comprehensive history of the Veiled Prophet parade and ball, see Thomas Spencer, *The St. Louis Veiled Prophet's Celebration: Power on Parade, 1887–1995* (Columbia: University of Missouri Press, 2000).
96. Mitchell, *All on a Mardi Gras Day*, 192–201.
97. Mitchell, *All on a Mardi Gras Day*, 151.
98. Mitchell, *All on a Mardi Gras Day*, 182–91.
99. "Emma Tenayuca: La Pasionara de Texas," *La Voz de Aztlán*, March 13, 2000.
100. Jorge González, in discussion with the author, February 2007.

Notes to Chapter Six

1. Names of informants have been changed at their request.
2. This insight is from David Harvey.
3. Roberto Da Matta, "Carnival in Multiple Planes," in *Rite, Drama, Festival, Spectacle*, ed. John MacAloon (Philadelphia: Institute for the Study of Human Issues, 1984), 209–40. Here I am borrowing from Roberto Da Matta's analysis of the way Brazilian carnival merges the separate areas of home and street.
4. Most visitors to San Antonio will note that much of San Antonio's tourism is at street level as well. The most obvious example of a street-level downtown landmark is the Alamo. I make this distinction between river level and street level, however, to emphasize that it is easier to see the city's socioeconomic realities when walking on street-level sidewalks than on the Paseo del Río.
5. De Oliver, "Democratizing Consumerism," 215.
6. De Oliver, "Democratizing Consumerism," 218–20.
7. Miguel de Oliver, "Multicultural Consumerism and Racial Hierarchy: A Case Study of Market Culture and the Structural Harmonization of Contradictory Doctrines," *Antipode* 33, no. 2 (2001): 240. De Oliver cites that the inner-city neighborhoods surrounding downtown have a Latino population where 52.8 percent live below the poverty line.
8. De Oliver, "Democratizing Consumerism," 254. He writes: "For minorities, despite legal equality and high-profile participation in the marketplace of representations, contemporary multiculturalism results in continued *bodily* socioeconomic marginalization, but full citizenship in the *democracy of commodities*."
9. De Oliver, "Multicultural Consumerism," 241.
10. De Oliver, "Multicultural Consumerism," 241.
11. Homesley, *Hemisfair '68 and the Transformation of San Antonio*, 1.
12. Tom Frost in Homesley, *Hemisfair '68 and the Transformation of San Antonio*, 43.
13. Frank W. Jennings, *San Antonio: The Story of an Enchanted City* (San Antonio: San Antonio Express News, 1998), 294–96.
14. Peter Hennessy, in discussion with the author, June 2006.
15. International Festivals and Events Association and Birchhill Enterprises, "Section One-Executive Summary." It is difficult to know exactly how the ratio of residents to visitors breaks down at each Fiesta event, but these studies of the Fiesta parades indicated that for the biggest events, between 14 percent (at NIOSA) to 35 percent (at the Carnival and El Mercado) of the attendants came from more than fifty miles from the city.
16. In the 2002 economic study of the Fiesta parades, researchers noted the five most common zip codes of those attending. These ranged from the wealthiest to the poorest neighborhoods in the city, with the elite community of Alamo Heights having the highest number and one of the least prosperous west side neighborhoods at the fifth highest. I believe that the variety of these zip codes had more to do with the way the study organized the events—combining the demographic information from all the parades together rather than treating each parade separately. Thus, the attendants included not only those who went to the Battle of Flowers and Fiesta Flambeau parades, but also the River and King William parades, which from my observations seem to have more middle- and upper-

class participants. International Festivals and Events Association and Birchhill Enterprises, "Section One-Executive Summary: Fiesta San Antonio Parades."

17. I owe part of this insight to Sylvia Rodríguez's work on the Taos Fiesta. During that festival, she argues that the local Mexicano population reoccupies Taos plaza, its central public space. In daily commercial life, merchants and tourists occupy this plaza. "Fiesta Time and Plaza Space: Resistance and Accommodation in a Tourist Town," *Journal of American Folklore* 111, no. 439 (1998): 39–56.

18. Chuck Blische, in discussion with the author, June 2006. Blische is currently the executive director for the Fiesta San Antonio Commission. The executive director is particularly important in Fiesta, because while presidents change annually and are volunteer, the executive director, whom the commission pays, usually serves for several years. Thus, the director provides continuity as volunteers change.

19. This notion of being out of place is from Cresswell's study *In Place, Out of Place,* 23–25.

20. International Festivals and Events Association and Birchhill Enterprises, "Executive Summary: Fiesta San Antonio Carnivals—Fiesta del Mercado and Fiesta Carnival." This study combined the events at El Mercado and the Carnival and found that overall the number of visitors who came from more than fifty miles to attend was 35 percent.

21. International Festivals and Events Association and Birchhill Enterprises, "Executive Summary: Fiesta Carnivals." The estimated overall attendance for 2002 was 850,000. One of the main reasons for the high attendance is that the Fiesta Carnival and El Mercado run every day and night of the week, while other festivals last for two or three days.

22. *San Antonio Light*, August 17, 1959.

23. *San Antonio Daily Express*, April 17, 1900.

24. *San Antonio Daily Express*, April 18, 1900.

25. *San Antonio Daily Express*, April 18, 1920.

26. *San Antonio Express News*, August 18, 1959.

27. *San Antonio Express News*, September 1, 1959.

28. *San Antonio Express News*, August 23, 1959.

29. *San Antonio Express News*, August 23, 1959. At the time, respondents gave their names and home addresses along with their comments.

30. *San Antonio Light*, May 3, 1959.

31. *San Antonio Express News*, August 21, 1959.

32. Gracie Poe Griffin, interview with the author, November 6, 1998.

33. Stuart Hall and Tony Jefferson, *Resistance Through Rituals: Youth Subcultures In Postwar Britain* (New York: Harper Collins, 1976), 72.

34. Peter Hennessy, in discussion with the author, June 2006.

35. Ralph Lehr, in discussion with the author, June 2006. Lehr suggested that some city councilmen were loyal to Andricks, who made it difficult for the commission to get city permits during this era. He indicated that some of the opposition to the commission did have to do with resentment against the elite. In his view, however, the commission did more to expand access to Fiesta, while Andricks wanted to narrowly control the entire festival.

36. Ralph Lehr, in discussion with the author, June 2006.

37. Mario Salas, in discussion with the author, March 2007. Philips's death was actually the catalyst for the formation of the San Antonio chapter of SNCC, whose

philosophy was a hybrid of SNCC and the Black Panthers. Salas, one of the founders of the organization, now refers to it as a SNCC-Panther chapter.

38. *San Antonio Light*, April 22, 1969.

39. *West Side Sun*, April 27, 1969.

40. *San Antonio Light*, April 22, 1969.

41. *San Antonio Light*, April 22, 1969.

42. Mario Salas, in discussion with the author, March 2007.

43. *San Antonio Light*, April 26, 1969.

44. *San Antonio Light*, April 26, 1969.

45. *San Antonio Light*, April 22, 1969.

46. *San Antonio Light*, April 22, 1969.

47. *San Antonio Light*, April 23, 1969.

48. Salas indicates that the Dallas chapter of SNCC had come down that night for a joint meeting. In front of the offices, thirty-forty armed men stood on guard outside. This was the usual routine for their meetings and shows the influence of the Black Panthers, of course. The police claimed they were performing military drills and used this claim to break up the meeting.

49. *San Antonio Light*, April 22, 1969.

50. *San Antonio Light*, April 26, 1969.

51. Montejano, *Anglos and Mexicans in the Making of Texas*, 274–80.

52. For example, Mario Salas remembers having to go through the back door of San Antonio's Majestic Theatre through 1965.

53. Hall and Jefferson, *Resistance Through Rituals*, 74. They write of a tendency of "the dominant culture to seek and find, in 'youth,' the folk-devils to people its nightmare: the nightmare of a society which, in some fundamental way, had lost its sway and authority over its young."

54. Santiago García, "La Semana Alegre," from *Bus Side Stories*, unpublished poems, in the author's personal collection.

55. Santiago García, in discussion with the author, July 19, 2007.

56. The out of place metaphor is from Cresswell's analysis in *In Place, Out of Place*, 149.

57. *San Antonio Express News*, April 26, 1991.

58. José Limón, *Dancing with the Devil* (Madison: University of Wisconsin Press, 1994), 104.

59. David Montejano, "On the Future of Anglo-Mexican Relations in the United States," in *Chicano Politics and Society in the Late Twentieth Century*, ed. David Montejano (Austin: University of Texas Press, 1999), 235.

60. Harvey, *The Condition of Postmodernity*, 148.

61. Limón, *Dancing with the Devil*, 106.

62. Limón, *Dancing with the Devil*, 109.

63. Filmmaker Jim Mendiola came up with the term "adolescent playground" to describe La Semana. Jim Mendola, in discussion with the author, November 6, 1998.

64. *San Antonio Express News*, April 26, 1991.

65. *San Antonio Light*, April 23, 1990.

66. *San Antonio Light*, April 24, 1990.

67. *San Antonio Light*, April 26, 1990.

68. *San Antonio Light*, April 26, 1991.

69. *San Antonio Express News*, April 28, 1991.

70. *San Antonio Light*, April 27, 1991.

71. *San Antonio Express News*, April 19, 1999.

72. *San Antonio Express News*, September 13, 2003.

73. Gini Sikes, *Eight Ball Chicks: A Year in the Violent World of Girl Gangs* (New York: Doubleday, 1997), 98.

74. Sikes, *Eight Ball Chicks*, 98.

75. Sikes, *Eight Ball Chicks*, 100–101.

76. Sikes, *Eight Ball Chicks*, 100–101.

77. *San Antonio Express News*, December 29, 1996.

78. *San Antonio Express News*, January 27, 1997.

79. Chuck Blische, executive director of the Fiesta Commission, in discussion with the author, June 2006.

80. *San Antonio Express News*, October 27, 1996.

81. *San Antonio Express News*, April 13, 1997.

82. *San Antonio Express News*, April 13, 1997.

83. *San Antonio Express News*, April 13, 1997.

84. *San Antonio Express News*, July 31, 1998.

85. *San Antonio Express News*, August 14, 1998.

86. *San Antonio Express News*, November 29, 1998.

87. *San Antonio Express News*, March 24, 1997.

Notes to Conclusion

1. Maguire, *A Century of Fiesta in San Antonio*, vii.

2. Laura Codina, "The What, How y Qué Más of Fiesta," *La Voz de Esperanza*, April 1993.

3. José Limón, in *Dancing with the Devil*, makes this argument from the work of Robert Lee Maril in *The Poorest of Americans: The Mexican-Americans of the Lower Rio Grande Valley of Texas* (South Bend, IN: Notre Dame University Press, 1989).

BIBLIOGRAPHY

Appadurai, Arjun, and Carol A. Breckenridge. "Why Public Culture?" *Public Culture Bulletin* 1, no. 1 (Fall 1988): 5–10.

Babcock, Barbara. "A New Mexican 'Rebecca': Imaging Pueblo Women" *Journal of the Southwest* 32, no. 4 (1990): 400–437.

Bakhtin, Mikhail. *Rabelais and His World*. Bloomington: Indiana University Press, 1968.

Battle of Flowers Association Collection. Daughters of the Republic of Texas Library, San Antonio.

Baudelaire, Charles. *The Painter of Modern Life and Other Essays*. New York: Da Capo Press, 1986.

Bauman, Richard. "Performance and Honor in 13th Century Iceland." *Journal of American Folklore* 99, no. 392 (1986): 131–50.

Bederman, Gail. *Manliness and Civilization: A Cultural History of Gender and Race in the United States, 1880–1917*. Chicago: University of Chicago Press, 1995.

Beezley, William. *Judas at the Jockey Club*. Lincoln: University of Nebraska Press, 1987.

Berman, Marshall. *All That Is Solid Melts Into Air: The Experience of Modernity*. New York: Simon and Schuster, 1982.

Bordo, Susan. *Unbearable Weight: Feminism, Western Culture and the Body*. Berkeley: University of California Press, 1993.

Bourdieu, Pierre. *Distinction*. Cambridge: Harvard University Press, 1984.

Boyd, Elizabeth Bronwyn. "Southern Beauty: Performing Femininity in an American Region." PhD diss., University of Texas at Austin, 2000.

Brear, Holly Beachley. *Inherit the Alamo: Myth and Ritual at an American Shrine*. Austin: University of Texas Press, 1995.

Brundage, W. Fitzhugh. "White Women and the Politics of Historical Memory in the New South 1880–1920." In *Jumpin' Jim Crow: Southern Politics from Civil War to Civil Rights*, edited by Jane Dailey, Glenda Elizabeth Gilmore, and Bryant Simon, 115–39. Princeton: Princeton University Press, 2000.

Bushick, Frank. *Glamorous Days*. San Antonio: Naylor Publishing, 1934.

Chabot, Frederick C. *With the Makers of San Antonio: Genealogies of Early Latin, Anglo-American, and German Families with Occasional Biographies; Each Group*

Being Prefaced with a Brief Historical Sketch and Illustrations. San Antonio: Artes Gráficas, 1937.

Coffin, Alfred Oscar. "Land without Chimneys: or The Byways of Mexico." Cincinnati, OH: Editor Publishing Co., 1898.

Cohen, Abner. *The Politics of Elite Culture: Explorations in the Dramaturgy of Power in a Modern African Society.* Berkeley: University of California Press, 1981.

Cresswell, Tim. *In Place, Out of Place: Geography, Ideology and Transgression.* Minneapolis: University of Minnesota Press, 1996.

Da Matta, Roberto. "Carnival in Multiple Planes." In *Rite, Drama, Festival, Spectacle,* edited by John MacAloon, 209–40. Philadelphia: Institute for the Study of Human Issues, 1984.

Davis, Janet M. *The Circus Age: Culture and Society under the American Big Top.* Chapel Hill: University of North Carolina Press, 2002.

Davis, Susan. *Parades and Power.* Philadelphia: Temple University Press, 1986.

De Certeau, Michel. *The Practices of Everyday Life.* Berkeley: University of California Press, 1984.

De León, Arnoldo. *Mexican Americans in Texas: A Brief History.* Arlington Heights, TX: Harlan Davidson, 1993.

———. *The Tejano Community, 1836–1900.* Albuquerque: University of New Mexico Press, 1982.

Deloria, Philip. *Playing Indian.* New Haven: Yale University Press, 1998.

De Oliver, Miguel. "Democratizing Consumerism: Coalescing Constructions of Subjugation in the Consumer Landscape." *Gender, Place and Culture* 4, no. 2 (1997): 211–33.

———. "Historical Preservation and Identity: The Alamo and the Production of a Consumer Landscape." *Antipode* 28, no. 1 (1996): 1–23.

———. "Multicultural Consumerism and Racial Hierarchy: A Case Study of Market Culture and the Structural Harmonization of Contradictory Doctrines." *Antipode* 33, no. 2 (2001): 228–59.

Delpar, Helen. *The Enormous Vogue of Things Mexican: Cultural Relations between the United States and Mexico, 1920–1935.* Tuscaloosa: University of Alabama Press, 1992.

Deutsch, Sarah. *No Separate Refuge: Culture, Class and Gender on an Anglo-Hispanic Frontier in the American Southwest, 1880–1940.* Oxford: Oxford University Press, 1987.

Deverell, William. *Whitewashed Adobe: The Rise of Los Angeles and the Remaking of Its Mexican Past.* Berkeley: University of California Press, 2004.

Diehl, Kemper, and Jan Jarboe. *Cisneros: Portrait of a New American.* San Antonio: Corona Publishing Co., 1985.

Dilworth, Leah. *Imagining Indians in the Southwest: Persistent Visions of a Primitive Past.* Washington, D.C.: Smithsonian Institution Press, 1996.

Douglas, Ann. *The Feminization of American Culture.* New York: Knopf, 1977.

Edmondson, Belinda. "Public Spectacles: Caribbean Women and the Politics of Public Performance." *Small Axe* 13 (March 2003): 1–16.

Edmundson, Munro. "Carnival in New Orleans." *Caribbean Quarterly* 4, nos. 3, 4 (1956): 233–45.

Edwards, Emily. Oral History Transcripts. San Antonio Conservation Society Library, San Antonio.

Elizondo, Virgil. *The Future is Mestizo: Life Where Cultures Meet*. Revised edition. Boulder: University Press of Colorado, 2000.

Evans, Sara. *Born for Liberty*. New York: Free Press, 1989.

Everett, Donald. "San Antonio Welcomes the 'Sunset'-1877." *Southwestern Historical Quarterly* 65, no. 1 (1961): 46–60.

Fenstermaker, Rowena Green. Oral History Transcripts. San Antonio Conservation Society Library, San Antonio.

Fiesta San Antonio Commission Records. Archives and Special Collections, University of Texas at San Antonio.

Fisher, Lewis F. *San Antonio: Outpost of Empires*. San Antonio: Maverick Publishing Company, 1997.

———. *Saving San Antonio: The Precarious Preservation of a Heritage*. Lubbock: Texas Tech University Press, 1996.

Flores, Richard R. *Los Pastores: History and Performance in the Mexican Shepherd's Play of South Texas*. Washington, D.C.: Smithsonian Institution Press, 1995.

———. *Remembering the Alamo: Memory, Modernity and the Master Symbol*. Austin: University of Texas Press, 2002.

Foley, Neil. *The White Scourge: Mexicans, Blacks and Poor Whites in Texas Cotton Culture*. Berkeley: University of California Press, 1997.

Frankenberg, Ruth. *White Women/Race Matters: The Social Construction of Whiteness*. Minneapolis: University of Minnesota Press, 1993.

García, Ignacio M. "Backwards from Aztlan: Politics in the Age of Hispanics." In *Chicanas and Chicanos in Contemporary Society*, edited by Roberto M. De Anda, 191–204. Boston: Allyn and Bacon, 1996.

García, Mario T. *Mexican Americans: Leadership, Ideology, and Identity, 1930–1960*. New Haven: Yale University Press, 1989.

García, Richard A. *The Rise of a Mexican American Middle Class: San Antonio 1929–1941*. College Station: Texas A&M Press, 1991.

Glassberg, David. *American Historical Pageantry: The Uses of Tradition in the Early Twentieth Century*. Chapel Hill: University of North Carolina Press, 1990.

———. *Sense of History: The Place of the Past in American Life*. Amherst: University of Massachusetts Press, 2001.

Gómez-Quiñones, Juan. *Chicano Politics: Reality and Promise, 1940–1990*. Albuquerque: University of New Mexico Press, 1990.

Gould, Steven. *The Alamo city guide, San Antonio, Texas. Being a historical sketch of the ancient city of the Alamo, and business review; with notes of present advantages, together with a complete guide to all the prominent points of interest about the city, and a compilation of facts of value to visitors and residents*. New York: Macgowan & Slipper, Printers, ca. 1882.

Graham, Henry. "History of the Texas Cavaliers." 1976. Texana Collection, San Antonio Main Library, San Antonio.

Grayson, George. *The United States and Mexico: Patterns of Influence*. New York: Praeger, 1984.

Griffin, Larry J. "The American South and the Self." *Southern Cultures* 12, no. 3 (2006): 6–28.

Guss, David M. *The Festive State: Race, Ethnicity and Nationalism as Cultural Performance*. Berkeley: University of California Press, 2000.

Hale, Grace Elizabeth. *Making Whiteness: The Culture of Segregation in the South, 1890–1940.* New York: Vintage, 1999.

Hall, Stuart, and Tony Jefferson. *Resistance Through Rituals: Youth Subcultures In Postwar Britain.* New York: Harper Collins, 1976.

Harvey, David. *The Condition of Postmodernity.* Cambridge: Blackwell, 1990.

———. "From Space to Place and Back Again." In *Mapping the Futures,* edited by Jon Bird, Barry Curtis, Tim Putnam, George Robertson, and Lisa Tickner, 3–29. London: Routledge, 1993.

Haynes, Michaele. *Dressing Up Debutantes: Glamor and Glitz in South Texas.* Oxford: Berg, 1998.

Hobsbawm, Eric, and Terence Ranger, eds. *The Invention of Tradition.* Cambridge: Cambridge University Press, 1983.

Hoelscher, Steven. *Heritage on Stage: The Invention of Ethnic Place in America's Little Switzerland.* Madison: University of Wisconsin Press, 1998.

Homesley, Sterling. *Hemisfair '68 and the Transformation of San Antonio.* San Antonio: Maverick Publishing Company, 2003.

Hosmer, Charles. *The Presence of the Past.* New York: G. P. Putnam's Sons, 1965.

———. *Preservation Comes of Age, From Williamsburg to the National Trust, 1926–1949.* Charlottesville: University of Virginia Press for the Preservation Press, 1981.

House, Boyce. *City of Flaming Adventure: The Chronicle of San Antonio.* San Antonio: Naylor Publishing, 1949.

Hoy, Suellen. *Chasing Dirt: The American Pursuit of Cleanliness.* New York: Oxford University Press, 1995.

International Festivals and Events Association and Birchhill Enterprises. "Section One-Executive Summary: Fiesta San Antonio." 2002. Fiesta San Antonio Commission Records. University of Texas at San Antonio.

International Festivals and Events Association and Birchhill Enterprises. "Section One-Executive Summary: Fiesta San Antonio—Night in Old San Antonio." 2002. Fiesta San Antonio Commission Records. University of Texas at San Antonio.

Jennings, Frank W. *San Antonio: The Story of an Enchanted City.* San Antonio: San Antonio Express News, 1998.

Johns, Michael. *The City of Mexico in the Age of Diaz.* Austin: University of Texas Press, 1997.

Johnson, Benjamin. *Revolution in Texas: How a Forgotten Rebellion and Its Bloody Suppression Turned Mexicans into Americans.* New Haven: Yale University Press, 2003.

Johnson, David R., John A. Booth, and Richard Harris, eds. *The Politics of San Antonio: Community, Progress and Power.* Lincoln: University of Nebraska Press, 1983.

Jones, Anne Goodwyn. *Tomorrow is Another Day: The Woman Writer in the South 1859–1936.* Baton Rouge: Louisiana State University Press, 1981.

Kinser, Samuel. *Carnival, American Style: Mardi Gras at New Orleans and Mobile.* Chicago: University of Chicago Press, 1990.

Lang, Clarence. "Between Civil Rights and Black Power in the Gateway City: The Action Committee to Improve Opportunities for Negroes, 1964–1975." *Journal of Social History* 37, no. 3 (Spring 2004): 725–54.

Lavenda, Robert. "Festivals and the Creation of Public Culture: Whose Voice(s)?" In *Museums and Communities: The Politics of Public Culture,* edited by Ivan Karp,

Christine Mullen Kreamer, and Steven D. Levine, 76–104. Washington, D.C.: Smithsonian Institution Press, 1992.

———. "'It's Not a Beauty Pageant!' Hybrid Ideology in Minnesota Community Queen Pageants." In *Beauty Queens on the Global Stage: Gender, Contests and Power*, edited by Colleen Ballerino Cohen, Richard Wilk, and Beverly Stoeltje, 31–46. New York: Routledge, 1996.

Limón, José. *American Encounters: Greater Mexico, The United States and the Erotics of Culture*. Boston: Beacon Press, 1998.

———. *Dancing with the Devil*. Madison: University of Wisconsin Press, 1994.

Lorini, Alessandra. "Public Rituals and the Cultural Making of the New York African-American Community." In *Feasts and Celebrations in North American Communities*, edited by Ramón A. Gutiérrez and Geneviève Fabre, 29–46. Albuquerque: University of New Mexico Press, 1995.

Lott, Eric. *Love and Theft: Blackface Minstrelsy and the American Working Class*. New York: Oxford University Press, 1995.

Lowenthal, David. *The Past is a Foreign Country*. Cambridge: Cambridge University Press, 1985.

MacCannell, Dean. *The Tourist: A New Theory of the Leisure Class*. 2nd ed. New York: Schocken Books, 1989.

MacMillan, Esther. Oral History Transcripts. San Antonio Conservation Society Library, San Antonio.

Maguire, Jack. *A Century of Fiesta in San Antonio*. Austin: Eakin Press, 1990.

Maril, Robert Lee. *The Poorest of Americans: The Mexican-Americans of the Lower Rio Grande Valley of Texas*. South Bend, IN: Notre Dame University Press, 1989.

Marling, Karal Ann. *Debutante: Rites and Regalia of American Debdom*. Lawrence: University Press of Kansas, 2004.

Marquez, Benjamin. *LULAC: The Evolution of a Mexican American Political Organization*. Austin: University of Texas Press, 1993.

Mason, Kenneth. *African Americans and Race Relations in San Antonio, Texas, 1867–1937*. New York: Garland Publishing, 1998.

Mason, Phillip. "Soul in the Culture of African Americans." *Music Educators Journal* 79, no. 3 (November 1992): 49–52.

Matovina, Timothy M. *Tejano Religion and Ethnicity: San Antonio, 1821–1860*. Austin: University of Texas Press, 1995.

McClintock, William A. "Journal of a Trip through Texas and Northern Mexico in 1846–7." *Southwestern Historical Quarterly* 34 (October 1930): 141–58.

Mclean, Robert M. *That Mexican As He Really Is, North and South of the Rio Grande*. New York: Fleming H. Revell, 1928.

McWilliams, Carey. *North from Mexico: The Spanish-Speaking People of the United States*. Rev. ed. 1949. Reprint, New York: Greenwood Press, 1968.

Mitchell, Reid. *All on a Mardi Gras Day: Episodes in the History of New Orleans Carnival*. Cambridge, MA: Harvard University Press, 1995.

Montejano, David. *Anglos and Mexicans in the Making of Texas, 1836–1986*. Austin: University of Texas Press, 1987.

———. "On the Future of Anglo-Mexican Relations in the United States." In *Chicano Politics and Society in the Late Twentieth Century*, edited by David Montejano, 234–50. Austin: University of Texas Press, 1999.

Montgomery, Charles. *The Spanish Redemption: Heritage, Power and Loss on New Mexico's Upper Rio Grande*. Berkeley: University of California Press, 2002.

Mullin, Molly. *Culture in the Marketplace: Gender, Art, and Value in the American Southwest*. Durham, NC: Duke University Press, 2001.

Nájera-Ramírez, Olga. "Engendering Nationalism: Identity, Discourse, and the Mexican Charro." *Anthropological Quarterly* 67, no. 1 (January 1994): 1–14.

Omi, Michael, and Howard Winant. *Racial Formation in the United States from the 1960s to the 1980s*. New York: Routledge, 1986.

Order of the Alamo. *Courts of the Order of the Alamo 1909–1925*. San Antonio: Order of the Alamo, 1925.

———. *History of the Order of the Alamo, Volume Two, 1926–1939*. San Antonio: Order of the Alamo, 1939.

Ott, Katherine. *Fevered Lives: Tuberculosis in American Culture since 1870*. Cambridge, MA: Harvard University Press, 1996.

Penick, Monica Michelle. "A preservationist's dissonance: Maury Maverick and the restoration of La Villita, 1939–1941." Master's thesis, University of Texas at Austin, 2001.

Phelps, Christi. "A Tale of Two Kings." *San Antonio Monthly*, April 1986.

Ramsdell, Charles. *San Antonio: A Historical and Pictorial Guide*. Austin: University of Texas Press, 1959,

Rodríguez, Jacob I. Papers. LULAC Archives. Nettie Lee Benson Latin American Collection. University of Texas at Austin.

Rodríguez, Sylvia. "Fiesta Time and Plaza Space: Resistance and Accommodation in a Tourist Town." *Journal of American Folklore* 111, no. 439 (1998): 39–56.

———. "Tourism, Whiteness, and the Vanishing Anglo." In *Seeing and Being Seen: Tourism in the American West*, edited David M. Wrobel and Patrick T. Long, 194–222. Lawrence: University Press of Kansas, 2001.

Roediger, David. *The Wages of Whiteness: Race and the Making of the American Working Class*. New York: Verso, 1999.

Rosaldo, Michele Zimbalist. "Women, Culture and Society: A Theoretical Overview." In *Women, Culture and Society*, edited by M. Z. Rosaldo and Louise Lamphere, 17–42. Stanford: Stanford University Press, 1974.

Rosaldo, Renato. *Culture and Truth: The Remaking of Social Analysis*. Boston: Beacon Press, 1993.

Rosales, Rodolfo. *The Illusion of Inclusion: The Untold Political Story of San Antonio*. Austin: University of Texas Press, 2000.

Rubin, Louis. "Changing, Enduring, Forever Still the South." In *The Prevailing South: Life and Politics in a Changing Culture*, edited by Dudley Clendinen, 220–34. Atlanta: Longstreet Press, 1988.

Ryan, Mary P. *Women in Public: Between Banners and Ballots*. Baltimore: Johns Hopkins University Press, 1990.

Said, Edward. *Orientalism*. New York: Random House, 1979.

Sanders, Heywood. "Building a New Urban Infrastructure: The Creation of Postwar San Antonio." In *Urban Texas*, edited by Char Miller and Heywood Sanders, 154–73. College Station: Texas A&M Press, 1990.

Saxton, Alexander. *The Indispensable Enemy: Labor and the Anti-Chinese Movement in California*. Berkeley: University of California Press, 1975.

Scott, Anne F. *The Southern Lady: From Pedestal to Politics, 1830–1930*. Chicago: University of Chicago Press, 1970.

Sekul, Joseph D. "Communities Organized for Public Service: Citizen Power and Public Policy in San Antonio." In *The Politics of San Antonio: Community, Progress and Power,* edited by David R. Johnson, John A. Booth, and Richard Harris, 175–90. Lincoln: University of Nebraska Press, 1983.

Sierra, Christine Marie. "In Search of National Power: Chicanos Working the System on Immigration Reform, 1976–1986." In *Chicano Politics and Society In the Late Twentieth Century*, edited by David Montejano, 131–53. Austin: University of Texas Press, 1999.

Sikes, Gini. *Eight Ball Chicks: A Year in the Violent World of Girl Gangs*. New York: Doubleday, 1997.

Smith, Horace R. "History of Alamo Plaza from Its Beginning to the Present." Master's thesis, Trinity University, 1966.

Smith-Rosenberg, Caroll, ed. *Disorderly Conduct: Visions of Gender in Victorian America*. New York: Alfred Knopf, 1985.

Spencer, Thomas. *The St. Louis Veiled Prophet's Celebration: Power on Parade, 1887–1995*. Columbia: University of Missouri Press, 2000.

Sobré, Judith Berg. *San Antonio on Parade: Six Historic Festivals*. College Station: Texas A&M University Press, 2003.

Stallybrass, Peter, and Allon White. *The Politics and Poetics of Transgression*. New York: Routledge, 1986.

Stoeltje, Beverly. "The Snake Charmer Queen: Ritual, Competition, and Signification in American Festival." In *Beauty Queens on the Global Stage: Gender, Contests and Power*, edited Colleen Ballerino Cohen, Richard Wilk, and Beverly Stoeltje, 13–30. New York: Routledge, 1996.

Taylor, William R. *Cavalier and Yankee: The Old South and American National Character*. Cambridge, MA: Harvard University Press, 1979.

Trillin, Calvin. "New Orleans Unmasked." *The New Yorker*, February 2, 1998.

Trouillot, Michel-Rolph. *Silencing the Past: Power and the Production of History*. Boston: Beacon Press, 1995.

Turner, Victor. *Dramas, Fields and Metaphors: Symbolic Action in Human Society*. Ithaca, NY: Cornell University Press, 1974.

Von Phul, Helen. "The Battle of Flowers Association." 1931. Battle of Flowers Association Collection. Daughters of the Republic of Texas Library, San Antonio.

Wilson, Chris. *The Myth of Santa Fe: Creating a Modern Regional Tradition*. Albuquerque: University of New Mexico Press, 1997.

Woodward, C. Vann. *Burden of Southern History*. Baton Rouge: Louisiana State University Press, 1960.

Wu, Judy Tzu-Chuu. "'Loveliest Daughter of Our Ancient Cathay!': Representations of Ethnic and Gender Identity in the Miss Chinatown U.S.A. Beauty Pageant." *Journal of Social History* 31, no. 1 (Fall 1997): 5–31.

Young, Robert. *Colonial Desire: Hybridity in Theory, Culture and Race*. New York: Routledge, 1995.

INDEX

Page numbers in **bold type** indicate photographs.

African Americans, 58, 66, 185; denied rights of full citizenship, 5; and Juneteenth parades, 34; portrayal by white southerners, 12; and Queen of Soul, 143; and racial cross-dressing, 30–31; in San Antonio after Civil War, 27; and segregation, 15, 60, 64; in St. Louis, 137

Alamo, 3, 13, **19**, 28, 91, 133; annual pilgrimage to, **194–95**; later uses of, 18; as a male domain, 38; neglect of, 18; restoration of, 93; and stories of racial unity, 129; and tourism, 19

Alamo chapel, 56, **57**, 165

Alamo Concessions, 192

Alamo Plaza, 22, 25, 26, 50, 66, 68, 69, 70, 71, 178

Allison, Dwight, 121

Andricks, Reynolds, 103–34, **118**, 137, 180, 181; loses battle to control Fiesta, 123; maintained tight control over FSJA, 109

Anglos, 27, 60, 66, 69, 74, 81, 106, 128; changing power relations with Mexicanos, 14; conflicts with Tejanos, 4; and interethnic marriages, 5; and martyrdom at Alamo, 92; and Mexican mobility, 61; partnerships with German community, 26; playing with Mexican identity, 67; and Tejanos, 7

Aubrey, William H., 49

Austin, Stephen F., 132

Bakhtin, Mikhail, 13, 14

Ballard, W. J., 20

barbed wire: invention of, 26

Battle of Flowers, 1, 15, 18–44, 123, 163, 164; a chaotic display of social disorderliness, 21; and commercial interests, 47

Battle of Flowers Association, 1, 20, 30, 41, 55, 102, 105, 124, 158; and board of directors for Fiesta, 106; and elite women, 122; Elizabeth Ogden becomes president, 47; emulated Mexico City's flower parades, 76; an exclusively women's organization, 36, 48; and first parade, 104; friction with Businessmen's Club, 40; membership policy of, 119–20; and opposition to commercial culture, 49; resigns from FSJA, 119; and womanhood, 16

Battle of Flowers Parade, 1, 2, 21, 27, 28, 31, 33, 34, **37**, 41, 66–67, 69, 104, 111, 140, 163, 169, 177, 198; attendance, 170; expansion of, 39; and Fort Sam Houston, 29; and a new sociopolitical order, 43; as a women's event, 36

beauty pageants: criticism of, 142

Bernal, Joe, 151, 156

Bichsel (police chief), 183–84

Black Masons, 64

Boothe, Joyce, **87**

Bowie, Jim, 130

Boyd, Elizabeth, 54

Bozorgi, Diane Thiel, 117, 118

Brear, Holly Beachley, 13, 14

Briseño, Alex, 189

Burnett, Davis, 152, 158
Bush, Barbara, 167
Bushick, Frank, 48, 74, 75, 112

Canary Island fantasy, 96–98
Canary Islands, 4
Cantú, Elysiana Judith, 143
Cárdenas, José, 151
Carmichael, Stokely, 185
Carnival, 9–17, 104, 111, 126, 140, 174,
     175, 178, 180, 188, 197, 198; in New
     Orleans, 165–66; revenue from, 176,
     177; in St. Louis, 165–66
Carranza, Venustiano, 63
Carrington, John, 49, 52, 55, 56, 58, 59, 114,
     120
Carvajal, Esther, 96
Casey, Rick, 160
cattle drives: and African Americans, 27
cattle trails: closing of, 26
charros, 152–55
Chicano Movement, 149, 150, 185
Chicanos, 196
chili queens, 75, 76, 81, 101
chili stands, 73–75, 83, 84, 93, 99
Cisneros, Henry, 151, 159, 160, 166; as sym-
     bol of interethnic reconciliation, 161
Cisneros, Sandra, 167
City of Flaming Adventure: The Chronicle of
     San Antonio (House), 131
Codina, Laura, 196
Cody, Buffalo Bill, 12
Cohen, Abner, 51
Colquitt, Oscar, 91
Communities Organized for Public Safety,
     148, 150, 159
Connally, John, 172
Cornyation, 113, 114
coronation, 44–47, 45, 50–56, 66–72, 111,
     113, 114, 117, 142, 165, 198
coronation queens, 72
coronation rituals, 54
Cortés, Ernie, 148, 149
Cortez, Gregorio, 62
Crane, Stephen, 74
Creoles, 9
Crockett, Davy, 130
crowd rowdiness, 174
cultural nationalism, 77, 95

Daughters of the Republic of Texas, 38, 48,
     50, 56, 86, 91, 92, 105, 106, 122–25,
     133, 194
Davis, Richard Harding, 23
debutante rituals, 50
De León, Arnoldo, 33
Deloria, Phil, 97
deportation, 79
De Zavala, Adina, 92; as defender of land-
     marks, 90; and second battle of the
     Alamo, 91
De Zavala, Lorenzo, 132
Díaz, Porfirio, 32, 61–62, 63, 70, 153
Dickinson, Susanna, 47
diez y seis, 34
Dolenz, Mickey, 111
donkey brigades, 30
Doria, Ray, 158
Doria, Sam, 162, 164
Douglas, Ann, 39
Douglas, Mary, 59
Downtowners, 177, 178, 179, 181
Driscoll, Clara, 90–91, 92; chosen carnival
     queen, 49–50
Duchess Ann, 44–45, 46
Duncan, Ray, 134

Edwards, Emily, 86, 88, 90
elite women, 122; and Texas history, 20
Elizondo, Virgil, 163
El Mercado, 170, 176, 189, 197
Esparza, Gregorio, 130, 131
ethnic interchangeability, 156
ethnic separation, 7
Eureste, Bernardo, 151, 160–61
Everett, Richard, 7

fandangos, 7, 10
La Feria de Las Flores, 165
Fiesta Commission, 174, 181, 192, 193; city
     council oversight of selection process
     for awarding contracts and conces-
     sions, 192
Fiesta de Los Angeles, 10
Fiesta Flambeau, 111, 164, 175, 198
Fiesta Flambeau Parade, 121, 173
Fiesta River Parade, 158, 181, 186
Fiesta San Antonio, 3, 12, 35, 156, 173, 188; as
     an Anglo celebration, 133; beginnings
     of, 3; bringing order to, 33; commem-
     oration vs. leisure, 124; current size
     of, 3; de-centered, 137; disruption to,

182; distinct events of, 198; funded by Carnival, 181; and Los Angeles fiesta, 10; name changed to, 129; as racist celebration, 196; as secular Easter, 13; and theme of interethnic harmony, 130; varying concepts of board of directors and executive committee, 106

Fiesta San Antonio Commission, 122, 123, 177, 178, 197

Fiesta San Jacinto Association (FSJA), 48, 55, 67, 99, 103–34, 179; encourages wearing of costumes, 126; known as Spring Carnival until 1913, 178; organizations with privileged positions within, 105

Fiesta San Jacinto Commission, 133

Fiesta West, 138

Flores, Richard, 13, 26, 91

Flores, Roger, 192, 197

Flores Magón, Enrique and Ricardo, 62, 63

fly-swatting contest, 58, 59

Ford, O'Neill, 95

Fort Sam Houston, 29, 30, 63, 146, 169

Frost, J. H., 49

Frost, Joseph, 55

García, Ignacio M., 150

García, Richard, 80

García, Samantha, 167

García, Santiago, 186

Garza, Catarino, 61, 62

gender, 15, 22, 66, 76, 88, 137

geographical discrimination, 79

German Club, 119

German community, 6, 7, 14, 26, 27, 28, 34, 74, 94

Glassberg, David, 30, 35

González, Henry B., 172

González, Jorge, 167

Good Government League, 109, 146, 160; disintegration of, 150; fails to benefit Mexican American and African American populations, 108

Good Samaritan Center, 193

The Goose with the Golden Eggs, 88

Graham, Elizabeth, 99

Grant, Rachel, 190

Greek Revival market, 89

Green, Rena Maverick, 83, 84, 86, 88, 92, 96

Gregorio Esparza Day, 132, 133

Griffin, Gracie Poe, 136, 138, 141, 142, 180

Groos, Franz, 49

Guenther, Hilmer, 42

Guerra, Carlos, 193

Guerra, Peterie, **127**

Hale, Grace Elizabeth, 53, 101

Harris, Ethel, 99, 100–101

Harrison, Gail, 83

Harrison, William Henry, 20–21

Harvey, David, 187

Haynes, Michaele, 14, 158

Heis, Bettsie Guerra, 116

Hemisfair, 173, 181; and transformation of tourism, 172

Hemisfair Plaza, 172

Hennessey, Peter, 173

Henry, O., 74

heritage elite, 15, 71, 72, 104, 105, 117, 119, 122, 123, 133, 134, 137, 138, 148, 165–68, 195, 197

Hernández, Andy, 136–37, 155

Hoover, Herbert, 61

Hosmer, Charles B., 82

House, Boyce, 131

Houston, Sam, 5, 8

Huerta, Victoriano, 63, 70

Hull, Joanna, **87**

Huston, Felix, 5

hybridization of culture, 14

immigrants: relationship with native Tejanos, 4

inclusion, ethic of, 16, 133

inclusion, politics of, 136

Indian Harvest Festival, 85, 99

Indians, 3, 4, 11, 12, 26, 30, 41, 77, 99, 152; denied rights of full citizenship, 5; eviction from communal landholdings, 32

invented traditions, 8, 9

inversions, 14, 30, 70, 114, 144, 162

Jackson, Helen Hunt, 10

Jim Crow segregation, 10, 12, 16, 58, 166, 185, 186, 197

Johnson, Benjamin, 64

Johnson, Lyndon B., 146, 172

Juárez, Benito, 153

Juneteenth, 34

Junior Chamber of Commerce, 105, 119

juvenile delinquency, 178, 179, 180, 182, 188

Kampmann, Eda, 47, 54
Kampmann, H. D., Mrs., 46
Kefauver, Estes, 180
Kilday, Paul, 80
King Antonio, 144–45, 151, 152, 154, 155, 161, 162, 163, 166; as king of the Anglos, 165; as senior king of Fiesta, 158
King William Fair, 138
Kozmetsky, Rosemary, 138
krewes, 51, 137, 165–66
Kuykendall (mayor), 179

Lackland Air Force Base, 146
Lamar, Mirabeau, 5
Langston Hughes Center, 184
Latin Quarter, 58, 60
Lavenda, Robert, 115
La Villita, 94–96; disembodied cultural landscape of, 96
League of United Latin American Citizens (LULAC), 75, 132, 136, 149, 156, 158, 161, 162, 163, 179, 192; created Rey Feo, 145; first Mexican American organization to exert influence on San Antonio, 79; as largest Mexican American voluntary association in United States, 65; sought inclusion in San Antonio public culture, 17
Lee, Robert E., 8
Leighton, Ed, Mrs., 99
Limón, José, 187
Longoria, Eva, 174
Los Angeles fiesta, 31
Losoya, Jesús, 94
Losoya Street, 94
LULAC Rey Feo Scholarship Fund, 143
Lummis, Charles, 82–83

MacMillan, Esther, 99, 101
Madero, Francisco, 62, 63, 70
Maguire, Jack, 8, 195
Mailer, Norman, 128
Main Plaza, 24, 66
Manifest Destiny, 2, 10, 12, 28, 43, 53
Mardi Gras, 9, 14, 49, 50–51, 68, 114
Market House, 85
Martínez, Lizzie, 197
mass culture: effect on youth, 180
Maverick, Maury, 80, 95
McAllister, Walter, 147, 172, 173, 181
McKinley, William, 42
McLean, Robert, 84

McMillan, Jane Maverick, 101
McSween, Paul, 163
McWilliams, Carey, 10, 128
Mexicana housekeepers, 101
Mexican American activists, 17, 149
Mexican American–Hispanic generation, 150
Mexican American Legal Defense Fund, 151
Mexican Americans, 109, 180, 185; and lack of Fiesta participation, 158
Mexican Chamber of Commerce, 179
Mexican costumes, 126
Mexican Independence Day, 4, 25
Mexicanness, 69, 71, 76, 85, 93, 101, 102, 126, 152, 165, 171
Mexicanos, 12, 15, 30, 58, 62, 66, 74, 78, 85, 92, 93, 109; and development of separate town, 65; and segregation, 60, 64, 69
Mexican Revolution, 62, 64, 78
Mexican War, 5, 6, 28–29
Mexico City, 31, 32–33
Military Plaza, 24, 25, 74; as important social space, 33
Miss Black America Pageant, 140
Miss Fiesta, 114, 118, 119, 167, 174; comparison to coronation queen, 115–16; dress of, 116; and Mexican Americans, 135; and modern beauty pageant, 115; as subtle critique of coronation queen, 115
Miss Fiesta Pageant, 166
Montejano, David, 187
mooning contest, 174–75
moral panics, 180–81, 187
Moyé, Don, 138
Mullin, Molly, 77
Munguía, Rubén, 164
myth of the southern beauty, 54, 55

Nájera-Ramírez, Olga, 152
Navarro, José Antonio, 132
Negrón, Delís, 134
New Orleans: carnival in, 9, 165–66
Night in Old San Antonio (NIOSA), 16, 73–102, 113, 125, 189, 197, 198

Obregón, Álvaro, 77
Ochoa, María Luisa, 99–101, **100**
Ogden, Elizabeth, 47, 48
Order of the Alamo, **45**, 46, **46**, 50, 51, 56, 57, 59, 65, 104, 105, 106, 114, 119, 120,

123, 167, 196; queen's identity kept secret, 52
Order of the Alamo's coronation, 47, 52, 54

pageant queens, 114
parade route, 173
parades, 34–35
Paseo de la Reforma, 33
Los Pastores: confusing production of, 97–98
People's Parade, 164, 165
Philips, Bobbie Joe, 182
Político, Don, 120, 121, 122
Puro Party: Celebrating a Genocide (documentary), 196

Queen of Soul pageant, **139**, 140–43
Queen of the Order of the Alamo, 118, 152

race, 12, 22
railroads, 8, 9, 24, 26, 27, 32, 57
Ramírez, Socrates, 152
Ramona (Jackson), 10
Ramos, Basilio, 64
Reconstruction, 28
La Reina de la Feria de las Flores, 143
Rey Feo, 17, 135, 144, 145, 152, 156, 161, 166, 168, 174, 198; as inversion of King Antonio, 162; as king of the Hispanos, 165; and political and social inclusion, 163; as symbol of Anglo-Mexicano reconciliation, 155
Richards, Ann, 167
Richelieu, David, 187
Richter, Rudolph, **118**
ricos, 65, 78, 79
Rivera, Diego, 78, 86
Riverwalk, 124; and tourism, 107
Rockefeller, Nelson, 78
Rodríguez, Jacob I., 132, 133, 134
Roosevelt, Franklin D., 95
Roosevelt, Theodore, 12, 43
Rosaldo, Renato, 29
Rosales, Rodolfo, 109
Rose, G. Q. A., 47
rurales, 32
Russell, Raymond, 111
Ryan, Mary, 15

Said, Edward, 11
Salazars, 169, 170

San Antonio: and cattle empire, 8; core of city enclosed by freeways, 171; dual identities of, 107; economy of, 24; Fiesta. *See* Fiesta San Antonio; and gangs, 190–91; increasing stratification of, 57; integration into national economy, 28; and Mexicano population, 59–60; and poor public services, 107; and promotion of Mexican culture, 65; roadways of, 6; segregation by ethnicity and class, 6; shift in politics, 151; as Spanish-Mexican village, 29; street level and river level, 170, 171; as transportation center, 8
San Antonio Businessmen's Club, 47, 48
San Antonio Charro Association, 143–44, 152, 154, 155
San Antonio Club, 20, 34
San Antonio Conservation Society (SACS), 16, 73–102, 105, 114, 122, 126, 147, 148, 172, 189; puppet show, **89**; and reliance on Mexicana labor, 98; and unraveling of racial stratification of Texas Modern, 93
San Antonio Express News, 103, 110, 118, 121, 151, 159, 160, 179, 180, 182, 184, 187, 190, 191, 193
San Antonio German Club, 105
San Antonio Light, 159, 164, 179–80, 182–83
San Antonio Pioneers Association, 105
San Antonio Woman's Club, 105
San Antonio Zulu Association, 138
Sánchez, Graciela, 196
San Fernando Cathedral, **67**
Santa Anna, Antonio López de, 4, 129, 130, 132
Sayers, Joseph D., 48
Schenker, Herbert, 177, 179
Schreckenghost, Rollette, 189
Sea World, 161
segregation, 60, 61, 108, 146, 179, 181; reconciling city's inclusive rhetoric with, 128; and reformulation of southern womanhood, 101
Seguín, Erasmo, 132
Seguín, Juan, 5, 130, 132
La Semana Alegre: accused of being source of violence, 189; discontinued, 189
sentimentalism, 39
Sheridan, Philip, 191–92
Slayden, Ellen Maury, 20, 32, 61
Slayden, James, 32, 61
Smith, Harvey, 83

INDEX

social protest: not distinguished from social disorder, 184
Solís, Connie Peña, 96
soul, 140
Southern, Parker, 112, 119
Spaniards, 26
Spanish Governors' Palace: restoration of, 96
Spanish heritage fantasy, 16
Spice, William H., Jr., Mrs., 119, 120, 122; and manifesto of BFA's mission, 121
Spring Carnival, 9, 40, 48, 66, 68, 99; and rules for crowd and participants, 71
Spring Carnival Association, 40, 48, 49, 55, 67, 72
St. Louis: carnival in, 165, 166
stage rushing incident, 189
Stallybrass, Peter, 12, 14
Stappenbeck, R. W., 126
Steen, John, 159, 160
Steves, David, **157**, 163
Steves, Edward, 192
Stewart, Logan, 145, 155, 156, **157**, 158, 160, 162, 164, 178
Student Nonviolent Coordinating Committee (SNCC), 181, 184, 185, 186

Taft, William Howard, 63
Tejanos, 6, 9, 132; and Anglos, 7; conflicts with Anglos, 4; and El Gallo Corriendo, 7; relationship with new immigrants, 4
Tenayuca, Emma, 167
Texas Cavaliers, 57, 59, 65, 66, 68, 72, 104, 105, 106, 123, 151, 152, 156, 159, 165, 166, 167; Carrington establishes, 55; difficulty in becoming a member, 119–20
Texas Centennial, 75, 80
Texas dip, 44
Texas Historical Landmarks Association (THLA), 90, 92
Texas history: teaching of, 52
Texas Modern, 13, 22, 26, 56, 66, 68, 72, 76, 92, 93, 102, 105, 195
Texas pioneers, 106
Texas Rangers, 27
Texas Republic, 132
Texas Revolution, 4, 106, 130, 132; assured continuance of slavery, 28
Thompson, Paul, 109, 112, 120, 121
tourism, 31, 35, 74, 82, 83, 89, 90, 93, 95, 96, 104, 106, 123, 125, 153, 170, 174, 195; and Battle of Flowers Parade, 38; cattle ranching and Mexicanos, 29; chili stands and, 75; dependent upon

images of Mexican culture, 12–13; and the invention of traditions, 8; and local audience, 14; Mexicano behavior, dress, and cultural productions and, 84; rivaled military as top industry, 172; Riverwalk and, 107; San Antonio Businessmen's Club and, 47; San Antonio elite women and, 16; second largest source of income, 147
Tournament of Roses, 14, 56, 111, 117
Tower of the Americas, 17, 172
traffic interruptions, 174
Travis, William, 130
tuberculosis, 59, 60, 78
Turner, Frederick Jackson, 11

Vásquez, Alfred, 109
vendedores, 29
Villa, Pancho, 63
Virgil, Máximo, 154
Volksfests, 34
Von Phul, Helen, 20, 36, 40
La Voz de Esperanza, 196

Walker, Cindy, 167
waterways, 3
Wayne, John, 129
Wertham, Fredric, 180
Western costumes, 126
White, Allon, 12, 14
White, Jack, 107
Wilson, Ricks, 158
Wilson, Woodrow, 63
Witte Museum, 85
women, 37; African American, 141; and Alamo Plaza, 39; and appeal to patriotism, 42; and Battle of Flowers Parade, 36; and changing power relations with men, 14; coronation as attempt to control power of, 54; and domestication of death, 39; and "going public," 15; and language of cultural custodianship, 36; and preservation of monuments, 38; and San Antonio Conservation Society, 75. *See also* elite women
Woodward, C. Vann, 11
Woodward, Sam H., 30

Yarborough, Ralph, 172
youth: as scapegoats, 180
youth violence, 176

Zapata, Emiliano, 63
Zarzamora Street, 94
Zottarelli, Prospero, 112

INDEX